CHARTING THE
END TIMES

nding God's Plan for the Ages

His will, according to His kind intention which He purposed in Him with a view to an administration suitable
, the summing up of all things in Christ, things in the heavens and things on the earth" (Eph 1:9-10).

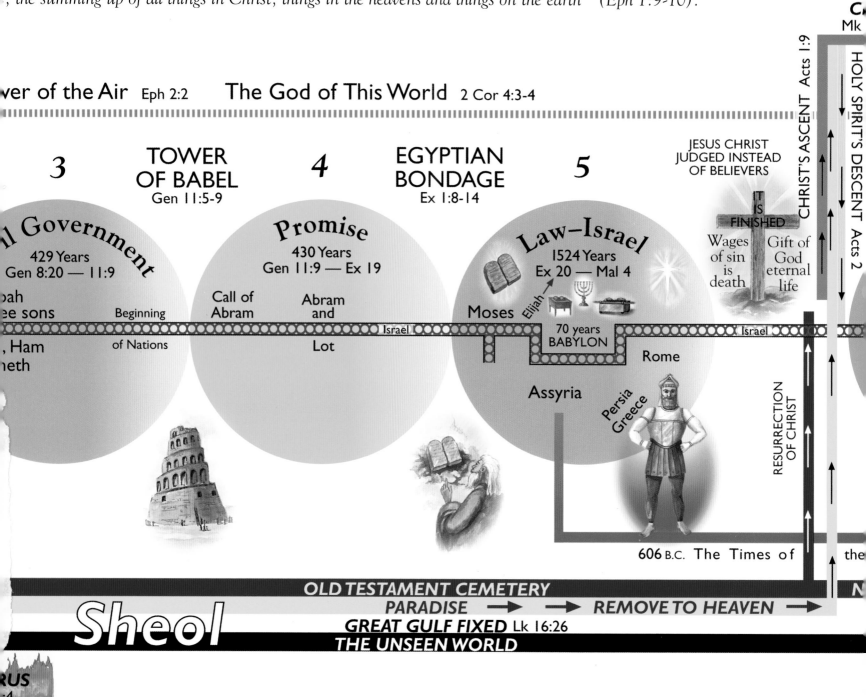

wer of the Air Eph 2:2   The God of This World 2 Cor 4:3-4

C.
Mk

HOLY SPIRIT'S DESCENT Acts 2

CHRIST'S ASCENT Acts 1:9

3

**TOWER
OF BABEL**
Gen 11:5-9

4

**EGYPTIAN
BONDAGE**
Ex 1:8-14

5

JESUS CHRIST
JUDGED INSTEAD
OF BELIEVERS

IT
IS
FINISHED

Wages | Gift of
of sin | God
is | eternal
death | life

l Government
429 Years
Gen 8:20 — 11:9

Promise
430 Years
Gen 11:9 — Ex 19

Law–Israel
1524 Years
Ex 20 — Mal 4

ah
e sons

, Ham
eth

Beginning

of Nations

Call of
Abram

Abram
and

Lot

Moses   Elijah

Israel

70 years
BABYLON

Israel

Rome

Assyria

Persia
Greece

RESURRECTION OF CHRIST

606 B.C. The Times of   the

N

OLD TESTAMENT CEMETERY

PARADISE → → **REMOVE TO HEAVEN** →

Sheol

GREAT GULF FIXED Lk 16:26
THE UNSEEN WORLD

RUS
:4

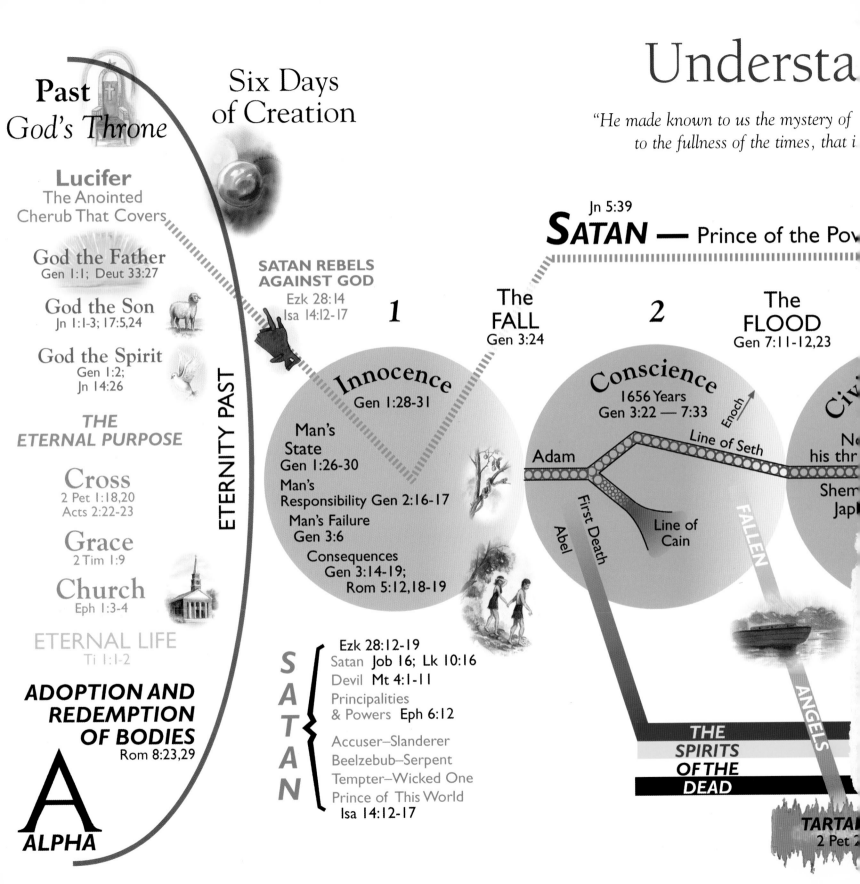

Past
God's *Throne*

Six Days of Creation

Understa

"He made known to us the mystery of
to the fullness of the times, that i

Lucifer
The Anointed
Cherub That Covers

God the Father
Gen 1:1; Deut 33:27

God the Son
Jn 1:1-3; 17:5,24

God the Spirit
Gen 1:2;
Jn 14:26

THE
ETERNAL PURPOSE

Cross
2 Pet 1:18,20
Acts 2:22-23

Grace
2 Tim 1:9

Church
Eph 1:3-4

ETERNAL LIFE
Ti 1:1-2

ADOPTION AND
REDEMPTION
OF BODIES
Rom 8:23,29

A
ALPHA

ETERNITY PAST

SATAN REBELS
AGAINST GOD
Ezk 28:14
Isa 14:12-17

1

Innocence
Gen 1:28-31

Man's
State
Gen 1:26-30

Man's
Responsibility Gen 2:16-17

Man's Failure
Gen 3:6

Consequences
Gen 3:14-19;
Rom 5:12,18-19

S A T A N
Ezk 28:12-19
Satan Job 16; Lk 10:16
Devil Mt 4:1-11
Principalities
& Powers Eph 6:12

Accuser–Slanderer
Beelzebub–Serpent
Tempter–Wicked One
Prince of This World
Isa 14:12-17

Jn 5:39
SATAN — Prince of the Pow

The
FALL
Gen 3:24

2

The
FLOOD
Gen 7:11-12,23

Conscience
1656 Years
Gen 3:22 — 7:33

Enoch

Line of Seth

Adam

First Death

Line of
Cain

Abel

FALLEN

Civ

No
his thr

Shem
Jap

ANGELS

THE
SPIRITS
OF THE
DEAD

TARTA
2 Pet 2

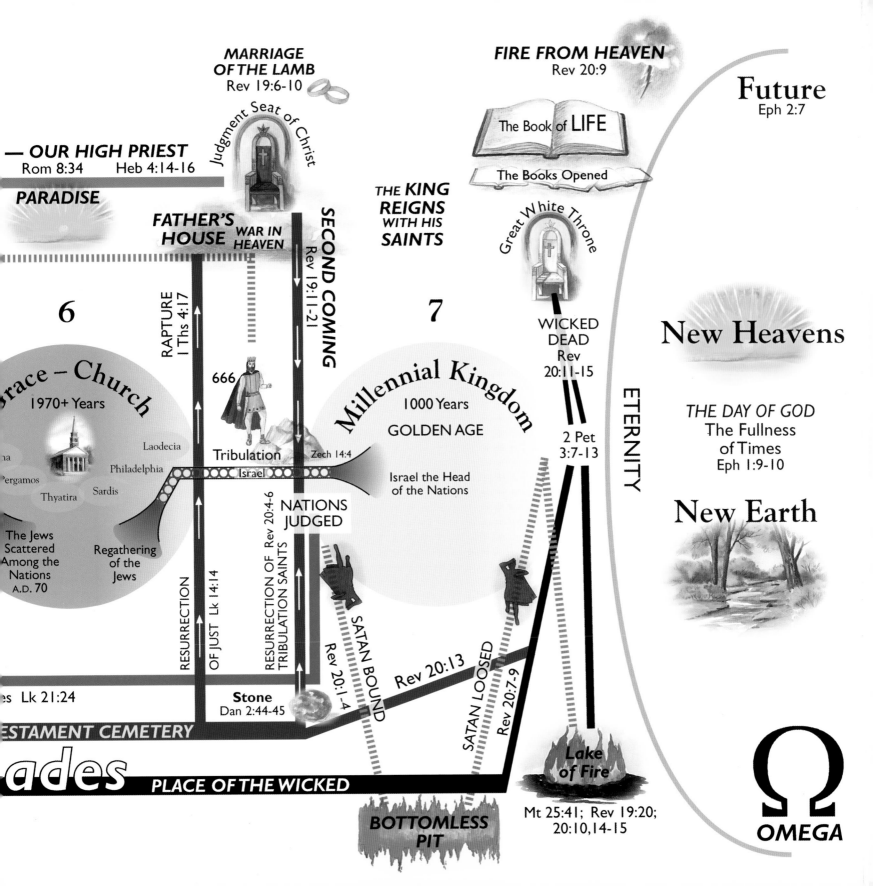

CHARTING THE END TIMES

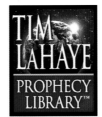

Tim LaHaye
Thomas Ice

Harvest House Publishers
Eugene, OR 97402

Unless otherwise indicated, all Scripture quotations are taken from the New American Standard Bible, © 1960, 1962, 1963, 1968, 1971, 1972, 1973, 1975, 1977, 1995 by The Lockman Foundation. Used by permission.

Verses marked KJV are taken from the King James Version of the Bible.

Verses marked NIV are taken from the Holy Bible: New International Version®. NIV®. Copyright © 1973, 1978, 1984 by the International Bible Society. Used by permission of Zondervan Publishing House. The "NIV" and "New International Version" trademarks are registered in the United States Patent and Trademark Office by International Bible Society.

Edited by Steve Miller

Cover design by Terry Dugan Design, Minneapolis, Minnesota

Interior design by Legacyroad Solutions, Colorado Springs, Colorado
Illustrations by Norma Lane; charts by Jeff Lane, Scott Johnson,
and Kelly Robinson

CHARTING THE END TIMES

Copyright © 2001 by Tim LaHaye and Thomas Ice
Published by Harvest House Publishers
Eugene, Oregon 97402

Library of Congress Cataloging-in-Publication Data

LaHaye, Tim F.
    Charting the end times / Tim LaHaye and Thomas Ice.
        p. cm. — (Tim LaHaye prophecy library series)
    Includes bibliographical references.
    ISBN 0-7369-0138-8
    1. Bible—Prophecies—End of the world. 2. End of the world—Biblical teaching.
    3. Bible—Prophecies—End of the world—Charts, diagrams, etc. 4. End of the
    world—Biblical teaching—Charts, diagrams, etc. I. Ice, Thomas. II. Title. III. Series.

BS649.E63 L34 2001
236'.9—dc21   2001024465

Printed in Hong Kong.

06 07 08 / NG / 15 14

In Memory of

Clarence Larkin, a mechanical engineer and architect turned minister at 34 years of age, who in 1920 published the seminal chart book of the twentieth century, *Dispensational Truth*. It has helped more ministers, Bible teachers, and earnest students who desire to rightly divide the Word of truth than any book of its kind.

Also, Dr. David L. Cooper, Th.M., Ph.D., founder and president of the Biblical Research Society, whose masterful chart book *The World's Greatest Library Graphically Illustrated*, published in 1942, has helped mold the thinking of both authors.

Dedicated to

The millions of readers of the *LEFT BEHIND*® series of end-times novels who want to study more in-depth the many prophetic scriptures upon which those stories are based…and to Christians everywhere who want to know the wonderful Holy Scriptures. Prophecy is history written in advance. Only the Bible has dependable prophetic truth. These charts are the culmination of many years of careful study by the authors and their many prophecy-scholar colleagues in the Pre-Trib Research Center.

And of course, this book is primarily dedicated to our Lord and Savior Jesus Christ, who alone is "the spirit of prophecy" (Revelation 19:10b). Only a study of prophecy gives Him His rightful place in history, both past and future.

ACKNOWLEDGMENTS

We wish to express our gratitude to Harvest House Publishers for their faith in our vision for this huge project—Bob Hawkins, Jr., who believed in our idea; Carolyn McCready, LaRae Weikert, and Betty Fletcher, who took our ideas and gave them feet; and Steve Miller, without whose persistence and assistance this book would have never been completed. Also, this project benefited tremendously from the creative expertise of Karl Schaller, Jeff Lane, and the rest of the team at Legacyroad Solutions. All these people were a joy to work with!

CONTENTS

WHY A CHART BOOK ON BIBLE PROPHECY?

There's a popular proverb that suggests "a picture is worth a thousand words." If that is true, a good chart is worth a thousand words about Bible prophecy. The value of charts is that they help us to see the timing of prophetic events and their relationship to each other. With a chart, we can summarize a subject or theme that, in written form, might take pages to explain. In this book, you will find virtually all the key themes of Bible prophecy in chart form.

One of the distinctives of biblical Christianity is that God knows and reveals the future (Isaiah 46:8-11). Only God can do that. Thus, the future is settled, and not open to change. We can look at the charts in this book with an assurance that the biblical teachings they portray are guaranteed to take place. We can have confidence that God will continue to carry out His plan for the ages, and we who are Christians have a significant part in that plan.

Our prayer is that *Charting the End Times* will enable anyone interested in Bible prophecy to learn the prophetic teachings of Scripture in a more meaningful way.

1.
UNDERSTANDING GOD'S PLAN FOR THE AGES

For reasons known only to God, He determined to populate eternity with a race of human beings who choose to worship Him by obeying His will. He created man in His own image with a mind superior to that of any other living creature, and He breathed into that man "the breath of life and he became a living soul." From that first man, named Adam, God extracted a rib and made it into a woman, whom Adam named Eve, to be a complementary companion to Adam. Together, by the Creator's design, they possessed the capability of procreating additional human beings like themselves with an eternal soul and a free will, enabling them also to obey or disobey God as they choose. Perhaps the most incredible part of this creation miracle is that they would also have the ability of passing the gift of procreation and free will on to their children for thousands of generations.

The Creator God then put man and his wife in a beautiful garden, which He called Eden. There He placed two special trees, which He designated "the tree of life" and "the tree of the knowledge of good and evil." They were expressly forbidden to eat of the latter tree or they would die, but they were not forbidden to eat of the tree of life. It is thought by many that if they had eaten of the tree of life first, before eating of the forbidden tree, their test would have been over and sin would not have entered the human race. Instead, they heeded the voice of the tempter and disobeyed God by eating of the forbidden tree. By this act, sin entered the human race.

God, in His marvelous grace, began revealing His will to man right from the beginning, in Genesis 3:15, which is the first prophecy related to God's redemptive plan for the salvation of mankind. From there onward, through the pens of many writers, God continued to reveal more of His plan, which we find in the Bible.

THE ORIGIN OF EVIL

At some point in the past, one of God's special angelic creations, Lucifer, the "anointed cherub" (Ezekiel 28:14), who was originally created perfect in all his ways (as were the other angels and man), became rebellious. Lucifer later enticed one-third of the angels of heaven and Adam and Eve to do the same. They had all received a free will and they used it to rebel against God. We are given only scant details of this rebellion, which resulted in Lucifer (also called Satan) being cast out of heaven along with the angels that joined his rebellion (Revelation 12). He came down to the earth, which was designated as his special province, where he became the "prince of the power of the air" (Ephesians 2:2) and "the god of this world" (2 Corinthians 4:4). This ignited the conflict of the ages between God and Satan as both sought the worship of each man and woman on earth. As prophecy teaches,

Satan, the master deceiver of mankind, will eventually be totally expelled from heaven along with all those who follow him, both angelic and human. After the Millennial kingdom of Christ and Satan's final rebellion, they will all be thrown into "the lake of fire" (Revelation 20:14).

Why God placed mankind on this earth—where fallen Satan had access to people's minds and will—we are not told. Given the Creator's objective to develop a race of people with a free will who voluntarily choose to worship and serve Him for eternity, this world then became a proving ground or testing place where every person must make his or her choice as to who they would follow—God or Satan. Satan, described by Jesus Christ as "the deceiver" and "a liar," is not honest in the way he approaches men. He never specifically asks mankind to be his servant or to worship him (but he will in the Tribulation period). Instead, he entices man with ideas like, "Do your own thing" or "You can be like God." His temptation of Eve in Genesis 3 is a perfect example of the dishonest way he deceives all people. By contrast, God is truth; He always approaches men and women honestly. In every age He forthrightly asks people to obey and serve Him. In the Old Testament He gave commandments to the children of Israel, and He promised to bless them if they kept the commands and curse them if they did not. The entire history of Israel is an illustration of the fulfillment of God's promises according to the people's choices and their behavior.

THE CONFLICT OF THE AGES

Satan's hatred for mankind becomes clear as we examine the conflict of the ages as it is revealed in the Bible. In every age, Satan has attempted to destroy mankind, whereas God has sought to save people. Adam and Eve had something Satan did not have—an eternal spirit that was able to respond to God. When Satan enticed them to sin by disobeying God, that spirit died. This necessitated the redemption of mankind through the shedding of innocent blood. Eventually God sent His Son to earth to become man's redeemer, the only means of eternal salvation for man by the sacrifice of that Son on the cross. From then on all mankind could, by choosing to receive Christ and trusting Him, have their spirit "born again" (John 3:3,7).

The complete story of the conflict of the ages between God and Satan for the souls of mankind is too lengthy to include here, but there are some key points in that story. For example, we read about the Flood in Genesis chapters 6–8. Prior to the Flood, people lived to great ages (some lived for 800 or even 900 years). Little is known of this period except that eventually the people on earth rebelled against God and became so morally corrupt and violent that God sent the Flood to destroy all but Noah and his family, who were deemed righteous.

After the Flood, God sent the rainbow as a permanent reminder that He would never again destroy the world by flood. While we have had and still have local floods, some of great severity, God, in His mercy, has kept His word, and we have never again had a worldwide flood.

Soon after the great Flood, Satan raised up Nimrod and his mother to establish idolatry in the city of Babel, which is second only to Jerusalem as the most influential city in the world. Every false religion, particularly pagan forms of idolatry, can be traced back to Babel, a city that is now being rebuilt (according to prophecy) and will one day be destroyed forever. Because of man's wrong intentions in building the tower of Babel, God brought confusion upon the people by causing them to speak different languages. This resulted in the dispersion of people throughout the earth according to language groups.

THE NATION OF ISRAEL

Later, God called Abraham from the idolatrous city of Ur and promised him a new land and his own people. Abraham and his wife Sarah did not have their promised first child until both were too old to have children. God clearly brought about a miracle when they gave birth to Isaac, who was the start of a new nation called *Israel*. Through their seed God would bless the peoples of the world; it was through Israel that God would send the Messiah to be the lamb of sacrifice and to bring redemption to all who call on His name.

God also planned to bless the people of the world through the Hebrew nation *if* they would obey Him. To them God gave the commission of being the torchbearers of the Old Testament, and He placed them in what today is known as the Holy Land. This land acted as a bridge between the continents to the north and south. It was here that the merchants and kings of Israel could be a witness to the polytheistic nations of the world. God promised that those who worshiped and served Him would be incredibly blessed beyond anything known in other nations, so that visitors could take the message of God back to their homelands—much like the Queen of Sheba did during the reign of Solomon. Because of Israel's access to the silk trade route in the Orient, the Hebrews could have even influenced China and the Orient if they had remained faithful.

God wanted to be Israel's king, and He provided His leadership through priests, prophets, and judges, many of whom wrote the revelation of His will for the Israelites and for future generations. This revelation is what we now know as the Holy Scriptures. These holy writings contain man's only truly authentic record of history, instructions on how to live, and prophecies for the future. All Israel had to do to experience incredible blessing was to worship God alone and manifest that worship by obeying and serving Him. Instead, the Israelites were duped by Satan to seek a king from among their own people—a king who eventually turned the people away from depending on God and serving Him to depending on and serving an earthly king and the physical government he provided. God then chose another man to become king—King David, "the man after God's own heart." During David's reign and the first part of the reign of his son Solomon, the nation of Israel went back to obeying God and received His unprecedented blessings.

Eventually both the ten northern tribes of Israel and the two southern tribes of Judah turned from worshiping God, and the majority of the people became idolaters. It was because of their sin of idolatry that God raised up King Nebuchadnezzar to take the Jews captive and transport them to Babylon for 70 years. He did this to prove once and for all that He alone was God and He alone could predict the future, as taught by the Hebrew prophets.

> One of the affirmations that Satan is a defeated enemy is God's prophetic plan for the second coming of Jesus Christ.

FROM JESUS CHRIST ONWARD

Approximately 400 years after the close of the Old Testament, the greatest of all fulfilled prophecies occurred: the birth, life, death, and resurrection of the Messiah. At least 109 prophecies were fulfilled in His 33-year life, fulfilling God's promise of almost 4000 years earlier that the seed of the woman (Eve) would bruise Satan's head. That happened through Jesus' death on the cross for the sins of the whole world. When Jesus cried out on the cross, "It is finished," He did not mean the conflict of the ages was over. He meant that the temporary sacrificial system of the Old Testament was no longer needed and that now a permanent way of escaping the deception of Satan and the consequences of sin had opened up—the way of salvation by grace through faith in Christ. In addition, Jesus promised to send His Holy Spirit to indwell believers. This would not make them impervious to the deceptions of Satan and the world, but it did mean believers would have a supernatural power with which to combat the power and deception of Satan if they walked with God and depended on Him.

This world has not become a perfect place since then; in every generation, people have had to choose whom they will serve. Those who choose to follow God have the benefit of the New Testament, which contains further revelations and prophecies inspired by the Holy Spirit. And, with the help of the indwelling of that same Spirit, believers have been able to experience victory over Satan and his legions of demons.

By contrast, the world has continued along its same destructive path. Satan has indwelt kings, dictators, presidents, and other governmental leaders. Many of these leaders have been among the sources of man's earthly struggles. And the progress of time has not seen the progress of mankind. In the recent twentieth century, our so-called civilized society distinguished itself as the most barbaric in the history of mankind. Modern-day governments and their wars have caused the deaths and murders of almost 180 million souls in this century alone—more deaths than in all the previous wars of history combined! Even today, the nightly news is filled with expressions of man's inhumanity to his fellow man through oppressive and dictatorial governments or government leaders.

The new birth in Christ and the indwelling Holy Spirit, together with the 27 New Testament books of divine revelation that help Christians to grow spiritually, seem to have lessened somewhat the plight of man during this conflict of the ages. Millions of Christians have used the help of these resources and the church. In reference to the church, Jesus said, "The gates of Hades will not overpower it" (Matthew 16:18). Thus Christians are protected to the extent that Satan's "wiles" cannot destroy them. One of the affirmations that Satan is a defeated enemy is God's prophetic plan for the second coming of Jesus Christ. In the first three centuries of its existence, the church had such a zeal and spiritual fire because of its belief in Christ's return to establish His kingdom on this earth that Christianity became the dominant religion and was adopted as the state religion by the emperor of Rome in A.D. 313.

Emperor Constantine meant well when he merged religion and government, but Satan quickly discovered that what he could not halt by persecution he was able to stifle by indulgence. At first Constantine ordered 50 new copies of the Holy Scriptures to replace those that the persecutors of the faith before him had burned. Then he gave church leaders the former pagan temples as places of worship.

By the fourth century, the Church of Rome began to accept some of the traditions and teachings of the Babylonian paganism that had been the official religious practices of Rome prior to and after the time of Christ. In the fifth century, Augustine and his Greek followers, who were educated in pagan humanism and fatalism, brought in the most powerful enemy of true Christianity, the allegorizing of Scripture. It is interesting that the Greek "Christian" theologian, Origen, was branded a heretic by the third-century church for allegorizing Scripture, whereas the fifth-century church officially accepted this same method for teaching prophecy from Augustine. This acceptance of allegorizing prophecy was eventually applied to all of Scripture. This opened the door to the eventual elevation of pagan religion to the same level as scriptural truth. This, in turn, ushered in the Dark Ages, an 1100-year period during which the Bible was kept from the common people. Not until the Protestant Reformation during the sixteenth century did the tide turn. By the providence of God, the invention of the printing press and the work of translating the Bible into the languages of the common people throughout Europe once again ignited the church. Chief among the reasons for the amazing growth of the church during the past four centuries has been the revival of interest in end-times prophecy, which naturally resulted as people began reading the Bible for themselves and believing it literally. To this day, churches and Christians who take the Bible literally tend to be premillennial, believing that God will win the conflict of the ages when His Son Jesus returns to this earth as the "King of kings and Lord of lords" (Revelation 19:16). He will then set up His righteous kingdom on earth for 1000 years, and that will be followed by an eternity best described as heaven.

LOOKING TO ETERNITY

There are many other details of the prophetic future that we will examine in this book. We would be remiss, however, if we did not point out two important truths about the time of man on this earth. One is that all mankind has two things in common. First, every person must make his or her own choice about God during their lifetime. From Adam and Eve to the last person living during the final rebellion described in Revelation 20:11-15, each person must decide who they will worship and serve—God, or the gods of this world (including idols, money, fame, or fortune).

The second fact is that there are only two places to spend eternity: heaven, where Jesus Himself is preparing a place for Christians, or hell, which was prepared for the devil and his angels. If you have not made your choice yet, we would urge you to believe that Jesus died for your sins according to the Scriptures, that He rose again the third day, and that you can be saved by confessing your sins to Him and inviting Him to come into your life through His Holy Spirit. Like all the other people who have heard this message, you have a choice to make. Please remember that your eternal destiny will be determined by that choice.

2.
WHAT IS BIBLE PROPHECY?

A *prophet* is defined as "one who speaks on behalf of another," and a *prophecy* is the message that he conveys. Bible prophecy is God's infallible message to man, spoken or written by prophets specially chosen by God. Today, many people think prophecy deals only with predictions about the future, but that is not the case. In a broad sense, prophecy includes any aspect of God's revelation to man as recorded in the 66 books of the Bible. However, in this book, our focus will be upon predictive prophecy, especially that which is still future in relation to our own day.

Prophecy is history written in advance. The Lord said through Isaiah the prophet, "Remember the former things long past, for I am God, and there is no other; I am God, and there is no one like Me, declaring the end from the beginning, and from ancient times things which have not been done, saying, 'My purpose will be established, and I will accomplish all My good pleasure'; calling a bird of prey from the east, the man of My purpose from a far country. Truly I have spoken; truly I will bring it to pass. I have planned it, surely I will do it" (Isaiah 46:9-11). The Lord determines what will happen in history and then He brings it to pass. Considering that God can do this, it is not difficult for Him to tell us, in advance, what will take place.

The apostle Peter wrote, "We did not follow cleverly devised tales when we made known to you the power and coming of our Lord Jesus Christ, but we were eyewitnesses of His majesty" (2 Peter 1:16). False religions and superstitions are built upon clever tales, but Christianity is built upon nothing less than God's revelation of Himself to mankind as found in the Bible. Peter went on to call biblical prophecy "the prophetic word made more sure, to which you do well to pay attention as to a lamp shining in a dark place" (2 Peter 1:19). Why can we place all our trust in God's prophetic Word? Because, as Peter concludes, prophecy is not a matter of the human interpretation of historical events: "Know this first of all, that no prophecy of Scripture is a matter of one's own interpretation, for no prophecy was ever made by an act of human will, but men moved by the Holy Spirit spoke from God" (2 Peter 1:20-21).

Prophecy provides Christians with an outline of God's program of the future. And because hundreds of specific prophecies have already been literally fulfilled—most of them in relation to the first coming of Christ—we know that all the prophecies about the future will be fulfilled literally in the end times, and Christ's return will be fulfilled literally as well. A faithful believer is to be found watching and waiting for our Lord's coming.

WHY CHRISTIANS SHOULD STUDY BIBLE PROPHECY

God must have wanted Christians to study Bible prophecy because He put so much of it in His divine revelation to mankind, which we call the Bible. Fully 28 percent of the Bible was prophetic in nature at the time that it was written. Dr. John Walvoord, dean of prophecy at Dallas Theological Seminary, teaches that half of the 1000 Bible prophecies documented in the last century have already been fulfilled. This assures us that the rest of Bible prophecy, which has so much to do with our own future, will also be fulfilled.

Tragically, many pastors today know little or nothing about Bible prophecy because it wasn't taught in their seminary; consequently, they do not teach about prophecy from the pulpit. This leaves many Christians ignorant of the exciting plans God has for the future. This is unfortunate, for there are several reasons God's people should study prophecy.

1. PROPHECY ACQUAINTS US WITH THE MOST IMPORTANT SUBJECT OF THE AGES, GOD'S PLAN FOR MAN

We are not isolated creatures living in a vacuum without cause or purpose (as secular thinkers who attribute man's existence to the accident of evolution would have us believe). We were created body, soul, and spirit by a loving God who has a detailed plan for our future, which is revealed only in the Bible. Not knowing that prophetic plan makes all people—even Christians—vulnerable to false teachings about our present day and the future. The only way to answer the convincing arguments of false teachers is to be armed with the truth about God's plan for the future.

Our foldout chart in the front of this book, titled "Understanding God's Plan for the Ages," gives an overall picture of what some Bible teachers call "the heart of the Bible" or "the backbone of the Bible." We like to think of the elements in this chart as the very foundation of Scripture and that everything in the 66 books of the Bible adds details to this basic framework. If you memorize these basic elements, it will make the chronology and history of the Bible easier to remember. We believe this chart and the rest of the charts in this book will help you better understand God's basic blueprint for man—past, present, and future.

2. STUDYING BIBLE PROPHECY CONVINCES US THAT THERE REALLY IS A GOD

Only God can reveal the future! And that is what prophecy is—history written in advance. In this book, we will affirm that many specific prophecies in the Bible have already been fulfilled. In fact, every prophecy that has been fulfilled was fulfilled at its proper time. What's more, the Bible teaches that the test of a prophet is whether his prophecies come to pass and whether they accord with the rest of the Bible (Deuteronomy 18:22). The many charts in this book are intended to convince you of the prophetic truth that "there is a God in heaven who reveals mysteries" (mysteries about the future—Daniel 2:28).

No other book or person has ever predicted the future with perfect accuracy. The fact that God alone can do so is an affirmation that He is all that He claims to be.

3. THE LITERAL FULFILLMENT OF PROPHECY TEACHES US THAT PROPHECY SHOULD BE INTERPRETED LITERALLY

Many teachers today are confusing Christians by teaching that Scripture was never intended to be interpreted literally. Instead, they call for a spiritualizing or allegorizing of the Bible's prophecies. This only leads to confusion! Did God mean what He said and say what He meant? The study of fulfilled prophecy says a resounding yes. Our study of already-fulfilled prophecy inspires us to trust God to fulfill the prophecies that will be fulfilled in the future.

4. THE STUDY OF PROPHECY PREPARES THE CHRISTIAN TO AVOID THE DECEPTIONS OF THE MANY FALSE PROPHETS THAT ARE ARISING IN OUR DAY

While there have always been false teachers, as we approach the end times there will be an increase in the numbers of those who lead people astray with their erroneous teachings. The best defense is to "put on the full armor of God so that you can take your stand against the devil's schemes" (Ephesians 6:11 NIV). Our Lord predicted that false christs and false prophets will appear in the end times, some of whom will be able to perform great signs and miracles and will deceive those who do not know the Scriptures—particularly Bible passages that relate to future things. The best way to avoid being deceived by the false teachers is to know the prophetic teachings of God's Word.

5. THE STUDY OF PROPHECY PROMOTES AN EVANGELISTIC CHURCH

The most evangelistic periods of church history have been the times when the church actively studied prophecy. The early church as a whole was evangelistic. From the time that our Lord said, "I will come again, and receive you to Myself" (John 14:3) all the way through most of the next three centuries, the early church had an evangelistic fire. It may seem the church's enthusiasm resulted from being a persecuted church, but part of the reason it was persecuted was because of its evangelistic fire—and that, in turn, was due to the fact that our Lord's soon return was a prominent part of the church's teachings.

By the fourth century A.D., paganism had crept into the church and the Bible was no longer taught widely. It became an object of worship, and all through the Dark Ages, the Bible was seldom taught and even fewer read it (or could read it). In the fourteenth century Englishman John Wycliffe (1330-1384) determined to translate the Word of God into the common language so that everyone could read it for himself. This was the starting point of the Reformation, and people began to read the Bible again.

In the nineteenth century came the rediscovery of the study of prophecy, or the study of last things. At the same time, the greatest missionary and evangelistic emphasis of the modern church era was born. During the past century some of the most evangelistic and missionary-minded churches have been those that taught prophecy, and that is true of our day as well.

6. THE STUDY OF PROPHECY TENDS TO PURIFY THE BELIEVER

It is no secret that we live in an unholy age. Unfortunately, too much of that unholiness is found even in the church. One tool the Holy Spirit uses to motivate believers to live holy lives is the study of prophecy, particularly those passages that relate to our Lord's soon return. The apostle John said this about those who hold to the promise of the Lord's second coming in their hearts: "Everyone who has this hope fixed on Him purifies himself, just as He is pure" (1 John 3:3).

Many a believer has, in a moment of temptation, thought, *Do I want to be doing this when Christ returns?* When the answer is no, it is easier to reject the temptation. We are challenged to live in such a way that we will not feel ashamed when our Lord returns.

7. PROPHECY OFFERS CONFIDENT HOPE IN A HOPELESS AGE

Human beings can absorb many pressures in life, but a lack of hope is not one of them. The world in which we live has no hope. Looking back, we see an unending history of war, hatred, and cruelty, all of which reveals the inhumanness of mankind. The very study of history is a study of war and man's inhumanity to his fellow man. The whole world yearns for peace, but knows no peace. Mankind's problems continually worsen, leaving many people without hope.

Prophecy students, however, not only know what our loving God has planned for the future of this planet and the billions who live on it, but they also have a firm confidence toward the future and are not afraid. They not only know what the future holds; they also know the One who holds the future.

What's sad is that the worst days in world history are not behind us, but are still ahead of us. Our Lord Himself warned that toward the end of human history there would be a time of "great tribulation, such as has not occurred since the beginning of the world until now, nor ever will" (Matthew 24:21). When we study the context of that passage in detail, we see that this future terror will be unparalleled in human history. Yet this is of no great personal concern for the Christian who rightly understands God's prophetic plan, for he knows his secure place in God's future plan.

This confidence or hope is not automatic; it comes in response to the study of the Word of God in general as well as those passages that pertain to prophecy. And when we speak of hope, we're not talking about a casual hope that says, "We hope things will turn out all right." No, we who are Christians are *confident* that the future will happen exactly as Christ predicted. We do not merely wish that Jesus will come again; we are *confident* that He will come again because He promised He would. The more we know about God's prophetic promises, the more convinced we will become of their future fulfillment. Those who are familiar with Bible prophecy are the only ones who can face what seems to be an uncertain future with peaceful confidence.

THE WORLD'S GREATEST LIBRARY
4.

The Bible is the world's greatest library (for it is not a single book but a library of 66 books). It is the revelation of God's plan for man, his history, and his future. It is one of the oldest books in the world and was put together unlike any other, written over a period of 1500 years by over 40 authors from all walks of life. And yet when we read from Genesis to Revelation, we see an incredible harmony that cannot be attributed to 40 different men, but rather to a supernatural God using them to reveal both His long-range plan and His will for humanity. As the apostle Peter said, God's revelation came not by "an act of human will, but men moved by the Holy Spirit" (2 Peter 1:21).

THE RELIABILITY OF THE BIBLE

The Holy Spirit has preserved the accuracy of the Bible, which has stood the test of more careful scrutiny than any other book in history. Archaeologists have also dug up irrefutable evidence that lines up with the statements of Scripture. In the past the Bible was ridiculed by skeptics for including Assyria, the city of Nineveh, and the names of kings not mentioned elsewhere in ancient history. But

The World's Greatest Library

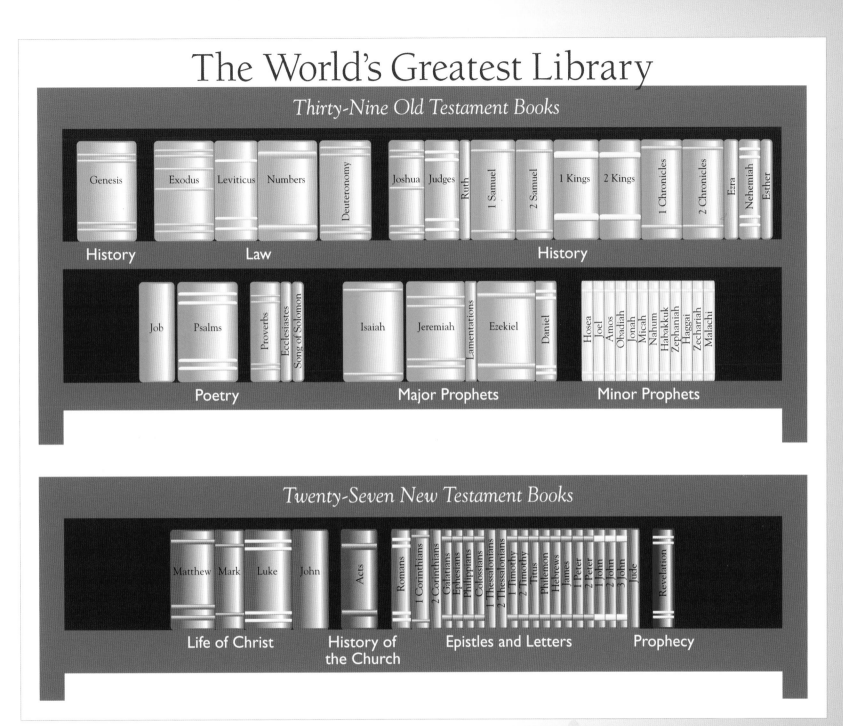

Thirty-Nine Old Testament Books

Genesis | Exodus | Leviticus | Numbers | Deuteronomy | Joshua | Judges | Ruth | 1 Samuel | 2 Samuel | 1 Kings | 2 Kings | 1 Chronicles | 2 Chronicles | Ezra | Nehemiah | Esther

History — Law — History

Job | Psalms | Proverbs | Ecclesiastes | Song of Solomon | Isaiah | Jeremiah | Lamentations | Ezekiel | Daniel | Hosea | Joel | Amos | Obadiah | Jonah | Micah | Nahum | Habakkuk | Zephaniah | Haggai | Zechariah | Malachi

Poetry — Major Prophets — Minor Prophets

Twenty-Seven New Testament Books

Matthew | Mark | Luke | John | Acts | Romans | 1 Corinthians | 2 Corinthians | Galatians | Ephesians | Philippians | Colossians | 1 Thessalonians | 2 Thessalonians | 1 Timothy | 2 Timothy | Titus | Philemon | Hebrews | James | 1 Peter | 2 Peter | 1 John | 2 John | 3 John | Jude | Revelation

Life of Christ — History of the Church — Epistles and Letters — Prophecy

archaeological discoveries have confirmed and are continuing to affirm what the skeptics have dismissed. When properly considered, all the evidence leads to the conclusion that the Bible is not only the world's greatest library, it is also the most reliable.

The late Dr. David L. Cooper, one of the most outstanding Bible scholars in the world, said of the Scriptures:

Abundant and overwhelming is the proof that the

Scriptures are God-breathed. No open-minded truthseeker can weigh the evidence for the divine origin of the Scriptures and can arrive at the conclusion that the books of the Bible were written by uninspired men.[1]

There are many lines of proof that lead to this conclusion, but because of space limitations, we will consider only one. There is an absolute unity that pervades these 66 books, which were written over a period of 1500 years by 40 or more different writers who came from very dissimilar backgrounds and experienced a wide variety of circumstances. Such a unity is humanly impossible—clearly it was God who orchestrated this unity. Dr. Cooper wrote:

> A careful examination of all the Scriptures shows that the plan which is announced in Genesis 3:15 is consistently carried through the Scriptures. This verse is the text of the Bible. All that follows is but the unfolding of that one divine purpose which runs through the ages and which

will culminate in the "dispensation of the fullness of the times" when God will head up all things under the Lord Jesus Christ (Ephesians 1:10). There are no contradictions in the Scriptures. To the superficial reader there appear some disagreements, but upon thorough investigation, those things which seem to be discrepancies prove to be glorious, convincing harmonies.[2]

Prophecy, or "history written in advance," provides an outline of God's program for the future before it occurs. And only God can know the future! Thus prophecy not only serves as a preview of the future, but fulfilled prophecy affirms God's supernatural hand on Scripture. Since hundreds of prophecies have already been fulfilled literally, we can be fully confident that all the prophecies yet to be fulfilled—particularly those about Christ's second coming—will be fulfilled literally as well. That's why a faithful believer is one who will be found watching for and awaiting His return—which will hopefully be in our lifetime.

5.

HOW WE GOT OUR BIBLE

The Bible is the most detailed revelation of God and His wonderful plan for the future of mankind. There are other ways He has revealed Himself—through the heavens, through the Lord Jesus Christ, and through the power of the cross to change lives today—but the most detailed revelation He has given is the Bible itself. This amazing book was compiled in the most unusual manner of any book ever written. God the Holy Spirit inspired over 40 holy men, mostly prophets, to write the 66 books in this library of God. It contains what we need to know about salvation, how to live the Christian life, the nature and plan of God, the second coming of Christ, and the end times.

No other book has ever been so loved or so hated. The Bible has been loved by multitudes through the years, many of whom have had a life-changing experience reading, studying, and following its timeless principles for living. It has been hated by atheists, freethinkers, and other secularists who start their belief system assuming there is no God. If there is no God, then there is no divine inspiration.

Never mind that they cannot explain the remarkable accuracy and consistency of the Bible, which was written over a 1500-year period, for the most part by ordinary men. It has been the subject of more persecution and book burning than any book in history, yet it is the all-time bestselling book in history. It is also the only reliable source of prophecy. In fact, the ability of God to write history in advance, which is the definition of prophecy, is one of the proofs of the divine origin of Scripture. Dr. John Walvoord, the dean of prophecy scholars in the twentieth century, has identified 1000 prophecies in Scripture, 500 of which have been fulfilled literally. The obvious conclusion is that the 500 yet to be fulfilled, which deal with future end-time events, will also be fulfilled literally.

Since the Bible is the source of all the prophecies described in this chart book, it's important to understand how the Bible came to be, how it was preserved through the centuries, and how we can be confident that it is the same revelation God gave to man thousands of years ago when it was first written.

AN OVERVIEW OF THE BIBLE

The Bible has two major sections: the Old Testament and the New Testament. Let's look first at the Old Testament.

The Old Testament

There are five basic categories of books in the Old Testament:

1. Law . . . . 5 books—Genesis to Deuteronomy
2. History . . . . 12 books—Joshua to Esther
3. Poetry . . . . 5 books—Job to Song of Solomon
4. Major Prophets . . . 5 books—Isaiah to Daniel
5. Minor Prophets . . 12 books—Hosea to Malachi

The account of God, creation, man, his origin and fall, the Flood, and the earliest civilizations is presented simply and clearly in the 50 chapters of Genesis, the first book of the Bible, which has been a prime target of critics for years. Their greatest attack has been on the authorship of Genesis, saying, "Moses was too far removed from the original events to speak accurately." These objections dissolve when we understand that "all Scripture is given by inspiration of God" (2 Timothy 3:16 KJV) and it was God who wrote the book through Moses. Since archaeological discoveries have indicated that "writing is as old as man," it is highly probable that Moses had received written accounts of many of these events from those who actually participated in them.

The other 38 books of the Old Testament were written during or just after the time they describe. God selected men from various walks of life through whom He "breathed" His Word. Among the writers were priests, prophets, herdsmen, kings, and judges. All worked faithfully, largely without ever having met the others, and yet the whole Bible is one consistent, unique message of salvation. Due to the passage of time and the primitive or fragile writing materials of clay, papyrus, or leather, we do not have the original writings produced by these men, but we do have numerous ancient copies of these writings that are considered extremely reliable. The accuracy of the Bible's text has been significantly confirmed by the Dead Sea scrolls, which, when compared to our Bibles today, reveal a near-perfect match.

The word *canon*, which means "measuring rod" or "rule," is the title given to those religious writings that have met the exacting standards required for inclusion in the Old Testament. The work of canonizing the Old Testament was done during the days of Nehemiah, Haggai, Zechariah, and Malachi. After Israel's captivity in Babylon, a council of 120 men was formed, with Ezra as its president, for the purpose of reconstructing the worship and religious life of the people after their return from Babylon. It's possible that this group of spiritual leaders, or certainly their successors, brought together the many religious writings that now comprise the Old Testament. Josephus, a noted Jewish historian, mentions 22 books which this group believed to be divine, and he listed those books. It is significant that the list corresponds exactly with the Old Testament in today's Bibles—our 39 books are exactly the same in content as their 22 books! (back then, they combined several books, such as 1 and 2 Kings).

Before a book could be included in the Old Testament, the canonizers asked, "Is it divinely inspired?" "Was it written by a prophet or spokesman for God?" "Is it genuine, and can it be traced back to the time and place as well as the writer?" It's worthwhile to note that Jesus and the apostles quoted from the Old Testament over 600 times, indicating their approval of the selected texts. It is with utmost confidence, then, that we can accept the Old Testament as God's divinely inspired Word.

Between the Testaments

The first translation of the Hebrew Old Testament into another language was called the *Septuagint*. Seventy scholars were brought to Alexandria, Egypt, to create this Greek translation (hence the name the *Septuagint*, or LXX, or 70). The work began around 280 B.C. and was completed about 100 years later. This work is significant to us because it proves the Old Testament was canonized by this time. It is also important because its agreement with the original Hebrew text shows that the translators took great care to create an accurate work.

When our modern-day Bibles are compared with the ancient Hebrew texts and the Greek Septuagint and Greek texts, very few differences are found, which suggests the Bible has been accurately preserved like no other ancient book.

The *Apocrypha* is the title given to 14 books that are included in the Roman Catholic Bible. These books were written in the era between the Old Testament and the New Testament. They contain fanciful stories and contradictory statements that immediately reveal that they are not on the same par as Scripture. They have never been accepted by the Jews as inspired writ, were not quoted by Jesus nor any of the apostles, and were not recognized by the early church. They were "slipped in" with a translation of the Greek Septuagint during the fourth century A.D. and were recognized by the Catholic church at the Council of Trent in 1546. They have never been accepted by the Protestant church.

> It has been the subject of more persecution and book burning than any other book in history, yet it is the all-time bestselling book.

The New Testament

The New Testament is not arranged chronologically. Our chart on pages 20–21 lists the 27 books as they were written, beginning with James about A.D. 50.

The New Testament is divided into five sections:

1. The Gospels . . . . . 4 books—Matthew, Mark, Luke, and John
2. The History of the Early Church . . 1 book—Acts
3. Paul's Epistles . . . . . 14 books—Romans to Hebrews
4. General Epistles . . . 7 books—James to Jude
5. Prophecy . . . . 1 book—Revelation

THE NEW TESTAMENT'S AUTHORITY

From the start, the early church used the Old Testament in their services with the same authority as did the Jews in their synagogues. As the New Testament books were completed, they were given the same respect as the prophets or Moses and were used right along with the Old Testament Scripture. In fact, in 1 Timothy 5:18, the apostle Paul quotes from Luke 10:7, citing it as "Scripture." He evidently regarded Luke's Gospel as Scripture before he wrote his great message on biblical inspiration in 2 Timothy 3:16. In 2 Peter 3:1-2, the apostle Peter placed his and the other apostles' writings on par with those of the Old Testament prophets. He also showed in 2 Peter 3:15-16 that he was familiar with Paul's writings and regarded them with the same degree of authority reserved for the Old Testament writers. This seems to be the common perspective of all the early church leaders.

THE ORIGINAL NEW TESTAMENT MANUSCRIPTS

The original manuscripts of the New Testament books were written on papyrus, which is the name of an aquatic plant in Egypt. The manuscript material came from this plant, and its fragile nature made it difficult for these manuscripts to survive. During the fourth century, vellum came into use, a much-improved writing material. There are several copies of the New Testament from this era that have survived through today.

ANCIENT TRANSLATIONS OF THE NEW TESTAMENT

The New Testament was originally written in Greek, and the work of translating it into other languages began early.

The Peshito or Syriac translation was written in Syrochaldaic, or Aramaic. Translated before A.D. 150, it has always been regarded with utmost respect and became the official Scriptures of the Eastern churches. From it, translations have been made into Arabic, Persian, and Armenian.

The Latin Vulgate, translated by Jerome in the fourth century, became the Bible of the Western churches and, for more than 1000 years, was the chief source of nearly every version of the Scriptures made in the West.

There are two important facts confirmed by these ancient translations: One, the New Testament was completed by the second century; and two, the authenticity of our New Testament can be traced back to within 100 years or less of the apostles. Even the book of the Revelation, written by John on Patmos in A.D. 95, was given instant acceptance by the early church as the fitting conclusion to the library of God.

Hundreds of other manuscripts—both versions and translations written into still other languages—appeared during the second and third centuries. These were destroyed by the Roman emperors, particularly Diocletian, who ordered the destruction of the sacred writings of the Christians.

When Emperor Constantine professed Christianity in A.D. 312, he authorized Eusebius, known as the father of church history, to prepare 50 copies of the Scriptures to be used in the churches. The question naturally arose: Which religious books are regarded to be Scripture? Through his research the answer become obvious: the 27 books of the New Testament, because they had been universally accepted since the earliest days of the church. Constantine also found that the books about which there had been some questions did not seem to be such that they should be omitted, for usage had long established their being recognized as inspired Scripture along with the other books. The tests of canonicity were much the same as they were for the Old Testament: Was this written by an apostle or a close associate of an apostle? Does it agree with the doctrine of the Lord and His apostles? Is it genuine in regards to facts, the date of writing, and the author? And, was it accepted for use in the early church? The 27 New Testament books we use today were formally ratified by the Council of Carthage in A.D. 397, which only recognized the books that had already been used by the church for over three centuries.

THE ANCIENT MANUSCRIPTS OF THE BIBLE

The most ancient existing manuscripts of the entire Bible are shown on the "How We Got Our Bible" chart. They comprise only a fraction of those in existence. It has been stated by scholars that we have more than 4000 Greek manuscripts of the New Testament, 8000 of the Latin Vulgate, and at least 1000 of other ancient versions. Add those up, and we have more than 13,000 manuscripts of all or parts of the New Testament, not to mention the 1700 fragments of the Hebrew Old Testament and the 350 copies of the Greek Septuagint.

No other ancient document comes even close to having such numbers back up its authenticity.

Sinaitic Manuscript—A.D. 340

This manuscript, written in Greek, is now in the British Museum. In 1844, Dr. Constantin Tischendorf discovered this manuscript by accident in the Monastery of St. Catherine at Mount Sinai. He saw some pages of it in the hall waiting to be used to light the monastery fires and recognized they might have significance, so he rescued them. Eventually the manuscript was given to the Czar of Russia and, after the Revolution of 1917, it was sold to the British Museum for the sum of $500,000.

Vatican Manuscript—A.D. 350

This manuscript, written in Greek, is in the Vatican Library in Rome, Italy. Revealed for the first time in a Vatican Library catalog in 1481, it was not opened to the public until after Tregelles, a

How We Got Our Bible

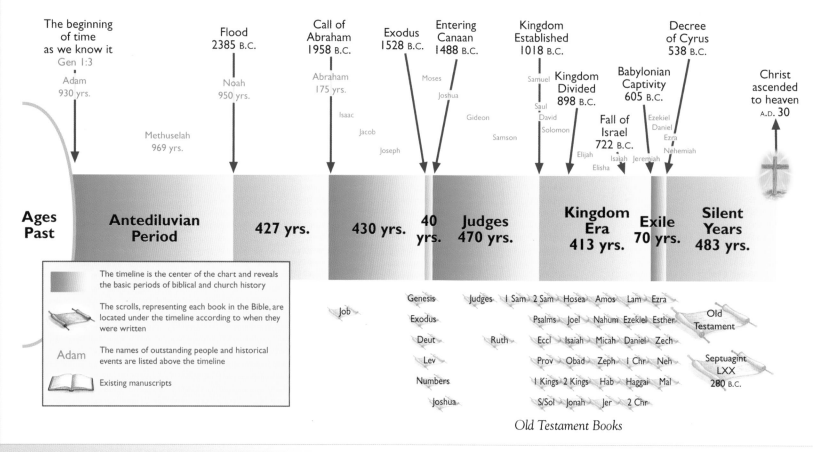

The beginning of time as we know it
Gen 1:3
Adam
930 yrs.

Flood
2385 B.C.

Noah
950 yrs.

Methuselah
969 yrs.

Call of Abraham
1958 B.C.

Abraham
175 yrs.

Isaac

Jacob

Joseph

Exodus
1528 B.C.

Entering Canaan
1488 B.C.

Moses

Joshua

Gideon

Samson

Kingdom Established
1018 B.C.

Samuel

Saul

David

Solomon

Kingdom Divided
898 B.C.

Fall of Israel
722 B.C.

Elijah

Elisha

Isaiah Jeremiah

Babylonian Captivity
605 B.C.

Ezekiel
Daniel
Ezra
Nehemiah

Decree of Cyrus
538 B.C.

Christ ascended to heaven
A.D. 30

Ages Past

Antediluvian Period

427 yrs.

430 yrs.

40 yrs.

Judges 470 yrs.

Kingdom Era 413 yrs.

Exile 70 yrs.

Silent Years 483 yrs.

The timeline is the center of the chart and reveals the basic periods of biblical and church history

The scrolls, representing each book in the Bible, are located under the timeline according to when they were written

Adam — The names of outstanding people and historical events are listed above the timeline

Existing manuscripts

Job

Genesis   Judges   1 Sam 2 Sam Hosea Amos Lam Ezra
Exodus   Psalms Joel Nahum Ezekiel Esther
Deut   Ruth   Eccl Isaiah Micah Daniel Zech
Lev   Prov Obad Zeph 1 Chr Neh
Numbers   1 Kings 2 Kings Hab Haggai Mal
Joshua   S/Sol Jonah Jer 2 Chr

Old Testament

Septuagint LXX
280 B.C.

Old Testament Books

---

famous English biblical scholar, was permitted to study it for several days. He revealed that he had memorized it and could reproduce it. Then the pope, in 1889, permitted it to be photographed and released to the libraries of the world.

Alexandrian Manuscript—A.D. 450

This was written in Greek, probably in Alexandria, Egypt. It is currently in the British Museum. It was presented to King James I of England in 1627.

Ephraem Manuscript—A.D. 450

Written in Greek and located in the National Library of Paris, France, this manuscript is thought to have been written in Alexandria. It was scrubbed clear by someone who did not recognize its worth, and the discourses of Ephraem, a Syrian father of the fourth century, were copied on it. It was given to the French Library in Paris, where a student noticed the faint writings underneath the Syrian text. Later, chemicals were applied that helped bring out much of the original writing.

From this point onward in time, we have many other Bible manuscripts, including the Beza Manuscript of A.D. 550, which is in the Cambridge University Library, Cambridge, England. The Claromontanus Manuscript (A.D. 550) is in the National Library of Paris. The Washington Manuscript (A.D. 550) is now

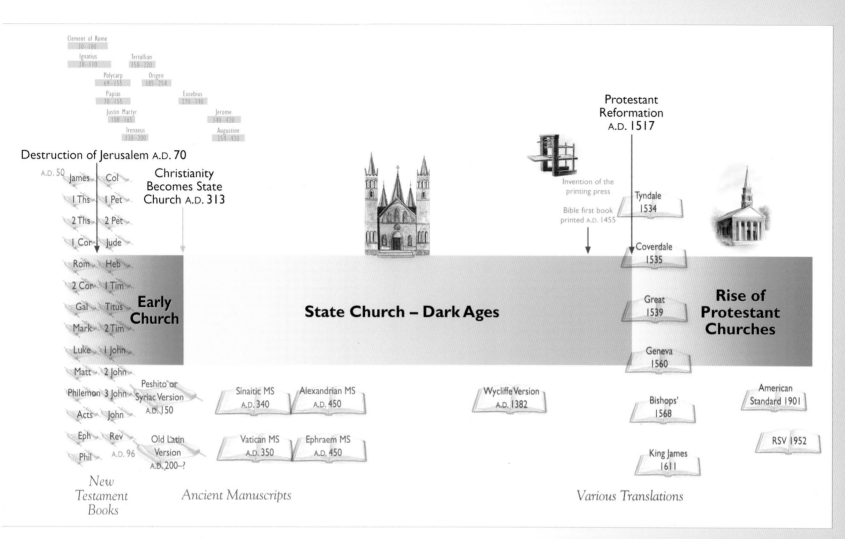

Clement of Rome 30–100
Ignatius 30–110
Tertullian 150–220
Polycarp 69–155
Origen 185–254
Papias 70–155
Eusebius 270–340
Justin Martyr 100–165
Jerome 340–420
Irenaeus 130–200
Augustine 354–430

Protestant
Reformation
A.D. 1517

Destruction of Jerusalem A.D. 70

A.D. 50

James Col
1 Ths 1 Pet
2 Ths 2 Pet
1 Cor Jude
Rom Heb
2 Cor 1 Tim
Gal Titus
Mark 2 Tim
Luke 1 John
Matt 2 John
Philemon 3 John
Acts John
Eph Rev
Phil A.D. 96

Christianity
Becomes State
Church A.D. 313

Early Church

State Church – Dark Ages

Rise of Protestant Churches

Invention of the printing press

Bible first book printed A.D. 1455

Tyndale 1534

Coverdale 1535

Great 1539

Geneva 1560

Peshito or Syriac Version A.D. 150

Old Latin Version A.D. 200–?

Sinaitic MS A.D. 340

Alexandrian MS A.D. 450

Vatican MS A.D. 350

Ephraem MS A.D. 450

Wycliffe Version A.D. 1382

Bishops' 1568

King James 1611

American Standard 1901

RSV 1952

New Testament Books

Ancient Manuscripts

Various Translations

in the National Library, Washington, D.C.

The writings of the early church fathers comprise a great bridge between the ancient manuscripts and the original New Testament writings. These men were the earliest leaders of the Christian church after the days of the apostles. Some of the most important are listed on the chart along with the time they lived. For the most part they were well-educated men and voluminous writers. They quote repeatedly from the New Testament—for example, Clement referred to Matthew, Luke, Romans, Corinthians, Hebrews, 1 Timothy, and 1 Peter. Ignatius referred to the Gospels as "the word of Jesus." Polycarp, a disciple of the apostle John, in a very short letter that takes only ten minutes to read, quoted from two-thirds of the books in the New Testament. Irenaeus

quoted from the New Testament 1800 times, and Tertullian did the same 7200 times. In fact, even though only a small percentage of the writings of the early church fathers have survived to the present day, they still contain all but 11 verses of the New Testament. This indicates that we can trace the actual words of the New Testament to within a very few years of the original manuscripts.

VARIOUS TRANSLATIONS OF THE BIBLE

Latin Vulgate—A.D. 450

Translated by Jerome from Hebrew, Greek, and Latin manuscripts.

Wycliffe's Version—1382

John Wycliffe was the first person to translate the Bible into English. He is called "The Morning Star of the Reformation."

Coverdale Bible—1535

Translated by Miles Coverdale, this is the first version that was printed in English.

Geneva Bible—1560

This version is the work of William Whittingham, who was the first to use the verse and chapter divisions found in our modern-day Bibles.

The King James Version—1611

After King Henry VIII severed his country's ties with the Catholic church, a need arose for an English version of the Bible that could be used in the Protestant churches. On July 22, 1604, King James I announced that he had appointed 54 men as translators, the only qualification being that they should be "proficient as Bible scholars." The translation work was the most thorough ever done up to that date. Six different groups of scholars would first translate a given section of the Scripture, and then their translation was examined by the five other groups. A committee of six was selected from all the translators to be the final authority in translation matters.

The King James Version stood for many years in a class by itself. Its smooth-flowing older-style language, based heavily on Wycliffe's 1382 version, gave it a majestic note not shared by any other translation up to that time. Up through the latter half of the twentieth century, it was the most popular English Bible version available. We do not possess the manuscripts from which the King James Version was translated, but the ancient manuscripts that have been discovered since 1611 verify its accuracy and reliability.

The American Standard Version—1901

This Bible is a revision of the English Revised Version of 1895, which was a very thorough translation itself. The ASV is regarded by conservative Bible scholars as the most reliable and best translation available today. Since its translation it has been updated and retitled the New American Standard Bible, and it is the version many Greek scholars choose because they believe it comes the closest to the original languages.

Many Modern Translations—1950 to 2000

The last half of the twentieth century saw such a proliferation of English translations that there are too many to mention here—including the New King James Version (NKJV), the New International Version (NIV), and an extremely popular paraphrase called The Living Bible, an easy-to-read text that has sold many millions of copies.

It is significant that the prophecies we discuss in this book all come from the most reliably authentic book in the world. It was written by God through "holy men of old" and preserved supernaturally. So many of the prophecies in the Bible have already been fulfilled that the only feasible explanation for this accuracy is that the prophecies were inspired by God, which makes them a reliable resource for understanding the future.

6.
THE FOUR PIVOTAL EVENTS OF HISTORY

On the timeline of human history, there are four pivotal events that stand out and shine above everything else because of the tremendous impact they have had or will have on the world. Each of these most significant events in history has marked or will mark the end of an age or era of time. The first three events are the creation, the Flood, and the first coming of Christ, including His death and resurrection. The fourth event is Jesus' second coming. While many important events have taken place in history, none are of equal significance to these four.

Much of what we read in the Bible has to do with the history of man on earth. The Bible says very little about ages past or the ages to come. Nearly 50 percent of the Bible's 66 books cover man's history, 25 percent of the Bible contains instructions on how God wants us to live, and 28 percent of the Bible is prophecy, some of which has already been fulfilled.

FOUR EVENTS

It's interesting to note that each of the four pivotal events is part of a titanic conflict between God and Satan for the devotion of mankind. The first three events made a significant impact on the generations that followed. The fourth event, Christ's return, will do the same.

The first two chapters of Genesis highlight the creation of

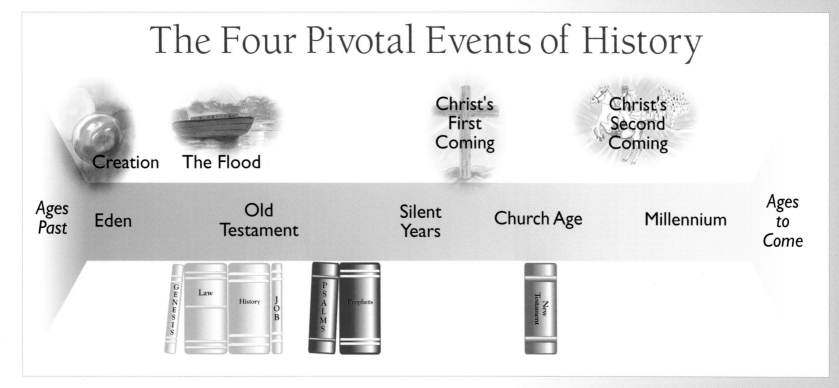

The Four Pivotal Events of History

Creation   The Flood   Christ's First Coming   Christ's Second Coming

Ages Past | Eden | Old Testament | Silent Years | Church Age | Millennium | Ages to Come

GENESIS | Law | History | JOB | PSALMS | Prophets | New Testament

Adam and Eve, who were composed of not only a body and mind but also an eternal soul. Right after creation, we have the fall, or the sin of Adam and Eve. They were created holy but were given a free will with which to choose to obey or disobey God. Their disobedience plunged the world into sin and corruption, and over the next 1000 years, the world became so corrupt that God used the Flood to destroy everyone except Noah and his family—a total of eight souls.

The worldwide flood, covered in detail in Genesis 8, is also mentioned in the literature of the various peoples of the ancient world. Some researchers have also found physical evidence of this flood—evidence that refutes some of what is advocated in the theory of evolution.

The third pivotal event was Christ's death on the cross. The cross, which is easily the most famous and recognized symbol in the world, speaks of more than just Christ's death. It also points to His sinless life and more importantly His resurrection, which has made our salvation possible. When Jesus gave Himself to die on the cross for the sins of the whole world, He ended the age of law and introduced the age of God's dealing with man in grace. That age will end with the next pivotal event, the second coming of Jesus Christ.

The second coming, and the many lesser events leading up to and following it, is primarily what prophecy is all about. It is doubtless the greatest story of the future to be found anywhere in our world. No religion, no culture, and no literature offers anything comparable. In fact, the Bible's teachings about the future have inspired many to turn from their sins to find Christ as their Lord and Savior.

This basic timeline of human history—with its four pivotal events—forms the basic skeleton upon which we will build many of the other charts in this book. Thus you'll want to remember these pivotal events and their significance. This timeline will be mentioned elsewhere in this book when introducing the many prophetic passages of Scripture that fill in the details of the future. It is most helpful to relate all prophetic teachings to this skeletal chart.

7.
THE ABSOLUTE CERTAINTY OF CHRIST'S RETURN

The most significant single truth in all biblical prophecy is the certainty of the second coming of Jesus Christ. And it well should be because His second coming is mentioned 329 times in the Bible, making it the second most frequently mentioned doctrine in all of Scripture. This event is the prophetic key that unlocks all other future events. It fulfills prophecies in both the Old and New Testaments, including many of Christ's own prophecies; it completes His work of salvation begun during His first coming; and it begins a chain of more than 15 events that will take place in the future. Yet the timing of His return is unknown, for Jesus said, "Of that day and hour no one knows, not even the angels of heaven, nor the Son, but the Father alone" (Matthew 24:36). Although we may speculate on the time when our Lord will reappear, absolutely no question exists that He *will* come again!

Before our Lord left the world, He gave an unconditional promise to His followers: "I will come again" (John 14:3). There is no way that promise can be set aside or explained away. Even if some ingenious scholar could make that promise mean something else, it is

The Certainty of the Second Coming

Matthew | Mark | Luke | John | Acts | Romans | 1 Corinthians | 2 Corinthians | Galatians | Ephesians | Philippians | Colossians | 1 Thessalonians | 2 Thessalonians | 1 Timothy | 2 Timothy | Titus | Philemon | Hebrews | James | 1 Peter | 2 Peter | 1 John | 2 John | 3 John | Jude | Revelation

All but four of the New Testament books contain teachings on the second coming of Jesus Christ. Three of those four are single-chapter letters.

repeated so many ways that it cannot be dismissed or nullified.

CHRIST'S COMING: A KEY DOCTRINE

If the value of a teaching were to be judged by the frequency of its mention, then the second coming of Christ would easily rank as one of the most important doctrines in the Bible. Only the subject of salvation is mentioned more frequently. The 216 chapters of the New Testament contain 318 references to the Lord's second coming, which means that one verse out of every 30 verses states this fact.

After the doctrine of salvation by grace through faith, the second coming of Jesus was the next most popular doctrine of the church for over 300 years. Note the chart "The Certainty of the Second Coming." Almost all the New Testament books contain teachings on the second coming, and three of the four books that don't mention Jesus' return were single-chapter letters to individuals.

That the second- and third-century church lived by and taught the second coming is seen in the fact that it was the driving force that produced sanctification, evangelism, and world missions—to the point that the early Christians turned the world upside down.

Christianity was so pervasive that Constantine made it the state religion in A.D. 313.

CHRIST'S COMING: A DOCTRINAL NECESSITY

Several key doctrines in the Bible are absolutely dependent on the coming again of Christ. For example, the doctrine concerning the resurrection of the human body cannot be fulfilled until Christ comes (1 Corinthians 15:53). The victory of Christ over Satan, as promised many times, beginning with Genesis 3:15, will not be completed until He comes again. And the most important doctrine in all the Scriptures, the one upon which all others depend, is the deity of Jesus Christ. He promised so many times to return that there is simply no way to vindicate His divine nature if He does not come again. God cannot lie or deceive. If Jesus does not come again, He will be guilty of fraud, to say the least. But since that is so incompatible with His earthly life, His promises, and His divine nature, it is beyond possibility. The fact remains that He said, "I will come again" (John

14:3). The second coming of Christ is not only certain, it is a doctrinal necessity.

What's remarkable is that 23 of the 27 books of the New Testament refer to our Lord's coming to earth again. Of the four books that don't—Philemon, 2 and 3 John, and Galatians—the reader should understand that three are single-chapter letters originally written to a particular person about a subject not involved with the second coming. And the fourth book, Galatians, does not specifically refer to Christ's return, although an implied reference to the event appears in 1:4.

The sheer weight of evidence leads to the conclusion that if one believes the Bible, he must believe in the second coming of Christ. Not only was the promise of our Lord's return a universal conviction and motivating factor of the early church, but all nine authors of the New Testament Scriptures mentioned it. Since they universally accepted so literally our Lord's promise, "I will come again," can we do less?

8.
THE MOUNTAIN PEAKS OF PROPHECY

There are some Old Testament prophecies that are difficult to understand because they contain, within one prophecy, information relevant to both comings of Christ. The Old Testament prophets did not see the long church age separating the two comings. More specifically, they did not see the two comings with clear understanding. In 1 Corinthians 2:9 Paul quoted Isaiah, who admitted he did not understand all that God had in store for mankind. Then Paul added, "But God hath revealed them unto us by his Spirit" (verse 10 KJV). Thus New Testament prophecies often clarify the end-times prophecies of the Old Testament. And that is why they should be studied together, as we do in this book.

The fact that the two comings of Messiah were inadvertently perceived as one event explains why so many Jews did not accept Jesus as their Messiah. They took Jesus' promises to overcome the world (promises that apply to His second coming) and applied those promises to His first coming. Thus the major reason many people rejected Jesus was not because He was not the most incredible miracle worker ever or the greatest teacher ever. It was because He had not thrown off the shackles of the Roman dictators. They wanted Him to free Israel, yet did not realize the prophecies related to His future kingdom would be fulfilled at His second coming, and not His first. He came instead to suffer for their sins, die on the cross, and rise again—without which there would be no forgiveness of sins or eternal life.

For example, Isaiah wrote, "For unto us a child is born, unto us a son is given: and the government shall be upon his shoulder: and

his name shall be called Wonderful, Counselor, the mighty God, the everlasting Father, the Prince of Peace. Of the increase of his government and peace there shall be no end, upon the throne of David, and upon his kingdom, to order it, and to establish it with judgment and with justice from henceforth even for ever" (Isaiah 9:6-7 KJV). He didn't realize two separate comings were described in those words. We who live in the church age have the benefit of looking back and seeing that some prophecies were fulfilled in Christ's first coming, and others won't be fulfilled until His second coming.

If we see the key prophecies of Jesus' two comings as mountain tops and other events like the church age and the Tribulation period as valleys, then much of what we read in Bible prophecy becomes clearer.

The importance of a chart locating the mountaintops of prophecy and history is made clear in a classic book written by

The Mountain Peaks of Prophecy

Our Viewpoint
We see the "Mountain Peaks" and the "Valleys" from the side, and we can separate the first- and second-coming prophecies.

Priest
Heb 4:14

The Three Appearings

"Now to Appear"

"Hath Appeared"

Glory
Heb 9:24

"Shall Appear"

The Holy City
Rev 21:2

Birth of Jesus
(Bethlehem)
Num 24:17;
Isa 7:14; Mic 5:2

Calvary
Isa 53:1-12

Antichrist
Dan 7:19-27

The Sun of
Righteousness
Mal 4:1-6

The
Kingdom
Dan 7:13-14
Isa 2:1-3
Mic 4:1-2
Hag 2:5-9

Destruction
of the Earth
by Fire
2 Pet 3:7-13

What the
Prophets Saw

The New
Heavens and
New Earth
Isa 65:17; 66:22;
Rev 21:1

The Old Testament
"Valley"—
The viewpoint
of the prophets

The Valley of the Church—
The prophets did not see this

The Valley of
the "Perfect Age"

Clarence Larkin:

...the prophet saw in a direct line along the "Peaks of Prophecy" and did not see the "Valley of the Church" in between. Our viewpoint is from the side. We face the "Valley" with the "First Advent" (the cross) to our left, and the "Second Advent" (the crown) to our right. All we have to do is to separate the prophecies of the "First Advent" from the prophetic references to Christ in the Old Testament, and apply the balance to His "Second Advent." This simplifies the study of prophecy.[3]

Isaiah's prophecies focus mainly on the Messiah and Israel. Jeremiah proclaimed Israel's return to their own land. Ezekiel spoke of the restoration of Israel to their own land as well as the Millennial land, the restored Temple, and the form of worship in that time. Daniel prophesied about the Gentiles and their final great leader, the Antichrist. Zechariah was most concerned about the events that will take place at the second coming of Christ:

Antichrist (the idol shepherd)—Zechariah 11:15-17
Armageddon—Zechariah 14:1-3
Conversion of Israel—Zechariah 12:9-14

Christ's return to Olivet—Zechariah 14:4-11
Old age in Jerusalem—Zechariah 8:3-8
Feast of Tabernacles—Zechariah 14:16-21

Notice that Zechariah does not see these events in their chronological order. All the major prophets and nine of the minor prophets emphasize the kingship of Christ in their prophecies. That's what confused the religious leaders of Christ's day. But today, in hindsight, we can separate the prophecies of the first coming from those of the second coming. That is appreciated most when you study the prophecies in the light of the above chart. This understanding will help you to become "a workman that needeth not to be ashamed, rightly dividing the word of truth" (2 Timothy 2:15 KJV) about the prophetic future.

9.
ISAIAH'S OUTLINE OF THE MESSIAH'S MINISTRY

This prophecy of the ministry of the Messiah, Jesus Christ, is one of the most significant prophecies in the Bible, for it outlines in advance His entire ministry. It mentions both His first and second comings, separated by a period of tribulation called the "day of vengeance of our God" and followed by His Millennial reign over the earth.

UNDERSTANDING ISAIAH 61

The prophet Isaiah, under the inspiration of the Holy Spirit (2 Peter 1:21), impersonated the Messiah in the first three verses. This is evidenced by his use of the personal pronouns "I" and "me" within a prediction that describes things no human could accomplish. As we will see, Jesus fulfilled all of the predicted events in His first coming and will fulfill the rest in His second coming. We need to keep in mind that the first coming of Jesus did not fulfill the entirety of God's wonderful plan for mankind. Instead, it accomplished the work of providing salvation to mankind through Jesus' death and resurrection. The second coming will finish God's plan, which is to bring His people into His kingdom and His eternal heaven.

During Jesus' first coming, the Holy Spirit was to come upon Jesus after His baptism by John. Afterward, Jesus would preach, heal, and "proclaim liberty to the captives" (Isaiah 61:1 KJV). Jesus is still considered the greatest teacher and preacher who ever lived, and He is the greatest healer in the history of the world. His works were a testimony that He had been sent by God (John 5:36). Just before His ascension to heaven, He descended into Sheol to "set the captives free" (Ephesians 4:9-10). (See chart "Where the Dead Are Now" on page 132.)

The phrase "proclaim the acceptable year of the Lord" (KJV) refers to the fulfillment of Jesus' prophecy in Matthew 16:18-19 to build His church, which would be victorious over "the gates of Hades." The church age began on the day of Pentecost and will extend until the Rapture of the church from the earth.

Proclaiming "liberty to the captives" (Isaiah 61:1 KJV) is thought by some Bible teachers to refer to the gift of salvation that is offered freely to mankind during this present church age. This could well be true, which is why we refer to this present period as the age of grace. Others believe it has reference to the Old Testament saints delivered from Sheol, for their sins had only been covered by the blood of animals. They were not yet "cleansed" and

Isaiah's Outline of the Messiah's Ministry

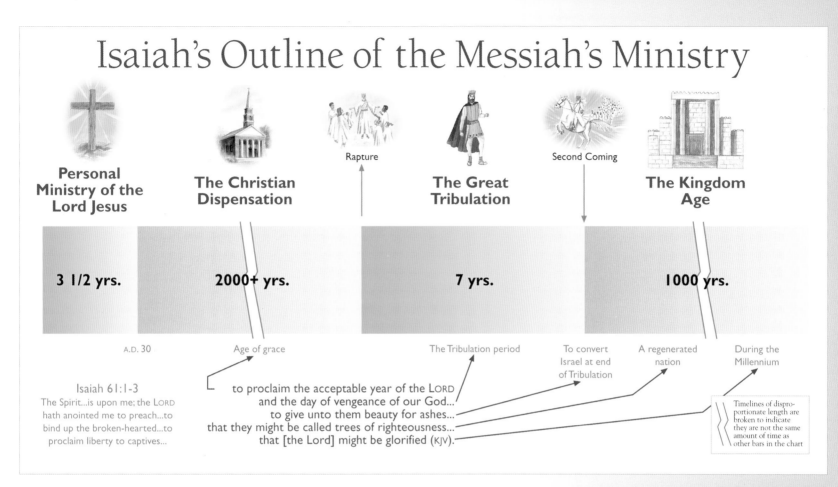

Personal Ministry of the Lord Jesus	The Christian Dispensation	Rapture	The Great Tribulation	Second Coming	The Kingdom Age
3 1/2 yrs.	2000+ yrs.		7 yrs.		1000 yrs.
A.D. 30	Age of grace		The Tribulation period	To convert Israel at end of Tribulation	A regenerated nation · During the Millennium

Isaiah 61:1-3
The Spirit...is upon me; the LORD hath anointed me to preach...to bind up the broken-hearted...to proclaim liberty to captives...

to proclaim the acceptable year of the LORD
and the day of vengeance of our God...
to give unto them beauty for ashes...
that they might be called trees of righteousness...
that [the Lord] might be glorified (KJV).

Timelines of disproportionate length are broken to indicate they are not the same amount of time as other bars in the chart

---

thus eligible for heaven until Christ finished the work of salvation by the sacrifice of Himself on the cross. From the time of the cross onward, spiritual captives in bondage to sin have been delivered by repenting of their sins and receiving Him, by faith, as their personal Lord and Savior. Thus they are eligible for heaven at death.

JESUS' CLAIM TO BE THE MESSIAH—LUKE 4

It is impossible to exaggerate the importance of Jesus' claim to be the Messiah, for it proves beyond all doubt the validity of using Old Testament Messianic prophecies to prove His identity. And Jesus clearly stated this claim in Luke 4:16-30, where He quotes from Isaiah 61 while visiting a synagogue.

As was His custom, Jesus entered the synagogue in His hometown of Nazareth on the Sabbath day. When He stood up to read,

He read from Isaiah 61. He read only verses 1 and 2, ending with the words "to preach the acceptable year of the LORD," a reference to the church age. Then He closed the book of Isaiah and said, *"Today this scripture is fulfilled in your hearing"* (Luke 4:21) and sat down. In saying that, Jesus was claiming He was the fulfillment of Isaiah's Messianic prophecy. This phenomenal statement, which officially launched His three-and-a-half-year ministry, would have been blasphemous if He were not the Son of God and the Messiah the Jews had looked for ever since the days of the prophet Moses 1500 years earlier. The townspeople of Nazareth, where Jesus had grown up, did not misunderstand what He was saying. They refused to believe His claim; they took Him to the edge of a cliff with the intent of pushing Him to His death. At that point they did not have sufficient evidence to believe He was the Messiah. The evidence, of course, was given during the next three-and-a-half years, during which Jesus fulfilled all of the 109 first-coming prophecies, including those having to do with His death and resurrection. Jesus was not just a man in history; He was indeed the fulfillment of all the Old Testament prophecies, and He made it clear that He recognized that fact.

Now, when Jesus read the prophecies about Himself in Isaiah 61, why did He stop at the beginning of verse 2? Because He was announcing the reasons for His first coming and because He was to "proclaim the acceptable year of the LORD" (KJV). That's a reference to the church age, often called the age of grace, a time when sinners can freely call on the name of the Lord to be saved (Romans 10:13). Jesus stopped at the words "and the day of vengeance of our God," which speaks of the Tribulation period, mentioned by the Hebrew prophets as "the day of wrath" and "the time of Jacob's trouble," and by Jeremiah as "a day of vengeance" (46:10). That's because the purpose of His first coming was to announce the period of grace and salvation we are living in, not the time of judgment that is yet to come.

Jesus had much to say about the church age but little about the Tribulation period. In Matthew 13 and some parallel passages, He outlined the whole dispensation of the church age in a series of parables. To premillennial scholars who take the Bible literally, including the prophecies, whenever possible, these parables are a pictorial presentation of the church age. They also bear an amazing parallel to the description of the church age found in Revelation 2–3. Jesus talked about the Tribulation in Matthew 24, but most of what we read about the Tribulation comes from the apostles Paul and John.

ISAIAH'S OUTLINE COMPARED WITH DANIEL'S 70 WEEKS

Daniel, another of the noted Hebrew prophets, wrote a panoramic overview of the time of the Gentiles. He did not have much to say about the church age, for his vision had to do with the governments of the Gentile nations, particularly those who would rule the world. Daniel also prophesied the time that the Messiah would first appear, and stated that He would be "cut off." This prophecy was fulfilled when Jesus was crucified.

As you study this chart in connection with the one on Daniel's 70 weeks of years on page 90, you will see that beginning with the decree to rebuild Jerusalem, 483 years would pass till the time of Messiah's death. In Daniel's prophecy of 70 weeks, each "week" means seven years, and because 69 weeks were to pass until "Messiah the Prince" (see Daniel 9:25 and Luke 19:28-38), that gives us 483 years. The seventieth week of years, or the final seven years, is the Tribulation period mentioned by Jesus, Paul, and John. Jesus predicted in Matthew 24:15 that the Temple would be desecrated during that seventieth week. The Temple will be rebuilt and then desecrated by the Antichrist at the midpoint of the Tribulation. He will set himself up as God and demand that the world worship him (2 Thessalonians 2:1-8).

The Tribulation period does not begin right after the Rapture, as many Christians think. According to Daniel 9:27, it will begin with Antichrist's signing of a covenant with Israel for seven years—a covenant that he breaks "in the midst of the week." This will begin the greatest time of trial the world has ever seen or ever will see, according to Jesus (Matthew 24:21). That persecution will target not only the Jews, but will include all believers in Christ. Those who are martyred will go in spirit to the presence of the Lord, awaiting the second phase of the resurrection (Revelation 20:4). Those who endure to the end (Matthew 24:13) will be delivered from the Tribulation by going directly into the Millennial kingdom.

10.
SATAN:
HIS PAST, PRESENT, AND FUTURE

Satan is not just an evil force or "principle of evil" as some believe. Rather, he is a supernatural being who leads a kingdom of fallen angels and demons. His presence and power in the world are so extensive that we would do well to understand how he works so we can protect ourselves from him. Peter said, "Be sober, be vigilant; because your adversary the devil, as a roaring lion, walketh about, seeking whom he may devour" (1 Peter 5:8 KJV). The names ascribed to him in the Bible describe him well: "Satan," "devil," "dragon," "the serpent," "your adversary," and, as our Lord called him, "a liar from the beginning." Anyone who does not understand that his major work is deception will likely be deceived by him, particularly as we approach the end of the age.

THE ORIGIN OF SATAN

No one knows for sure when Satan was created. But we can be sure of this: he is a created being. He may think he is God, but only God can create, and Satan is not God. Some Bible scholars believe he was created before the earth in ages past. However, Satan and the angels were likely created during the six days of creation.

Ezekiel gives this description of Satan:

You were in Eden, the garden of God...on the day that you were created.... You were the anointed cherub who covers.... You were on the holy mountain of God; you walked in the midst of the stones of fire. You were blameless in your ways from the day you were created until unrighteousness was found in you. By the abundance of your trade you were internally filled with violence, and you sinned; therefore I have cast you as profane from the mountain of God. And I have destroyed you, O covering cherub, from the midst of the stones of fire. Your heart was lifted up because of your beauty; you corrupted your wisdom by reason of your splendor. I cast you to the ground; I put you before kings, that they may see you (Ezekiel 28:13-17).

Evidently Satan was the most beautiful creature in heaven. He was placed in "the garden of God" (or the mineral garden of God, not to be confused with the Garden of Eden). His assignment was to be "the anointed cherub who covers." Many believe he commanded the angels before the throne of God. Still others believe he was given dominance over this earth, for he is called "the god of this world." He had a free will, beauty, and wisdom, but somehow evil arose in him. Instead of worshiping God he craved to be worshiped as God, and this led to his downfall:

How art thou fallen from heaven, O Lucifer, son of the morning! How art thou cut down to the ground, which didst weaken the nations! For thou hast said in thine heart: I will ascend into heaven, I will exalt my throne above the stars of God: I will sit also on the mount of the congregation, in the sides of the north: I will ascend above the heights of the clouds; I will be like the most High (Isaiah 14:12-14 KJV).

Even though Satan fell somewhere between Genesis chapters 2 and 3, he still has access in the heavenly realm (Job 1–2). In the middle of the Tribulation, he will be expelled from heaven and cast down to earth:

> There was war in heaven: Michael and his angels fought against the dragon; and the dragon fought and his angels, and prevailed not; neither was their place found any more in heaven. And the great dragon was cast out, that old serpent, called the Devil...he was cast out into the earth, and his angels were cast out with him (KJV).

From that time onward the conflict of the ages has raged between God and Satan for the souls of men. While we do not know exactly why God permitted this conflict, we do know how it will end. Christ will come again to establish His kingdom, and Satan will be bound in the bottomless pit for a thousand years (Revelation 19:11–20:7).

THE PRESENT WORK OF SATAN

Satan's desire is to get people to follow him instead of God. Just as he led one-third of the angels of heaven to follow him in rebellion, he has led billions of people on earth to do the same.

In the Garden of Eden

It was Satan who told Eve, "Has God said, 'You shall not eat from any tree of the garden?...You surely will not die!'" (Genesis 3:1,4). Satan caused Eve to question whether God keeps His word. Adam and Eve ate of the forbidden tree, bringing the first sin and its consequences into the world. Their sin was then passed on to their children and will continue on from them through all generations up to the end of the Millennial kingdom of Christ. It was Adam and Eve's sin that led God to promise to send a Savior (Genesis 3:15) for the sins of all mankind.

Polluting the Bloodline of Adam

In the days from Adam to the Flood (about 1000 years), during a time of rapid population growth, Satan attempted to pollute the pure bloodline of Adam. He did this by allowing the cohabitation of fallen angels with women whom they found appealing, and thus producing "Nephilim," or fallen ones, in an attempt to corrupt the "seed of the woman" and thwart the redemptive plan of God. We read about this in Genesis 6:1-4 and Jude 7, and this is likely the reason God resorted to the extreme measure of sending a flood to destroy the whole human race, with the exception of Noah's family. Through Noah's family God preserved the purity of the original bloodline of humans; the sin of mixing "strange flesh" with human flesh cannot happen again because God imprisoned these fallen angels in Tartarus (2 Peter 2:4-10).

Rebellion at the Tower of Babel

The Tower of Babel (Genesis 11:1-9) was a satanically inspired attempt to establish a universal, idolatrous religion in Babel, the largest city in the world in that day, and to keep mankind from worshiping the one true God. God brought an end to this by confounding their language, which caused the people to separate and scatter around the world.

The Temptation of Job

Evidently Satan has access to the throne of God on some occasions, as in the case of Job. We can take comfort in the fact that Satan cannot take a believer's life unless God permits, and that God will indeed give us grace and strength when we are tempted by Satan.

Attempting to Kill the Hebrew Race

When Satan recognized that the Messiah would come through the Hebrew race, he decided to destroy all Jews while they were confined in one place—Egypt. At the time of Moses' birth, Pharaoh ordered that all the male Hebrew babies be killed. Yet God brought deliverance through Moses, saving the Hebrew race and preserving the promised bloodline of the Messiah.

Attempting to Kill the Messiah

Satan launched an attack on the infant Jesus by having Herod kill all the babies in Bethlehem. But Joseph and Mary fled to Egypt, and didn't return until all danger was past. His subsequent temptations and attempts on Jesus' life failed as well, and Jesus was able to

Satan: His Past, Present, and Future

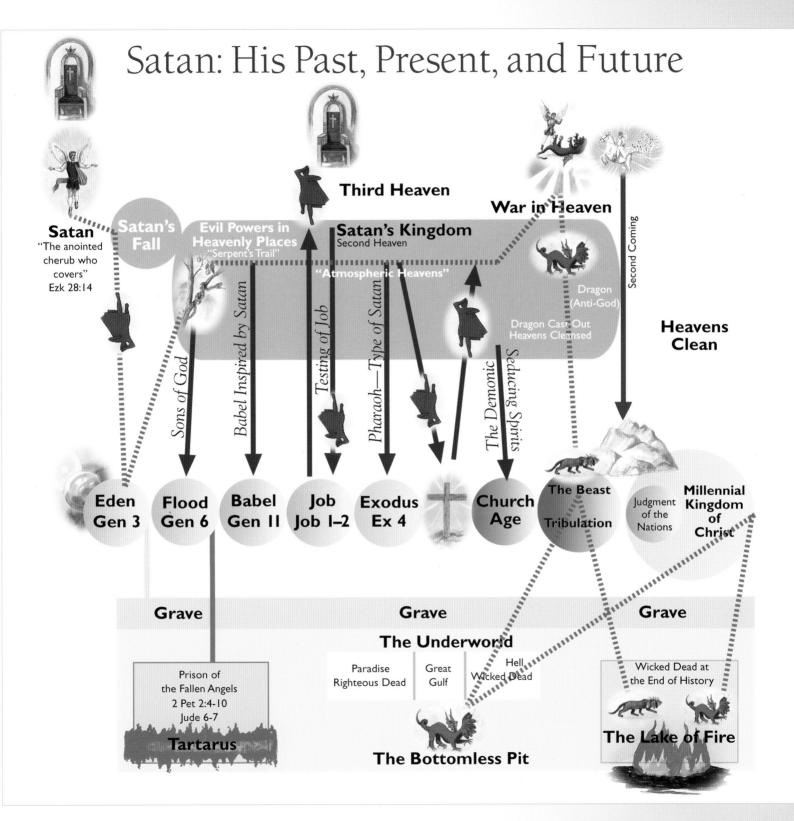

Third Heaven

War in Heaven

Satan
"The anointed cherub who covers"
Ezk 28:14

Satan's Fall

Evil Powers in Heavenly Places
"Serpent's Trail"

Satan's Kingdom
Second Heaven

"Atmospheric Heavens"

Second Coming

Dragon (Anti-God)

Dragon Cast Out
Heavens Cleansed

Heavens Clean

Sons of God

Babel Inspired by Satan

Testing of Job

Pharaoh—Type of Satan

The Demonic

Seducing Spirits

| Eden Gen 3 | Flood Gen 6 | Babel Gen 11 | Job Job 1–2 | Exodus Ex 4 | | Church Age | The Beast Tribulation | Judgment of the Nations | Millennial Kingdom of Christ |

Grave

Grave

Grave

The Underworld

| Paradise Righteous Dead | Great Gulf | Hell Wicked Dead |

Wicked Dead at the End of History

Prison of the Fallen Angels
2 Pet 2:4-10
Jude 6-7

Tartarus

The Bottomless Pit

The Lake of Fire

defeat Satan through His crucifixion and resurrection.

Attempting to Destroy the Church

Throughout church history Satan has busied himself trying to destroy the church. His two principal methods of attack have been persecution and false teaching. When it comes to persecution, no religious organization has been attacked as much as the church. One estimate is that 500 million believers have been martyred during the past 2000 years, yet the church is still the largest religious body in the world. As for false teachings, Satan attempts to deceive human beings into disbelieving God and doing their own thing. During the coming Tribulation period, Satan will use both persecution (Revelation 6:9-11) and false teachers (Matthew 24:23-26) in his endeavor to deceive people about God and Christ.

THE FUTURE OF SATAN

During the seven-year Tribulation, Satan will persecute the people of God unmercifully. Through many false teachers who perform signs and wonders, he will deceive millions on earth into worshiping him.

Satan knows and understands prophecy; therefore he knows that Christ will return again. But his extreme egotism causes him to think he can thwart Christ's coming. At the end of the Tribulation, Satan will bring the armies of the world together to do battle with Christ in what promises to be the greatest battle in the history of the world. After the battle, which Satan loses, he will be thrown into the "bottomless pit" where he will be "bound...a thousand years" so that he can "deceive the nations no more, till the thousand years should be fulfilled" (Revelation 20:1-3 KJV).

It is interesting that at this same time, God will throw the Antichrist and the false prophet immediately into "the lake of fire which burns with brimstone" (Revelation 19:20). The reason Satan won't suffer that same fate is that God won't be finished with him yet. At the end of the Millennial kingdom, Satan will be released one last time to deceive mankind and lead one last rebellion against God. After this final rebellion, Satan will be "cast into the lake of fire and brimstone, where the beast and the false prophet are" (Revelation 20:10 KJV). Notice they are still alive and suffering in that Lake of Fire after being there 1000 years. This proves that lost souls are not annihilated. Rather, they all will "be tormented day and night for ever and ever" (verse 10).

Many have wondered why God will allow Satan one more time to deceive the nations. If God did not do this, all the people who are born and live during the Millennial kingdom would be exempt from the decision to follow God or follow Satan. By releasing Satan one more time, all men are given equal standing before God. Indeed, because your eternal destiny is involved, the decision to either receive or reject Jesus the Christ is the most important decision you will make in your life.

11.
THE OLIVET DISCOURSE

The Olivet Discourse, delivered shortly before Jesus' crucifixion, is the most important single passage of prophecy in all the Bible. It is significant because it came from Jesus Himself immediately after He was rejected by His own people and because it provides the master outline of end-time events. Studied in relation to Daniel 2, 7, 8, and 9 and Revelation 2–20, it gives more information about the major events that yet await mankind than will be found in the writings of any religion in the world. We like to think of this outline as a clothesline from which all the other prophecies about the end times can either be hung at the appropriate time or, in the case of Daniel 2, 7, 8, and 9 and Revelation 2–20, can run parallel to it. This discourse must be of great significance because it is mentioned in all three synoptic Gospels. The most complete version of the discourse is in Matthew 24–25, with the parallel passages appearing in Mark 13 and Luke 21.

One common mistake many Christians make when they study this discourse is that they try to find the Rapture in this message. They look in vain, for not only is it not there, but the church itself was not founded until after this message was delivered to Israel following their rejection of Christ as the Messiah. This message predicts the events of Israel's future, though much of it is applicable to Christians because we share many of the same end-time events. The Rapture was not a major teaching of our Lord except in John 14:1-3. He left comments about the Rapture to be made by the apostles Paul and John.

THE DISCIPLES' QUESTIONS

The Olivet Discourse is a response to three questions asked by the disciples. Jesus had just predicted the destruction of the Temple in Jerusalem (which took place in A.D. 70). Because the disciples knew Daniel had predicted the Temple would be destroyed, they immediately assumed Jesus was talking about the end times that Daniel had mentioned. They had no idea Jesus was predicting a destruction that would take place in a little under 40 years. After Jesus made His statement, the disciples asked:

When will these things be?

What will be the sign of Your coming?
What will be the sign of the end of the age?

The whole discourse must be seen in the light of Jesus' response to those questions.

JESUS' ANSWER

The first thing our Lord wanted His disciples—and us—to know about the end times is that there will be many deceivers and false messiahs who lead people astray. In fact, there are at least nine warnings in this message about deceivers and false prophets misleading, if they could, even "the very elect." Historically the church age has seen many false religious teachers, but they will be even more pronounced just before the Tribulation and increasingly throughout it.

Jesus' answer to the first question really appears in Luke 21:20-24 and should be located between verses 6 and 7 of Matthew chapter 24. Matthew then gives the most detailed answers to the other questions, making Matthew the preferred account among Bible scholars.

The Signs of the Times

What are the signs of the end times? The first sign Jesus pointed to was war. Not just any war, of which the world has seen over 15,000 to

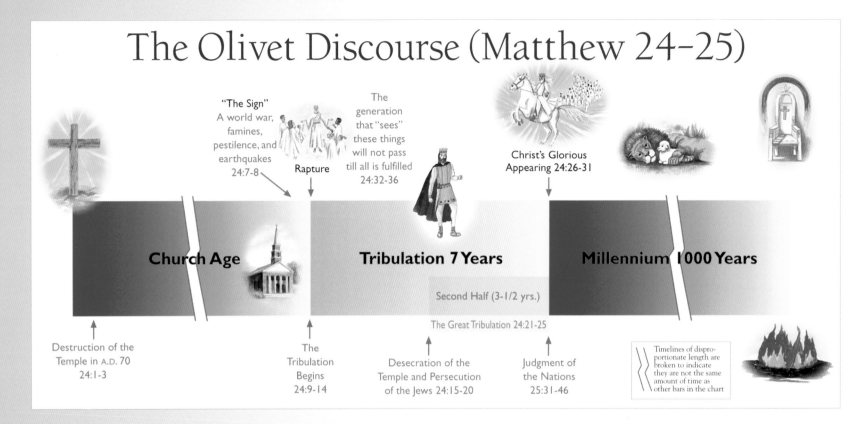

The Olivet Discourse (Matthew 24-25)

"The Sign"
A world war,
famines,
pestilence, and
earthquakes
24:7-8

Rapture

The
generation
that "sees"
these things
will not pass
till all is fulfilled
24:32-36

Christ's Glorious
Appearing 24:26-31

Church Age

Tribulation 7 Years

Millennium 1000 Years

Second Half (3-1/2 yrs.)

The Great Tribulation 24:21-25

Destruction of the
Temple in A.D. 70
24:1-3

The
Tribulation
Begins
24:9-14

Desecration of the
Temple and Persecution
of the Jews 24:15-20

Judgment of
the Nations
25:31-46

Timelines of dispro-
portionate length are
broken to indicate
they are not the same
amount of time as
other bars in the chart

---

date, but a special war started by two nations and joined by many other nations on either side until all the world is involved. It was to be the greatest world war in human history. That occurred with World War I in 1914–1918. Since then there have been a parade of "signs" (see chapter 44 on "The Signs of Christ's Return"), the most significant one being the regathering of the Jewish people back into the land of Israel and the recognition of Israel as a nation in 1948. Many other signs have occurred in fulfillment of Matthew 24:8: "These are the beginning of sorrows" (KJV) or "the beginning of birth pangs" (NASB), in the way that a woman, before the birth of her child, has birth pains that increase in frequency and intensity (Isaiah 66:7-8). This is why we consider the signs of our times to be setting the stage for the Tribulation.

The Tribulation

Beginning with Matthew 24:9 Jesus gives a brief description of

the Tribulation period, which is described in more detail in Revelation 4–19 and limited to seven years, according to both Daniel and John. Matthew 24:9-14 covers the first half of the Tribulation, and verses 15-26 describe the second half, also known as "the Great Tribulation." Obviously, the second half will be worse than the first half. One of the most significant means of identifying that period is our Lord's statement in verse 21—the events of that time will be worse than anything that has ever happened in the history of the world. Those who hold to the preterist viewpoint of prophecy believe all this trauma was fulfilled in the destruction of Jerusalem in A.D. 70, but there are three problems with their view, in addition to the fact that the Temple was not desecrated as Jesus said in verse 15. Though the destruction of the Temple and Jerusalem was bad, it does not compare to the two world wars that killed over 20 million people, as well as the Jewish Holocaust. Secondly, Jesus did not come physically in A.D. 70 as He promised or as the angels promised in Acts 1:9-11. And third, preterists cannot prove John wrote Revelation seven years before the fall of Jerusalem. Rather, he wrote Revelation in A.D. 95 while exiled to the Isle of Patmos, which is what the church has always believed. That alone renders preterism impossible, for Revelation is all about things to come, or a time yet future.

No, the worst time in human history is still ahead in the future. The description of this time is found in Revelation 6–19, charted and described on pages 44–45.

The Glorious Appearing

The disciples asked Jesus for the sign of His coming, and He gave very significant details in Matthew 24:27-31. All the other Bible passages about His glorious return—such as Revelation 19:11-16—should be considered in the light of this one. While no one knows the day or the hour of Jesus' Rapture of the church, we do know when the glorious appearing will occur—"immediately after the tribulation" (verse 29). It will be accompanied by cataclysmic happenings in the heavens and "then shall appear the sign of the Son of man in heaven" (verse 30 KJV). All of this will happen so quickly it will be too late for people to get ready for it. The decision whether to accept Christ as the resurrected Messiah must be made before He comes in power to set up His kingdom, for that decision alone determines who will go into the Millennial kingdom and who will be cast into everlasting punishment. This judgment of the nations will take place at the time of His coming and just before the beginning of the Millennial kingdom (Matthew 25:31-46).

The Generation That Sees These Things

Much confusion has resulted from many well-meaning people trying to identify the "generation [that] will not pass away until all these take place" (Matthew 24:34). Some start this generation at verse 31 and believe that it's talking about the generation beginning at the time Israel became a nation in 1948. The passage of time, of course, has disproved that idea. It's better to interpret this verse in its context: that is, the generation that sees the events of the Tribulation will also see the coming of Christ and the other events leading to the end of the age. This avoids harmful speculations about the future, for no man knows the day or the hour (Matthew 24:36). As soon as Antichrist and Israel sign a peace treaty, which he breaks in the middle of the Tribulation, there will be seven years until the coming of Christ. However, just as the people of Noah's day did not know the day or the hour when the Flood would come and take them all away into judgment, so will unbelievers not know or be prepared for the glorious appearing of Christ. That is why Jesus warned believers living before the Rapture, as well as the Tribulation saints, to "be...ready; for in such an hour as ye think not the Son of man cometh" (Matthew 24:44 KJV). All should learn from His story of the ten virgins who were to live every day in the light of His sudden and unannounced coming (Matthew 25:1-13).

Jesus' statement in Matthew 24:35 is as appropriate today as it was when it was given: "Heaven and earth shall pass away, but my words shall not pass away" (KJV). In other words, the events described by our Lord in His Olivet Discourse are more certain than the heavens above us and the earth we live on.

12.
PAUL AND THE SECOND COMING

Christians have long debated whether or not there is a single passage in the Bible that reveals the two phases of Christ's coming separated by the Tribulation period. We believe that, when properly understood, 2 Thessalonians 2:1-12 is such a passage. Titus 2:13 comes the closest to showing the two phases of His coming in a single verse, while the book of Revelation shows them in a single book. But 2 Thessalonians 2:1-12 reveals the entire outline of these significant events within just a few verses.

The subject is the whole second coming of Jesus Christ (verse 1). The Rapture phase is also seen in the words "our gathering together unto him" (KJV), and the glorious appearing is seen in verse 8 in the words, "the Lord shall consume with the spirit of his mouth, and shall destroy with the brightness of his coming" (KJV). Notice these two events are separated by "that Wicked [the Antichrist] ...whose coming is after the working of Satan with all power and signs and lying wonders, and with all deceivableness of unrighteousness" (verses 8-10 KJV). There can be no question this wicked one is the tool of Satan, often referred to as Antichrist. A complete description of his deeds during the Tribulation is provided in Revelation 11–13.

What's important to observe is that Antichrist's coming is clearly located between the two phases of Christ's coming—the Rapture in verse 1 and the glorious appearing in verse 8, when Christ will destroy Antichrist. As John tells us in Revelation 19:20, Christ throws Antichrist and the False Prophet into the Lake of Fire forever. This alone makes a clear case for the pretribulational Rapture sequence of events: first we have the Rapture, then the man of sin is revealed, and finally he is destroyed by the brightness of the glorious appearing of Jesus. That is similar to the apostle John's description of the Rapture in Revelation 4:1-3, the seven-year Tribulation period in Revelation 6–18, and the glorious appearing in Revelation 19:1-20.

WHAT IS THE FALLING AWAY?

This sequence of events is sufficient to affirm the accuracy of the pre-Trib Rapture truth. However, there is additional evidence found in a proper understanding of 2 Thessalonians 2:3: "that day shall not come, except there come a falling away first" (KJV). There is little agreement among scholars as to whether the Greek word *apostesia* ("falling away") refers to a physical departure (the Rapture) or a metaphorical one (departure from the faith). The first seven translations of the English Bible rendered it "departure." No one knows why the translators of the King James Version rendered it "falling away" or why others translate it "rebellion." A case can be made that all seven of the earliest translations of the English Bible were right in rendering it "departure," which could mean a physical departure or rapture. If "departure" is the more accurate translation, this passage would leave no doubt regarding a pretribulational Rapture, for it places the Rapture prior to the revelation of the man of sin. However, if the more popular view of "falling away" or "rebellion" is the true meaning, then *apostesia* would refer to the career of Antichrist during the Tribulation. The important truth here is "that day," or the glorious appearing, will not occur until the "son of perdition" has been revealed (see Revelation 12–13).

Those who disagree with the pre-Trib Rapture view prefer the King James rendering of the Greek word *apostesia* as "a falling away first," yet

Paul and the Second Coming

Pretribulation Rapture in One Chapter—2 Thessalonians 2:1-12

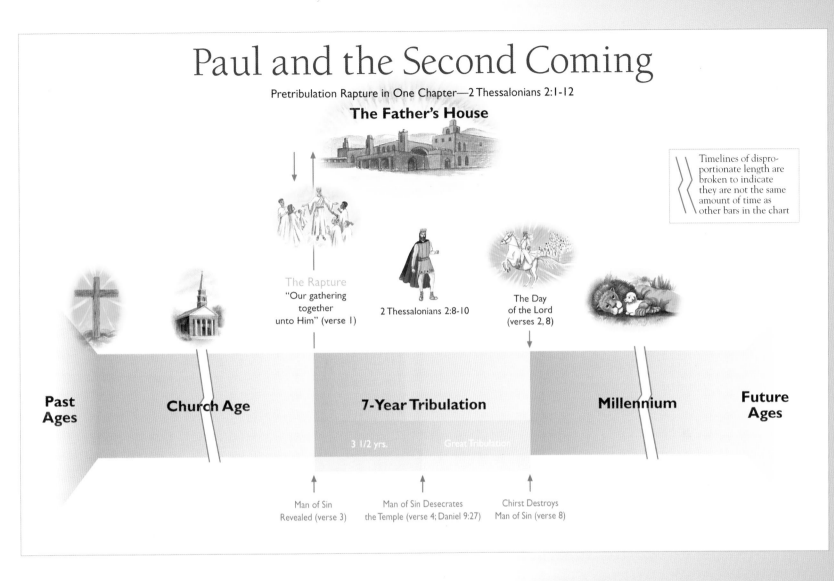

The Father's House

The Rapture
"Our gathering together unto Him" (verse 1)

2 Thessalonians 2:8-10

The Day of the Lord (verses 2, 8)

Timelines of dispro-portionate length are broken to indicate they are not the same amount of time as other bars in the chart

Past Ages	Church Age	7-Year Tribulation	Millennium	Future Ages

3 1/2 yrs.   Great Tribulation

Man of Sin Revealed (verse 3)

Man of Sin Desecrates the Temple (verse 4; Daniel 9:27)

Chirst Destroys Man of Sin (verse 8)

---

they may well be prejudiced, for they know that agreeing with the first seven translators of the English Bible would weigh very heavily in favor of the pretribulational Rapture position:

> 1384 Wycliffe Bible—"Departynge first"
> 1526 Tyndale Bible—"Departynge first"
> 1535 Coverdale Bible—"Departynge first"
> 1539 Cranmer Bible—"Departynge first"
> 1576 Breeches Bible—"Departing first"
> 1583 Beza Bible—"Departing first"
> 1608 Geneva Bible—"Departing first"

Dr. Kenneth S. Wuest, a Greek scholar, has this to say about the proper translation of *apostesia*:

> The root verb *aphistemi* is found fifteen times in the New Testament. It is translated "depart" eleven times. It is used once in connection with departure from the faith (1 Timothy 4:1). The very fact that the qualifying words "from the faith" are added, shows that in itself the word does not have the idea of a defection from the truth. Eight times it is used of a departure from a person, once in the sense of a departure from a place. In the other places where it is found it is translated "fall away," in the case of those in temptation (Luke

8:13), "drew away" much people (Acts 5:37), "refrain" from these men (Acts 5:38). The predominant meaning of this verb in the New Testament, therefore, is that of the act of a person departing from another person or from a place. The neuter noun, *apostasion*, is translated in its three occurrences by the word "divorcement," which in itself suggests a withdrawal of one person from another. Thayer translates the word, "a defection" of a freedman from his patron, "a divorce, a repudiation." The feminine form, *apostasia*, appears in Acts 21:21 where Paul is charged with teaching "all the Jews which are among the Gentiles to forsake Moses," "forsake" being the AV transla-

tion of the word. "To forsake" involves a departure. This word is found only here and in our Thessalonian passage.[4]

According to other Greek scholars, the secondary meaning of *apostasia* is "a departure" or "a disappearance." This provides far more reason to accept the original English translation of "a departure," such as the Rapture, rather than the KJV "falling away," or as some translators suggest, "rebellion." Actually, we see the statement "our gathering together unto Him" of verse 1 and *apostesia* of verse 3 as referring to the departure of the saints in the Rapture, which confirms our premise that both phases of our Lord's coming, separated by the Tribulation, are mentioned in 2 Thessalonians 2:1-12.

13.
PETER AND THE FUTURE

One of the last books in the New Testament to be written was 2 Peter. Like many of the other apostles, he was moved to warn the church that "there shall come in the last days scoffers" (2 Peter 3:3 KJV). He was right on target, for one of the many signs that we could be living in the last days is the enormous increase we've seen in false prophets, false teachers, scoffers (particularly in higher education), and others who deny that Jesus is coming back again.

The apostle Peter warns that one of the signs of the second coming is that scoffers will say: "Where is the promise of His coming? For ever since the fathers fell asleep, all continues just as it was from the beginning of creation." In other words, these scoffers say that things in the world have always continued in a state of uniformity. To the contrary, man has seen two major divisions of time, and there is a third to come. The first, which was terminated by the Flood, is called by Peter "the world that then was" (verse 6 KJV). The present world he calls "the heavens and the earth, which are now" (verse 7 KJV). The third, after the second coming of Christ, will see a new heaven and earth.

Peter very clearly teaches that this world has undergone one earthshaking catastrophe and will experience yet another. The first

one, the Flood of Noah's day, changed the order of nature in the atmosphere and on the earth. Consequently, the present order is not sufficiently similar to the one before the Flood to provide us with accurate indications of what that world was like. Scientists who draw conclusions from present conditions and apply them to conditions before the Flood inevitably arrive at wrong conclusions.

THE SCOFFERS
The Origin of the Scoffers

The theory of uniformitarianism, popularized in the mid-1800s by the English geologist Sir Charles Lyell, became a prominent foundation for Darwinism and evolution, Marxism and socialism, Freudianism and liberalism. In fact, it fostered many of the evils that

Peter and the Future (2 Peter 3:1-14)

Creation   **The Flood**   **Christ's First Coming**   **Christ's Second Coming**

Past Ages

Millennium   **Future Ages**

The World that Was (verse 6)   The World that Is (verse 7)   The World that Is to Come   New Heavens and New Earth (verses 10-13)

Catastrophe   Day of the Lord

beset our society today, and it is propagated by many of the most intellectually trained members of our culture.

Don't let the big word *uniformitarian* throw you. It simply refers to the idea that the present uniform processes of life are sufficient to account for the origin and development of all the earth's physical and biological phenomena. This, of course, dismisses any possibility of divine intervention via catastrophic events designed by God to judge His creature, man.

What's fascinating is that almost 2000 years ago Peter, an untrained Galilean fisherman, predicted that scoffers would say "all things continue as they were from the beginning of the creation" (2 Peter 3:4 KJV). That is exactly the philosophy of our day! "Gradual progression" from a spontaneous beginning through millions of years to the present order of things reflects what evolutionists teach. The moment one suggests a catastrophic interruption in their theory of uniformity, they scoff.

The Blindness of the Scoffers

When confronted with the growing evidence against uniformitarianism and Darwinian evolution, some of it supplied by non-Christian scholars such as Hapgood, Hooker, Sanderson, and Velikovsky, many people wonder why scoffers are so blind. In 2 Peter 3, the apostle Peter gives us two reasons.

The first is found in verse 5: "For this they willingly are ignorant of" (KJV). It is difficult for a student who trusts his professor to realize that his teacher may be willingly prejudiced, but such is the case! The unregenerated minds of unbelievers resist the idea of God's intervention in human affairs. Intellectuals pride themselves on being objective, but objectivity suffers when non-Christians encounter the Word of God. The problem is spiritual—a matter of the will—and the unbeliever is deliberately refusing to face the truth of a future judgment.

Long before geologist Lyell promoted his theory of uniformitarianism, he was an atheistic humanist. As such, he rejected the biblical record. It is not surprising, then, that he would arrive at conclusions opposed to the teachings of the Bible. Nor should we be surprised that Lyell's uniformitarianism, rejected by men like Pasteur, was accepted readily and advanced by the humanists of his day. All had one thing in common: They were willingly ignorant of the truth of God's Word.

Another reason for the intellectual blindness of scoffers is their "walking after their own lusts" (verse 3 KJV). They are focused solely on the pleasures of our fallen world. Voltaire and Rousseau, two French skeptics who had no small influence in the development of humanism, were moral degenerates. For example, Rousseau's mistress bore him five illegitimate children, all of whom he callously abandoned at the Paris General Hospital.

All the evidence in the world—scientific and rational—will not convince the man who is determined to reject Christ. Nor can a man bent on pleasure hear the voice of the Spirit. Only when such a person comes to the end of himself will he seek the real and ultimate truth.

The Judgment of the Scoffers

Those who reject God for the satisfaction of immediate lusts almost universally reject the idea of eternal judgment. No amount of rationalization, of course, will change the fact that God will indeed judge them at the Great White Throne judgment, a judgment that is for eternity. Peter stated that just as God exercised real judgment in Noah's day, He will mete out judgment again in the future (2 Peter 3:6-7). In verse 7 Peter also said that just as God's word sustains this world, which is hung in place on nothing, so will His word regarding judgment be fulfilled. Man may not like the idea of judgment, but that doesn't change its certainty.

THE LORD
The Mercy of the Lord

In 2 Peter 3:9, Peter said, "[God] is long-suffering...not willing that any should perish, but that all should come to repentance" (KJV). This is a foundational premise on the nature of God that should influence our understanding of Him. He does not want anyone to perish. He wants all men to come to Him, even the grossest of sinners. But they can only do so by faith in the finished work of His Son on the cross.

The Day of the Lord

In spite of God's long-suffering and mercy, the majority of mankind will reject Him, even during the Tribulation. However, when He comes in power, called by Peter the "day of the Lord" (2 Peter 3:10-12), He will destroy all those who have rejected His offer of free salvation. Isaiah 34 gives more detail, but this "day of the Lord" signals that time when, at the end of the Millennial kingdom, God will destroy this old sin-cursed earth. We know that a world catastrophe (the Flood) separates our present world from the previous one, and Peter uses this as a sign that another catastrophe will end this present order and usher in a new one, which he calls the "new heavens and a new earth" (verse 13).

In light of all this, we are challenged to "be diligent that ye may be found of him in peace, without spot, and blameless" (verse 14 KJV). When we remember to keep this eternal perspective, we live more holy lives out of concern for lost souls.

Those who scoff say things will continue as always, and that Jesus will not return. However, as Peter said, "The Lord is not slack concerning his promise, as some men count slackness" (2 Peter 3:9 KJV). God keeps His promises. Christ *will* come again!

14.
JOHN'S REVELATION OF THE FUTURE

The book of Revelation is without doubt the most exciting book ever written for two reasons: First, it presents Jesus Christ in His well-deserved splendor and glory. The first time He came to this earth it was as the suffering Messiah, which is why the Jews rejected Him. They did not want a Savior to forgive their sins and give them eternal life; they wanted a Messiah who would rid them of their Roman conquerors and give them the blessings promised by the prophets for the kingdom age. But the second time Christ comes, it will be in full glory.

The second reason this book is such a blessing is because it gives more definitive details about the future and our relationship to it than any other book or prophecy in the world. These details encompass the church age, the seven-year Tribulation period, the glorious appearing, the Millennial kingdom, heaven, and a myriad of other facts about the future. The importance of Revelation cannot be exaggerated, for without it, many Old and New Testament prophecies would not be understandable.

Unfortunately, many teachers and preachers never deal with the book of Revelation, even some who teach all the other books of the Bible. It is as though there is a satanic attack on the credibility of the book to keep God's people from understanding it and being motivated by it. Since the third and fourth century, the Greek form of reading the text allegorically or symbolically was espoused in search of more than one meaning for the words in the book. Because of this, traditionally, Revelation has been an enigma. The reason is simple: You cannot understand this book unless you take it literally, the way it was intended—literally, that is, unless the facts of the immediate context indicate otherwise. The literal method of interpretation should be applied to this book just as it is for the other books of Scripture. In fact, the only way the promise of a blessing to the reader and those who obey its commandments can be fulfilled is to take Revelation literally (Revelation 1:3). Otherwise it cannot be understood, and if you do not understand it, you cannot receive a blessing by reading it.

In Revelation 1, Jesus is seen walking among the lampstands, or churches. We already know that the church is to be the light of the world and is entrusted with one primary task: fulfilling the great commission to take the gospel to all the world. The threefold outline of Revelation is found in 1:19, where John is instructed to write about 1) "the things which you have seen"—the vision in its entirety; 2) "the things which are"—the church age; and 3) "the things which will take place after these things"—the future. We shall look briefly at the things that are and the things that will be.

THE THINGS THAT ARE

Revelation 2–3 have to do with the church age, beginning with the first century, which is called the apostolic age. Though the apostles were dead before the end of the first century, they are mentioned in the message to the church of Ephesus. The Lord's letters to the seven churches in Revelation 2–3 were written to more than just the seven churches listed, for there were thousands of churches by A.D. 95, when Revelation was written. Most literalist prophecy scholars believe that these letters apply to all the churches existing in that day and all through the ages. In each letter the Lord challenges all to "hear what the Spirit says to the churches." Notice the plural tense. These letters were to be circulated among all the churches, and indeed, we can see that they are applicable to churches in any age. There are also some who hold the view that

John's Revelation of the Future

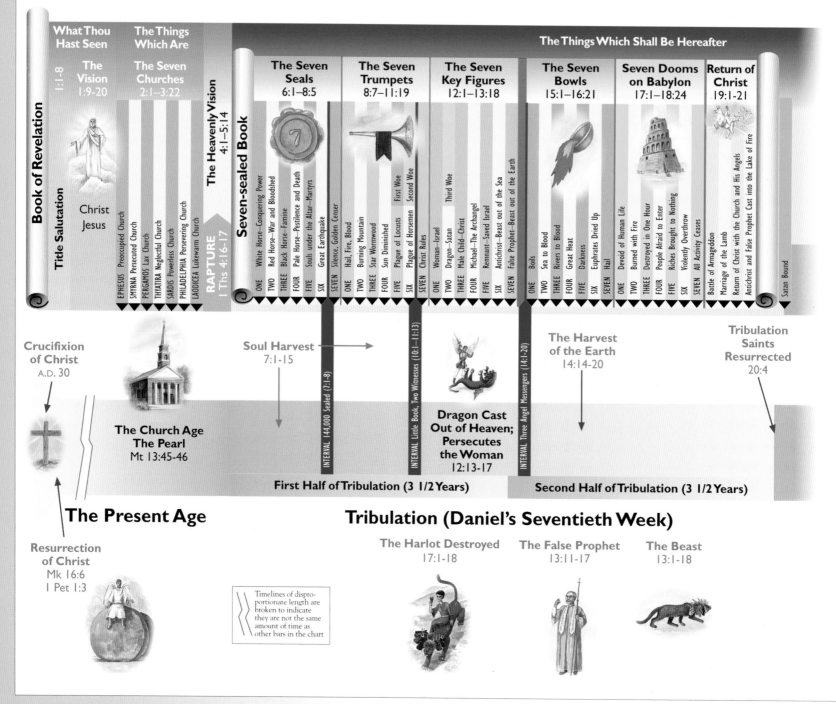

Book of Revelation

Title Salutation — 1:1-8 · Christ Jesus

What Thou Hast Seen — The Vision 1:9-20 · Christ Jesus

The Things Which Are — The Seven Churches 2:1–3:22
- EPHESUS Preoccupied Church
- SMYRNA Persecuted Church
- PERGAMOS Lax Church
- THYATIRA Neglectful Church
- SARDIS Powerless Church
- PHILADELPHIA Persevering Church
- LAODICEA Lukewarm Church

RAPTURE 1 Ths 4:16-17

The Heavenly Vision 4:1–5:14

The Things Which Shall Be Hereafter

Seven-sealed Book

The Seven Seals 6:1–8:5
- ONE White Horse—Conquering Power
- TWO Red Horse—War and Bloodshed
- THREE Black Horse—Famine
- FOUR Pale Horse—Pestilence and Death
- FIVE Souls under the Altar–Martyrs
- SIX Great Earthquake
- SEVEN Silence, Golden Censer

The Seven Trumpets 8:7–11:19
- ONE Hail, Fire, Blood
- TWO Burning Mountain
- THREE Star Wormwood
- FOUR Sun Diminished
- FIVE Plague of Locusts / First Woe
- SIX Plague of Horsemen / Second Woe
- SEVEN Christ Rules

The Seven Key Figures 12:1–13:18
- ONE Woman–Israel
- TWO Dragon–Satan / Third Woe
- THREE Male Child–Christ
- FOUR Michael–The Archangel
- FIVE Remnant–Saved Israel
- SIX Antichrist–Beast out of the Sea
- SEVEN False Prophet–Beast out of the Earth

The Seven Bowls 15:1–16:21
- ONE Boils
- TWO Sea to Blood
- THREE Rivers to Blood
- FOUR Great Heat
- FIVE Darkness
- SIX Euphrates Dried Up
- SEVEN Hail

Seven Dooms on Babylon 17:1–18:24
- ONE Devoid of Human Life
- TWO Burned with Fire
- THREE Destroyed in One Hour
- FOUR People Afraid to Enter
- FIVE Riches Brought to Nothing
- SIX Violently Overthrown
- SEVEN All Activity Ceases

Return of Christ 19:1-21
- Battle of Armageddon
- Marriage of the Lamb
- Return of Christ with the Church and His Angels
- Antichrist and False Prophet Cast into the Lake of Fire

Satan Bound

Crucifixion of Christ A.D. 30

The Church Age The Pearl Mt 13:45-46

Soul Harvest 7:1-15

INTERVAL 144,000 Sealed (7:1-8)

INTERVAL Little Book, Two Witnesses (10:1–11:13)

Dragon Cast Out of Heaven; Persecutes the Woman 12:13-17

INTERVAL Three Angel Messengers (14:1-20)

The Harvest of the Earth 14:14-20

Tribulation Saints Resurrected 20:4

First Half of Tribulation (3 1/2 Years)

Second Half of Tribulation (3 1/2 Years)

The Present Age

Tribulation (Daniel's Seventieth Week)

Resurrection of Christ Mk 16:6 1 Pet 1:3

> Timelines of disproportionate length are broken to indicate they are not the same amount of time as other bars in the chart

The Harlot Destroyed 17:1-18

The False Prophet 13:11-17

The Beast 13:1-18

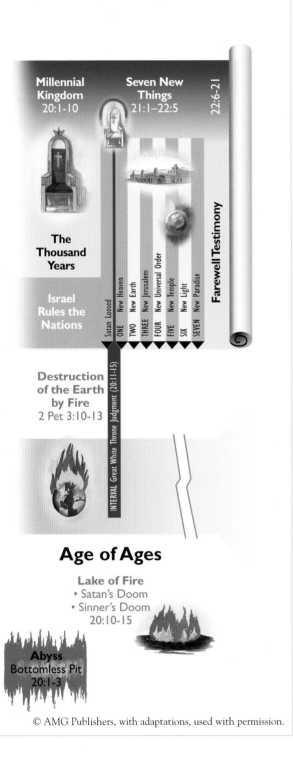

Millennial Kingdom 20:1-10

Seven New Things 21:1—22:5

22:6-21

The Thousand Years

Israel Rules the Nations

Satan Loosed

ONE New Heaven
TWO New Earth
THREE New Jerusalem
FOUR New Universal Order
FIVE New Temple
SIX New Light
SEVEN New Paradise

Farewell Testimony

INTERVAL Great White Throne Judgment (20:11-15)

Destruction of the Earth by Fire 2 Pet 3:10-13

Age of Ages

Lake of Fire
• Satan's Doom
• Sinner's Doom
20:10-15

Abyss Bottomless Pit 20:1-3

these seven churches represent a progression in the history of the church, beginning with the first century and continuing through today. Prophecy scholar and author Gary Cohen describes it this way:

> The theory that the seven churches of Revelation 2–3 are prophetical, that they represent seven consecutive periods in ecclesiastical history, seems to have first been suggested by some of the words of the martyr Victorinus, Bishop of Pettau (died circa A.D. 303). This belief as held today does not deny that at the same time the seven churches are also historical and representative. It asserts that the prophetical element is in addition to these other elements and wholly compatible with them. Thus it beholds the seven congregations 1) as historically existent at the time of John's writing in A.D. 95–96; 2) as representing the entire church through the seven types of local churches which shall exist throughout the dispensation; and 3) as prefiguring seven aspects of the professing church which would successively rise into prominence before Christ's second coming.[5]

The seven periods are generally given approximately as follows:

Ephesus—apostolic church (A.D. 30–100)
Smyrna—persecuted church (A.D. 100–313)
Pergamos—state church (A.D. 313–590)
Thyatira—papal church (A.D. 590–1517)
Sardis—reformed church (A.D. 1517–1730)
Philadelphia—missionary church (A.D. 1730–1900)
Laodicea—apostate church (A.D. 1900–?)

Although this time-honored belief that Christ's message to the seven churches takes a prophetic look at the seven stages of church history has never been held unanimously, it is held by most premillennialists. Even Phillip Schaff, the writer of the classic eight-volume set *History of the Christian Church*, accepts that position.

The first three churches have passed off the pages of history, but the last four are living concurrently, for we have these four kinds of churches in our world today. The message to all is the same: "Be thou faithful unto death" (KJV).

THE THINGS THAT WILL BE

Immediately after the seventh church is described and just before God's judgments are poured out, we see John, a member of the church, taken up into heaven

(Revelation 4:1-2). While we could not build the truth of the pretribulational Rapture on this single passage, it certainly fits in with the many other passages that describe it (1 Corinthians 15:50-58; 1 Thessalonians 4:13-18; see chapter 17 on the Rapture).

The events of the last days will include the destruction of Babylon—governmentally, religiously, and commercially. This will be followed by the glorious appearing of Jesus Christ, who will throw the Antichrist and the False Prophet into the Lake of Fire. Christ will then set up the Millennial kingdom, and Satan will be bound for 1000 years. At the end of that time he will be released to tempt the nations once again before being cast alive into the Lake of Fire—forever! Then comes the Great White Throne Judgment (Revelation 20:11-15), after which all unbelievers will be cast into the Lake of Fire.

Revelation closes with a vision of what heaven will be like. It is the most incredible picture of eternity ever presented, and it is all available to those who receive Jesus. More details about this will be given in a future chapter, but for now we call attention to the fact that Jesus will come "quickly" (meaning that His coming will be "suddenly") and He will reward every man according to his work (Revelation 22:12). Don't miss His coming or the reward for a lifetime of faithful service, for those rewards will last forever and ever!

15.
THE THREE GROUPS OF PEOPLE IN BIBLE PROPHECY

Scripture speaks of three classes of people throughout prophecy and history. We find all three in 1 Corinthians 10:32: "Give none offence, neither to the Jews, nor to the Gentiles, nor to the church of God" (KJV). Up until the time of Abraham, all people were Gentiles, including Adam, Enoch, and Noah. There were saved Gentiles, such as Adam, Seth, Noah, and Shem, and there were unsaved Gentiles, such as Cain, Lamech, and Nimrod. Thus, the first man was a Gentile, and Gentiles have continued to exist throughout the entire span of human history.

When God called Abraham to begin a new nation, Abraham became the first Hebrew, Jew, or Israelite. His grandson was Jacob, who had his name changed to Israel (Genesis 32:24-28). Jacob had 12 sons, who became the heads of the 12 tribes of Israel. They began the Jewish nation, and since then the human race has been divided into Jews and Gentiles. There are saved Jews and unsaved Jews, even though Israel is God's elect nation through whom He brought salvation to all mankind. Israel began with "Father Abraham" and will continue as a distinct entity throughout the rest of history.

The church is the body of Christ, which began on the Day of Pentecost and will go to heaven in the Rapture. Its makeup is different from Gentiles and Jews in that it is the only spiritually pure entity—it is composed of only saved Jews and Gentiles. While it's true that the human institution we know as the church contains an element of unbelievers, the true church is made up of only genuine believers in Christ, their Savior. The church is also a temporary entity; it did not exist before its birth at Pentecost, and it will come to an abrupt end at the Rapture. Thus, those saved during the Tribulation and Millennium are not a part of the church, even though these people will become saved by believing the same gospel that has brought church-age individuals to Christ.

End-times Bible prophecy includes mention of all three groups of people—Gentiles, Jews, and the church. God has a clear prophetic plan for all three. These three peoples are separate in many ways, but their paths have been interwoven together throughout history.

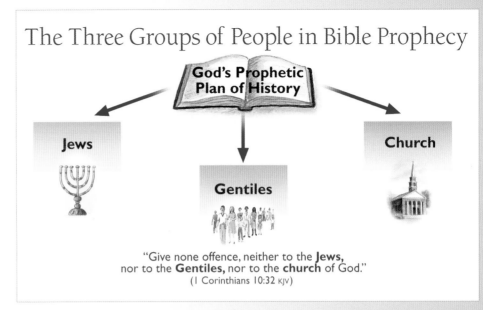

The Three Groups of People in Bible Prophecy

God's Prophetic Plan of History

Jews

Gentiles

Church

"Give none offence, neither to the **Jews,**
nor to the **Gentiles,** nor to the **church** of God."
(1 Corinthians 10:32 KJV)

16.
THE CHURCH'S PROPHETIC DESTINY

What is the prophetic future of the church? In order to answer that question, we must first understand that the church relates in two ways to the program of God. First, there's the true church, which is made up of Jews and Gentiles who genuinely know Christ as their Savior and have had their sins forgiven. Beginning on the Day of Pentecost in Acts 2 and continuing to the Rapture, all believers are part of Christ's body, or the church.

Second, there's the realm of the professing church's influence, which we will call Christendom. Christendom constitutes everything associated with the visible church, including all of her branches, such as Roman Catholicism, Eastern Orthodoxy, Protestantism, and even the cults. Christendom includes both true believers and mere professors, both the wheat and the tares (Matthew 13:24-30). These two aspects of the church—true believers and Christendom—have very different prophetic destinies.

The next event on the prophetic calendar for the true church is the Rapture (John 14:1-3; 1 Corinthians 15:51-52; 1 Thessalonians 4:13-18). In the Rapture, all living and dead believers "shall be caught up...in the clouds to meet the Lord in the air" (1 Thessalonians 4:17 KJV). This event could happen at any moment, without warning, and fits the motif of Christ as the Groom and the church as the bride. In this age the church is betrothed to Christ—totally committed, having been bought by His blood. The Groom has gone away to the Father's house to prepare a place for His bride. While He is away (during the church age) the bride's faithfulness is tested by the separation, and she is to remain faithful while constantly watching for the Groom's unannounced return. When God the Father gives the signal, the shout will go forth and the church age will be completed at the Rapture, and true believers will go to be with the Lord.

Christendom, by contrast, will be left behind to enter into the Tribulation period and is being prepared to serve as Satan's harlot—"the great harlot who sits on many waters" (Revelation 17:1). Christendom will help facilitate the great delusion of Antichrist in the form of the world church. This ecumenical and apostate church will pave the way for a one-world religion, which will include the worship of Antichrist and the reception of the mark of the Beast (Revelation 13:16-18). It is significant to note that Revelation 13:11-18 presents the False Prophet (the head of the one-world church during the Tribulation) as the one who advocates, on behalf of the Antichrist, the reception of the number 666. Just as the true church's role is to proclaim the truth of God, so Satan's harlot will have a role in fostering his deception.

The church is unique in the plan of God and separate from His plan for Israel. While the church partakes of the spiritual promises of the Abrahamic Covenant as fulfilled through Christ, Israel, and not the church, will fulfill her national destiny as a separate entity after the Rapture and Tribulation and during the Millennium. The New Testament teaches that the church was an unrevealed mystery in the Old Testament (Romans 16:25-26; Ephesians 3:2-10; Colossians 1:25-27), which is why she began suddenly, without warning, in Acts 2, and why this age will end suddenly and mysteriously, without warning, at the Rapture. Therefore, the church has no earthly prophetic destiny beyond the Rapture.

THE CHURCH ON EARTH

The church age is not characterized by historically verifiable prophetic events (except her arrival on the Day of Pentecost and her departure at the Rapture). But we do find the general course of this age in prophecy and can provide a general overview of what can be expected during this age. Keep in mind, however, that there are prophecies being fulfilled during the church age that relate to God's prophetic plan for Israel and not the church. For example, the prophesied destruction of Jerusalem and her Temple in A.D. 70 relates to Israel (Matthew 23:38; Luke 19:43-44; 21:20-24). Thus it's

appropriate that we see prophetic fulfillments relating to Israel's reestablishment as a nation in 1948 even though we are still living in the church age.

Let's look now at three sets of New Testament passages that reveal to us the general course of the church age.

Matthew 13

The parables in Matthew 13 survey the church age in terms of God's kingdom here on earth, which covers the time between Christ's first and second comings. Dr. J. Dwight Pentecost summarizes Matthew 13 this way:

> We may summarize the teaching as to the course of the age by saying: 1) there will be a sowing of the Word throughout the age, which 2) will be imitated by a false counter-sowing; 3) the kingdom will assume huge outer proportions, but 4) be marked by inner doctrinal corruption; yet, the Lord will gain for Himself 5) a peculiar treasure from among Israel, and 6) from the church; 7) the age will end in judgment with the unrighteous excluded from the kingdom to be inaugurated and the righteous taken in to enjoy the blessing of Messiah's reign.[6]

Revelation 2–3

Revelation 2–3 refers to the *program* of the church (rather than the kingdom). Thus its overview of seven churches begins at Pentecost and ends with the Rapture (as indicated by Revelation 4:1-3). These seven historical churches of the first century provide a pattern of the types of churches that will exist throughout church history.

The Epistles

The following is a list of the seven major passages in the epistles that deal with the church in the last days: 1 Timothy 4:1-3; 2 Timothy 3:1-5; 4:3-4; James 5:1-8; 2 Peter 2:1-22; 3:3-6; and Jude 1-25. Every one of these passages emphasizes over and over again that a dominant characteristic of the church in the last days will be that of *apostasy*.

The apostles repeatedly warned believers to be on guard against doctrinal defection, or apostasy. That we see so much defection

An Overview of the Church Age

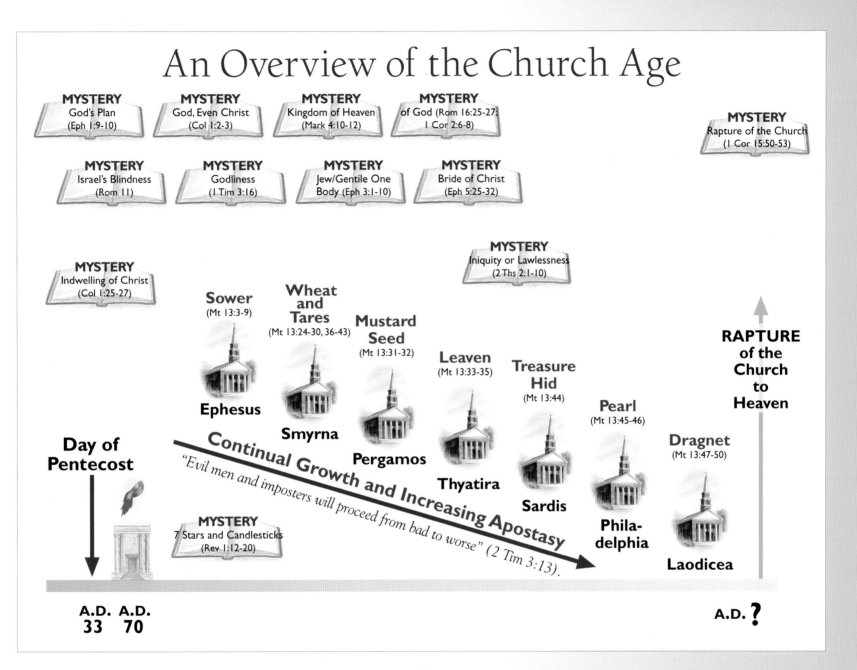

MYSTERY God's Plan (Eph 1:9-10)

MYSTERY God, Even Christ (Col 1:2-3)

MYSTERY Kingdom of Heaven (Mark 4:10-12)

MYSTERY of God (Rom 16:25-27; 1 Cor 2:6-8)

MYSTERY Rapture of the Church (1 Cor 15:50-53)

MYSTERY Israel's Blindness (Rom 11)

MYSTERY Godliness (1 Tim 3:16)

MYSTERY Jew/Gentile One Body (Eph 3:1-10)

MYSTERY Bride of Christ (Eph 5:25-32)

MYSTERY Iniquity or Lawlessness (2 Ths 2:1-10)

MYSTERY Indwelling of Christ (Col 1:25-27)

Sower (Mt 13:3-9)

Wheat and Tares (Mt 13:24-30, 36-43)

Mustard Seed (Mt 13:31-32)

Leaven (Mt 13:33-35)

Treasure Hid (Mt 13:44)

Pearl (Mt 13:45-46)

Dragnet (Mt 13:47-50)

RAPTURE of the Church to Heaven

Ephesus

Smyrna

Pergamos

Thyatira

Sardis

Philadelphia

Laodicea

Day of Pentecost

"Evil men and imposters will proceed from bad to worse" (2 Tim 3:13).

Continual Growth and Increasing Apostasy

MYSTERY 7 Stars and Candlesticks (Rev 1:12-20)

A.D. **33**   A.D. **70**

A.D. **?**

today is a clear sign that we are in the end times.

Even though the New Testament doesn't give specific prophecies concerning the church age, we have three sets of passages that paint a general picture of the course of this age. All three indicate that apostasy will characterize Christendom during the time that the Rapture takes place.

THE CHURCH IN HEAVEN

The New Testament teaches that the church will be removed by the Rapture before the Tribulation begins (1 Thessalonians 1:10; 5:9; Revelation 3:10) and taken by Christ to the Father's house (John 14:1-3). She will be in heaven during the Tribulation, as represented by the 24 elders (Revelation 4:4,9-11; 7:13-14; 19:4), and during the seven years will undergo the judgment seat of Christ in preparation (Revelation 19:4-10,19) for accompanying Christ at His second coming (Revelation 19:14). The heavenly preparation of the church during the Tribulation is seen in Revelation 19:7: "The marriage of the Lamb has come and His bride has made herself ready." This will take place at the beginning of the Millennium, after the second coming.

While the next event for the true church—the body of Christ—is its translation from earth to heaven at the Rapture, those unbelievers left in the organized church (the institution) will pass into the Tribulation and form the base of an apostate superchurch that the False Prophet will use to aid the worldwide rule of the Antichrist (Revelation 13; 17–18). The true church of Jesus Christ will not go through the Tribulation.

THE CHURCH IN THE MILLENNIUM

During the Millennium, all members of the church will reign and rule with Christ (Revelation 3:21). In Matthew 19:28, Jesus told His disciples, who are members of the church, that they would join Him in the kingdom and reign over the 12 tribes of Israel. Also, in 2 Timothy 2:12, Paul writes, "If we endure, we will also reign with Him." The primary purpose of the Millennium is the restoration of Israel and Christ's rule over it, but the church as the bride of Christ is not absent from Millennial activities.

Scripture is not clear as to whether Israel, the church, and the other believer groups of history will maintain their distinctions throughout eternity. There does not appear to be any biblical reason why they may not worship and serve God as distinct entities for all eternity.

17.
THE RAPTURE OF THE CHURCH

Ever since our Lord promised the early Christians that He was returning to His Father's house to prepare a place for them and that He would "come again, and receive [them] unto [Himself]; that where I am, there [they] may be also" (John 14:3 KJV), believers have looked forward to being raptured or translated rather than seeing death. In 1 Corinthians 15, Paul wrote, "I show you a mystery; we shall not all sleep [referring to death for the Christian], but we shall all be changed—in a moment, in the twinkling of an eye" (verses 51-52 KJV). As we shall see, this is called a "mystery," the Rapture, or "the blessed hope" of the church (Titus 2:13).

THE EXPECTATION OF CHRIST'S RETURN

The apostles and the church of the first three centuries wholeheartedly expected that Christ would return for His church during their lifetime. The blessed hope that motivated the first-century church was the imminent return or the sudden and unexpected coming of Christ at any moment.

Scripture indicates that some people in the church at Thessalonica became upset because someone claimed the appointed day had already taken place and they had been left behind. Paul's answer to them in 1 and 2 Thessalonians probably gave more impetus to the belief in the imminent return of Christ than any other single scripture on the matter. Most first-century Christians believed so intensely in Christ's at-any-moment coming that they were driven with a passion to share their faith everywhere, as we can see in 1 Thessalonians 1:6-10:

You also became imitators of us and of the Lord, hav-

EVENTS OF THE RAPTURE

1. The Lord Himself will descend from His Father's house, where He is preparing a place for us (John 14:1-3; 1 Thessalonians 4:16).

2. He will come again to receive us to Himself (John 14:1-3).

3. He will resurrect those who have fallen asleep in Him (deceased believers whom we will not precede—1 Thessalonians 4:14-15).

4. The Lord will shout as He descends ("loud command," 1 Thessalonians 4:16 NIV). All this takes place in the "twinkling of an eye" (1 Corinthians 15:52).

5. We will hear the voice of the archangel (perhaps to lead Israel during the seven years of the Tribulation as he did in the Old Testament—1 Thessalonians 4:16).

6. We will also hear the trumpet call of God (1 Thessalonians 4:16), the last trumpet for the church. (Don't confuse this with the seventh trumpet of judgment upon the world during the Tribulation in Revelation 11:15.)

7. The dead in Christ will rise first (the corruptible ashes of their dead bodies are made incorruptible and joined together with their spirits,

which Jesus brings with Him—1 Thessalonians 4:16-17).

8. Then we who are alive and remain will be changed (or made incorruptible by having our bodies made "immortal"—1 Corinthians 15:51,53).

9. We will be caught up (raptured) together (1 Thessalonians 4:17).

10. We will be caught up in the clouds (where dead and living believers will have a monumental reunion—1 Thessalonians 4:17).

11. We will meet the Lord in the air (1 Thessalonians 4:17).

12. Christ will receive us to Himself and take us to the Father's house "that where I am, there you may be also" (John 14:3).

13. "And so we shall always be with the Lord" (1 Thessalonians 4:17).

14. At the call of Christ for believers, He will judge all things. Christians will stand before the judgment seat of Christ (Romans 14:10; 2 Corinthians 5:10), described in detail in 1 Corinthians 3:11-15. This judgment prepares Christians for...

15. The marriage of the Lamb. Before Christ returns to earth in power and great glory, He will meet His bride, the church, and the marriage supper will take place. In the meantime, after the church is raptured, the world will suffer the unprecedented outpouring of God's wrath, which our Lord called "the great tribulation" (Matthew 24:21).

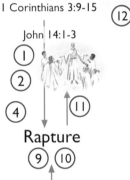

The Father's House

Judgment Seat
1 Corinthians 3:9-15

Marriage of the Lamb

John 14:1-3

Rapture

1 Thessalonians 4:16-17
1 Corinthians 15:51-58

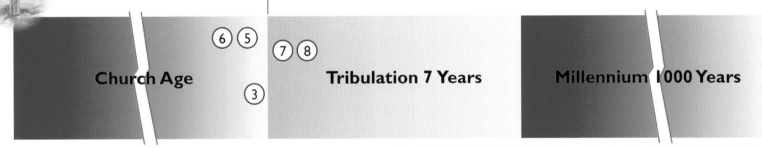

Church Age   **Tribulation 7 Years**   **Millennium 1000 Years**

ing received the word in much Tribulation with the joy of the Holy Spirit, so that you became an example to all the believers in Macedonia and in Achaia. For the word of the Lord has sounded forth from you, not only in Macedonia and Achaia, but also in every place your faith toward God has gone forth, so that we have no need to say anything.

For they themselves report about us what kind of a reception we had with you, and how you turned to God from idols to serve a living and true God, and to wait for His Son from heaven, whom He raised from the dead, that is Jesus, who rescues us from the wrath to come.

While the church of the first three centuries did not use the word *Rapture* to describe this resurrection of dead believers and translation of living Christians, they anticipated the event. Even during the Dark Ages, when literal interpretation of the Bible was eclipsed, some still anticipated the imminent translation of the church. Later Christian saints, such as Hugh Latimer (burned at the stake for his faith in 1555), expressed assurance of the Rapture: "Peradventure it may come in my days, old as I am, or in my children's days...the saints *'shall be taken up to meet Christ in the air'* and so shall come down with Him again" (emphasis added).

Since Latimer's time, the Bible has been translated into many languages. Wherever it has gone, this expectation of translation to be with Christ has become the anticipation of the church. The anticipation of this event has had a tremendous influence on the church during the past two centuries as millions of Christians have accepted the literal message of our Lord's promise to come for His church.

Modern Christians know this event as the Rapture—that moment when, in "the twinkling of an eye," Christ will shout from heaven and "the dead in Christ will rise first. Then we who are alive and remain will be caught up together with them in the clouds to meet the Lord in the air" (1 Thessalonians 4:16-17).

The Greek word for "caught up" is *harpazo*, which means "snatched up." The familiar word *Rapture* does not appear in the Greek New Testament, for it is a Latin word. Those who translated the Greek New Testament into Latin used *Rapture* to describe "snatched up" or "caught away" because it suggests a joyous exalta-tion—which is not the case when a person is snatched away by a kidnapper or someone who plans to harm him.

THE TWO PHASES TO CHRIST'S RETURN

When the 300-plus Bible references to the second coming are carefully examined, it becomes clear that there are two phases to Christ's return. These passages have far too many conflicting activities connected with His return to be merged into a single coming (fifteen key differences can be seen in the chart on page 112).

Since we know there are no contradictions in the Word of God, our Lord must be telling us something here. Most scholars who take the Bible literally whenever possible believe He is talking about one "coming" in two stages. First, He will come suddenly in the air to rapture His church and take believers to His Father's house, in fulfillment of His promise in John 14:1-3. There, they will appear before the judgment seat of Christ (2 Corinthians 5:8-10) and participate in the marriage supper of the Lamb (Revelation 19:1-10). Then Jesus will finish His second coming by returning to earth gloriously and publicly in great power to set up His kingdom.

Look now on page 51 at the passages that deal with the Rapture (the passages on the second coming are listed on page 65). The numbers inside the circles correspond with the numbered items listed on the chart.

THE JUDGMENT SEAT OF CHRIST
18.

Immediately after the Rapture, every Christian will stand before Christ to be judged by Him. This judgment has nothing to do with salvation, for only the saved will be there. Paul mentions our appearance before "the judgment seat of Christ" in 2 Corinthians 5:10, and Romans 14:10.

The most detailed passage of Scripture related to this coming event is 1 Corinthians 3:9-15:

> We are God's fellow workers; you are God's field, God's building. According to the grace of God which was given to me, like a wise master builder I laid a foundation, and another is building on it. But each man must be careful how he builds on it. For no man can lay a foundation other than the one which is laid, which is Jesus Christ. Now if any man builds on the foundation with gold, silver, precious stones, wood, hay, straw, each man's work will become evident; for the day will show it because it is to be revealed with fire, and the fire itself will test the quality of each man's work. If any man's work which he has built on it remains, he will receive a reward. If any man's work is burned up, he will suffer loss; but he himself will be saved, yet so as through fire.

GOOD WORKS

Since good works will receive rewards, we need to know what constitutes a good work. The following are some possibilities described in Scripture.

Witness. Matthew 5:16 says, "Let your light shine before men in such a way that they may see your good works, and glorify your Father...in heaven." A Christian is expected to let his light shine for the world to see. He represents the Lord Jesus Christ to a world that, for the most part, does not know Him. Part of a Christian's good works involves living a pure life and being a consistent witness for the Lord.

Worship. Jesus referred to the worship of Himself as a good work. When a woman anointed His head with precious ointment, He told His anxious disciples to leave her alone because she had "done a good deed to Me" (Matthew 26:10). Very often we limit our concept of worship to adoration of and praise to God. But the worship of Christ is a good work as well.

Generosity. First Timothy 6:18 says we learn that being "rich in good works" involves being generous and willing to share. Specifically the verse says we're to be "ready to share." In other words, it is primarily the attitude of generosity that comprises the good work. If we have the wrong attitude or motivation, our so-called generosity is not a good work. But all acts performed with the proper motives will stand the test of fire and receive a reward.

Jesus made it clear that nothing is too small to be considered a good work. In Matthew 10:42 He said, "Whoever in the name of a disciple gives to one of these little ones even a cup of cold water to drink, truly I say to you, he shall not lose his reward." Even a seemingly insignificant word or deed done for the glory of the Lord will receive divine compensation. So, virtually anything done for Christ with the right attitude and motive will receive a reward. In 1 Corinthians 3:12 these deeds are described as gold, silver, and precious stones.

WORKS WITH WRONG MOTIVES

By contrast, Jesus tells us that deeds done with the intention of impressing men are worthless in His sight. In Matthew 6:2 He states flatly that anyone who does a good work in order to receive praise from others will receive no reward from God. The earthly approval is the only reward that person will receive. These works, of course, are the wood, hay, and straw mentioned in 1 Corinthians 3:12. They will not survive the test of fire.

REWARDS THAT LAST

The two greatest enemies of Christian service, selfishness and laziness, have robbed many of God's children of rewards they should have received. Don't let these enemies overcome you lest you become a victim of the *judgment of loss* (1 Corinthians 3:15).

What kinds of rewards will we who are Christians receive when we are judged? In Scripture we find mention of five different crowns reserved for those who are faithful to do God's work. These crowns and their accompanying Scripture passages are shown in the chart "The Judgment Seat of Christ."

Incorruptible Crown. This crown, often called "the victor's crown," is conferred upon those who "keep under [their] body, and bring it into subjection" (1 Corinthians 9:27 KJV). That is, those who have purged themselves from the inducements and pleasures of the world in order to be of profitable service for the Lord Jesus Christ merit this crown.

Crown of Life. Often called "the martyr's crown" or "the sufferer's crown," this reward will rectify the many injustices Christians suffer in life. Those who have suffered much yet endured with a sweet Christian spirit will be given the "crown of life." The crown is also a special reward for those who have been "faithful unto death" as a witness for Christ (Revelation 2:10 KJV).

Crown of Glory. This is often called "the shepherd's crown" or "the pastor's crown." It is reserved for those who have given their lives to the teaching of the Word of God (1 Peter 5:1,4).

Crown of Righteousness. A special crown is reserved for those Christians who, inspired by the imminent return of Christ, have lived a very righteous and holy life. God does not demand talented vessels for His service. In fact, we need to remember that what comes from our lives is accomplished by His power, not our skills or talent. He simply lays down one major requirement: that a Christian be clean. Somehow the doctrine of the imminent return of Christ has a purifying effect upon the believer (Titus 2:12-14; 1 John 3:2-3).

Crown of Rejoicing. Often referred to as "the soul winner's crown," this crown is reserved for those who have devoted their primary attention to the salvation of lost souls. Often this service is rendered obscurely, unknown to other Christians. Those unsung heroes and all those who have given themselves to winning people to Christ will receive this crown (1 Thessalonians 2:19).

Crowns are a symbol of authority. As such, they denote the authority that will be granted to Christians during the Millennial period when they reign with Christ for 1000 years. Now, Christians will not be running around with one or more crowns upon their heads any more than the Queen of England wears a crown all the time. The fact that she is the queen entitles her to wear the crown, which gives her the authority to exercise her queenly prerogatives.

So it will be with believers during the Millennium. Christians are now earning their position of service for Christ during the Millennium. Knowing this should give us incentive to pursue better and more lasting heights of Christian service here on earth!

A FINAL EXHORTATION

In Revelation 3:11, Jesus said, "I am coming quickly [suddenly]; hold fast what you have, so that no one will take your crown." Second John 8 warns, "Watch yourselves, that you do not lose what we have accomplished." Many a Christian has served the Lord for many years only to capitulate to the enticement of carnality, sensuality, or some other temptation that turns him from serving Christ to reveling in the appetites of the flesh. Although such individuals will not lose their salvation, they will forfeit their rewards or they may lose the crowns they have already earned.

Every Christian who desires to serve Christ to the maximum during the Millennium is advised to heed our Lord's challenge to the church of Smyrna in Revelation 2:10: "Be faithful until death, and I will give you the crown of life."

Years ago a great Bible teacher, M. R. DeHaan, said, "To come to Christ costs you nothing, to follow Christ costs you something, to serve Christ will cost you everything."

As 1 Corinthians 3:15 says, "If any man's work is burned up, he will suffer loss; but he himself will be saved, yet so as through fire."

The Judgment Seat of Christ (The Bema)
Romans 14:10

Heaven

Christ Meets the Church
1 Ths 4:16-17

The Marriage of the Lamb
Rev 19:7-9

The Rapture
1 Ths 4:13-18

Gold, Silver, and Precious Stones

Judgment of Believers for Their Works
1 Cor 3:11-15; 2 Cor 5:10

Wood, Hay, and Stubble

The Glorious Appearing
2 Ths 1:7-10

Incorruptible Crown	**Crown of Life**	**Crown of Glory**	**Crown of Righteousness**	**Crown of Rejoicing**
The Victor's Crown	Martyr's Crown	Elder's Crown	For those who love His appearing	Soul Winner's Crown
1 Cor 9:25	*Rev 2:10*	*1 Pet 5:2-4*	*2 Tim 4:8*	*1 Ths 2:19-20*

"Every man that striveth for the mastery is temperate in all things. Now they do it to obtain a corruptible crown; but we an incorruptible" (KJV).

"Fear none of those things which thou shalt suffer: behold, the devil shall cast some of you into prison, that ye may be tried; and ye shall have tribulation ten days; be thou faithful unto death, and I will give thee a crown of life" (KJV).

"Feed the flock of God which is among you, taking the oversight thereof, not by constraint but willingly; not for filthy lucre, but of a ready mind; neither as being lords over God's heritage, but being examples to the flock. And when the chief Shepherd shall appear, ye shall receive a crown of glory that fadeth not away" (KJV).

"There is laid up for me a crown of righteousness, which the Lord, the righteous judge, shall give me at that day: and not to me only, but unto all them also that love his appearing" (KJV).

"For what is our hope, or joy, or crown of rejoicing? Are not even ye in the presence of our Lord Jesus Christ at his coming? For ye are our glory and joy" (KJV).

It is obvious the person's salvation is not jeopardized, for he is saved "so as through fire." The phrase "as through fire" is similar to our contemporary adage "saved by the skin of his teeth." These Christians will not lose their salvation, but they will have nothing to show for their life of Christian service.

19.
THE TRIBULATION

In His masterful Olivet Discourse, our Lord warned that this world has yet to see a time of "great tribulation, such as was not since the beginning of the world to this time, no, nor ever shall be" (Matthew 24:21 KJV). And those who take the Bible literally find it significant that the Tribulation period is given more space in Scripture than any other comparable event. There is more space allocated to the Tribulation than the 1000-year Millennial kingdom, heaven, hell, or any subject except salvation and the promise of Christ's second coming. It is mentioned at least 49 times by the Hebrew prophets and at least 15 times in the New Testament.

OLD TESTAMENT TRIBULATION REFERENCES

The Time of Jacob's Trouble . . . . . . Jeremiah 30:7

The Seventieth Week of Daniel . . . Daniel 9:27

Jehovah's Strange Work . . . . Isaiah 28:21

Jehovah's Strange Act . . . . Isaiah 28:21

The Day of Israel's Calamity . . . . . . Deuteronomy 32:35; Obadiah 12-14

The Tribulation . . . . Deuteronomy 4:30

The Indignation . . . . Isaiah 26:20; Daniel 11:36

The Overflowing Scourge . . . . Isaiah 28:15,18

The Day of Vengeance . . . . Isaiah 34:8; 35:4; 61:2

The Year of Recompense . . . . Isaiah 34:8

The Time of Trouble . . . . Daniel 12:1; Zephaniah 1:15

The Day of Wrath . . . . Zephaniah 1:15

The Day of Distress . . . . Zephaniah 1:15

The Day of Wasteness . . . . Zephaniah 1:15

The Day of Desolation . . . . Zephaniah 1:15

The Day of Darkness . . . . Zephaniah 1:15; Amos 5:18,20; Joel 2:2

The Day of Gloominess . . . . Zephaniah 1:15; Joel 2:2

The Day of Clouds . . . . Zephaniah 1:15; Joel 2:2

The Day of Thick Darkness . . . . . . Zephaniah 1:15; Joel 2:2

The Day of the Trumpet . . . . Zephaniah 1:16

The Day of Alarm . . . . Zephaniah 1:16

NEW TESTAMENT TRIBULATION REFERENCES

The Day of the Lord . . . . . 1 Thessalonians 5:2

The Wrath of God . . . . Revelation 14:10,19; 15:1,7; 16:1

The Hour of Trial . . . . Revelation 3:10

The Great Day of the Wrath of the Lamb of God . . . . . . Revelation 6:16-17

The Wrath to Come . . . . . 1 Thessalonians 1:10

The Wrath . . . . 1 Thessalonians 5:9; Revelation 11:18

The Great Tribulation . . . . Matthew 24:21; Revelation 2:22; 7:14

The Tribulation . . . . Matthew 24:29

The Hour of Judgment . . . . Revelation 14:7

The details provided in all these Bible passages make it obvious that this is a future event, for no such period has yet occurred in human

The Tribulation

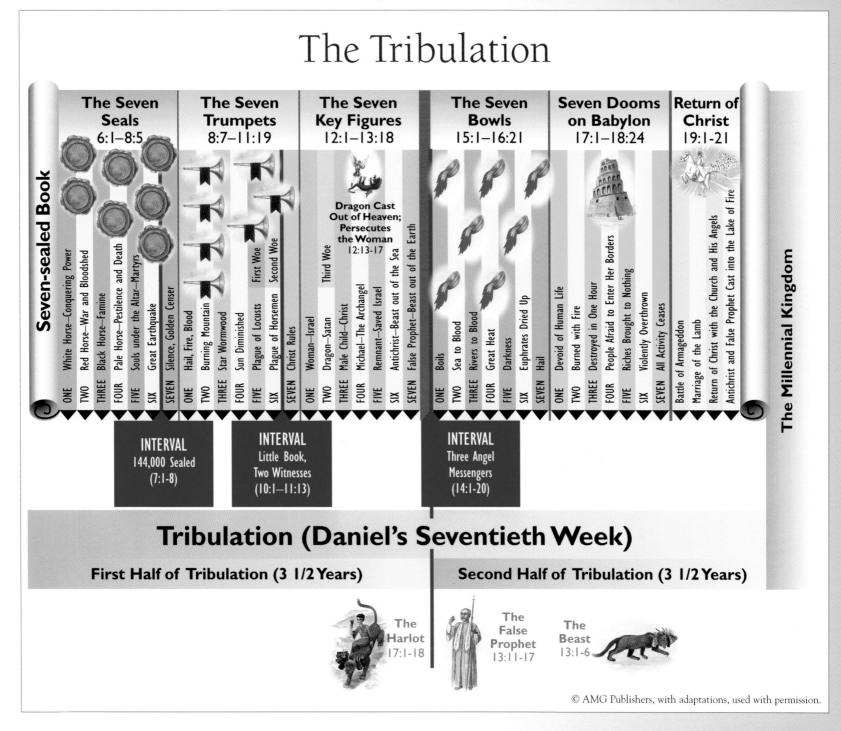

The Seven Seals 6:1–8:5	The Seven Trumpets 8:7–11:19	The Seven Key Figures 12:1–13:18	The Seven Bowls 15:1–16:21	Seven Dooms on Babylon 17:1–18:24	Return of Christ 19:1–21

Seven-sealed Book

The Seven Seals:
- ONE — White Horse—Conquering Power
- TWO — Red Horse—War and Bloodshed
- THREE — Black Horse—Famine
- FOUR — Pale Horse—Pestilence and Death
- FIVE — Souls under the Altar—Martyrs
- SIX — Great Earthquake
- SEVEN — Silence, Golden Censer

The Seven Trumpets:
- ONE — Hail, Fire, Blood
- TWO — Burning Mountain
- THREE — Star Wormwood
- FOUR — Sun Diminished
- FIVE — Plague of Locusts / First Woe
- SIX — Plague of Horsemen / Second Woe
- SEVEN — Christ Rules

The Seven Key Figures:
- ONE — Woman–Israel
- TWO — Dragon–Satan / Third Woe
- THREE — Male Child–Christ
- FOUR — Michael–The Archangel
- FIVE — Remnant–Saved Israel
- SIX — Antichrist–Beast out of the Sea
- SEVEN — False Prophet–Beast out of the Earth

Dragon Cast Out of Heaven; Persecutes the Woman 12:13-17

The Seven Bowls:
- ONE — Boils
- TWO — Sea to Blood
- THREE — Rivers to Blood
- FOUR — Great Heat
- FIVE — Darkness
- SIX — Euphrates Dried Up
- SEVEN — Hail

Seven Dooms on Babylon:
- ONE — Devoid of Human Life
- TWO — Burned with Fire
- THREE — Destroyed in One Hour
- FOUR — People Afraid to Enter Her Borders
- FIVE — Riches Brought to Nothing
- SIX — Violently Overthrown
- SEVEN — All Activity Ceases

Return of Christ:
- Battle of Armageddon
- Marriage of the Lamb
- Return of Christ with the Church and His Angels
- Antichrist and False Prophet Cast into the Lake of Fire

The Millennial Kingdom

INTERVAL
144,000 Sealed
(7:1-8)

INTERVAL
Little Book,
Two Witnesses
(10:1–11:13)

INTERVAL
Three Angel
Messengers
(14:1-20)

Tribulation (Daniel's Seventieth Week)

First Half of Tribulation (3 1/2 Years) | **Second Half of Tribulation (3 1/2 Years)**

The Harlot 17:1-18
The False Prophet 13:11-17
The Beast 13:1-6

© AMG Publishers, with adaptations, used with permission.

history. What's more, Jesus Himself said the Great Tribulation would take place just before His glorious appearing. He clearly said in His Olivet Discourse, "Immediately after the tribulation of those days...the sign of the Son of Man will appear in the sky, and then all the tribes of the earth will mourn, and they will see the Son of Man coming on the clouds of the sky with power and great glory" (Matthew 24:29-30).

The prophet Daniel predicted that the Tribulation would last seven years. Seventy *heptads* or seven-year periods were determined upon the people of God, the nation of Israel (Daniel 9:24-27), which means seventy times seven (or 490) years. This 490-year period has three divisions: seven *heptads*, or 49 years, to restore the wall of Jerusalem; 62 *heptads*, or 434 years, until "Messiah will be cut off" (Christ's crucifixion—Daniel 9:26); and then seven final years that have not yet been fulfilled. Israel has been on prophetic "hold" for almost 2000 years, but someday it will go through that final seven-year period!

Jesus predicted that, due to its severity, the Tribulation would be shortened. The reason the Tribulation will be a holocaust of major proportions is because it combines the wrath of God, the fury of Satan, and the evil nature of man run wild.

Take the horror of every war since time began, throw in every natural disaster in recorded history, and cast off all restraints so that the unspeakable cruelty and hatred and injustice of man toward his fellow men can fully mature, and compress all that into a period of seven years. Even if you could imagine such a horror, it wouldn't approach the mind-boggling terror and turmoil of the Tribulation.

WHY A PERIOD OF TRIBULATION?

Everything God does has one or more purposes, and that's true about the Tribulation. In Scripture we can find at least four purposes for the Tribulation.

To bring time to an end. When introducing the events that culminate with the Tribulation and return of Christ, Daniel spoke of the consummation of time as "bring[ing] in everlasting righteousness" (9:24). The Tribulation is a fitting consummation of the grand experiment of the ages from Adam to the second coming, which gave individuals an opportunity to worship God voluntarily.

To fulfill Israel's prophecies. Many prophecies about Israel have yet to be fulfilled. The Jewish people's return to the land during this last century and their recognition as a nation in 1948 is only one (described in detail in Ezekiel 36–37). Other prophecies, such as the rebuilding of the Temple and the renewal of the Temple sacrifices, will be fulfilled during the Tribulation. God is not done with Israel!

To shake man from his false sense of security. A stable world leads man to think that he can function independently of God. Earthquakes, plagues, and other physical phenomena from God will so shake man's natural confidence that, when he hears the gospel through the preaching of the 144,000 witnesses, he will be more open to its offer of forgiveness and grace.

To force man to choose Christ or Antichrist. One major purpose of the Tribulation is to give the billions of individuals living at that time seven years of opportunity in which to make up their minds to receive or reject Christ. That may be part of what Daniel meant in calling it "the consummation" (9:27). Billions of people will not have an opportunity to live out their normal lifespan, so amid these traumatic events, they will make an eternal decision. If they choose Christ, they will, as "servants of our God," receive the mark of the Father on their foreheads (Revelation 7:3). But they will then be "open season" for martyrdom at the hands of the religious system of Babylon, the government leaders headed by Antichrist, the False Prophet, and the people whose lust for sin is surpassed only by their hatred for Christians. It is doubtful that many Tribulation saints will survive to the Millennium. If, on the other hand, people accept the Antichrist, they will have the mark of the Beast placed on their foreheads and hands. This seems to be a final, irrevocable decision.

It is difficult for non-Christians to understand that a God of love would allow the Tribulation. But God wants to draw as many people as possible to Him before Jesus returns to set up His Millennial kingdom, and He will use the Tribulation to get their attention. In grace and love, He will give more supernatural signs and leadings of His Spirit than at any time in the history of the world, proving that He is "not willing that any should perish, but that all should come to repentance" (2 Peter 3:9 KJV).

Consider the incredible efforts God will expend to help man make the right decision:

He will pour out His Spirit on man as in the Day of Pentecost (Joel 2:28-32).

He will commission 144,000 Jewish witnesses like the apostle Paul (Revelation 7).

He will shake man's false sense of security through three massive earthquakes and many chaotic plagues.

He will send two Old Testament prophets to testify in Jerusalem with supernatural power (Revelation 11).

He will send an angel who proclaims the everlasting gospel "to preach to those who live on the earth, and to every nation and tribe and tongue and people" (Revelation 14:6). God will do this to make sure everyone hears the gospel and can make a deliberate choice to receive His Son and be saved. That is the only time in the Bible when an angel is used for such a task.

With all these loving efforts to draw people to salvation, the world will witness the greatest soul harvest in human history. Revelation 7:9 tells us that "a great multitude...from every nation, and all tribes and peoples, and tongues, [will be] standing before the throne and before the Lamb, clothed in white robes, [with] palm branches...in their hands." Who are these redeemed souls? An angel told the apostle John, "These are the ones who come out of the great tribulation, and they have washed their robes and made them white in the blood of the Lamb" (verse 14). So, during the Tribulation, God will mercifully lead huge numbers of people to faith in His Son and to eternal life.

THE LENGTH OF THE TRIBULATION

In his prophecy of the 70 weeks or 490 years, Daniel said the Tribulation would be "one week" and uses the Hebrew word designating a week of years, or seven years. The first 69 weeks of years, which started with the decree of Artaxerxes to restore the walls of Jerusalem and ended with the rejection of Jesus, was exactly 483 years. And the Tribulation, or the last week of years, will be seven years long (Daniel 9:24-27).

In Revelation, we find the seven years divided into two periods of 1260 days, or 42 months, or three-and-one-half years, or "time and times and half a time" (Revelation 11:2-3; 12:6,7,14; 13:5). Every one of those time spans totals up to seven years. The first half, or first 42 months, is the Tribulation, while the last half is called by our Lord "the great tribulation."

THE JUDGMENTS OF THE TRIBULATION

Our chart featuring the Tribulation on page 57 shows the three major judgments and how they interrelate. The seal judgments cover the first quarter or about 21 months, during which the Antichrist comes on the scene and conquers the world by diplomacy. Then the breaking of the seventh seal introduces the seven trumpet judgments, which will cause even greater catastrophes to come to the earth. When Satan indwells Antichrist in the middle of the Tribulation, that introduces the last 1260 days or three-and-one-half years, which is the "great tribulation." The seventh trumpet, like the seventh seal, does nothing but introduce the seven bowl judgments, which are the severest of all the judgments.

The Seal Judgments

During the Tribulation, the seal judgments come first (Revelation 6; 8:1). In the ancient world, seals were used to close up a scroll. Hot wax was dripped onto the closed scroll, then the sender's signet ring was pressed into the wax to form a mark. This seal assured

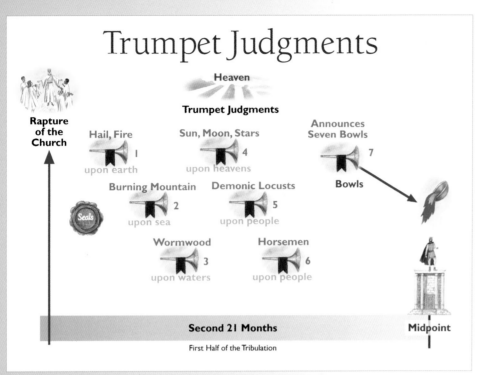

Trumpet Judgments

Heaven

Trumpet Judgments

Rapture of the Church

Hail, Fire — 1 — upon earth

Sun, Moon, Stars — 4 — upon heavens

Announces Seven Bowls — 7

Burning Mountain — 2 — upon sea

Demonic Locusts — 5 — upon people

Bowls

Wormwood — 3 — upon waters

Horsemen — 6 — upon people

Seals

Second 21 Months

Midpoint

First Half of the Tribulation

---

that the message would not be opened before it reached the individual to whom it was sent. A thorough study of Revelation 5 indicates that the sealed scroll is the title deed of ownership to planet Earth. Only Jesus Christ—the Lamb of God—is found worthy to open the seals and commence the judgments of the Tribulation.

First Seal (Revelation 6:1-2)—This is the white horse judgment or the first horseman of the Apocalypse. On the horse is Antichrist, who comes to conquer at the beginning of the Tribulation. We read that he is wearing a crown, but the fact that he does not have arrows for his bow indicates he will conquer the world's governments by peaceful diplomacy rather than military might. By contrast, Christ conquers at the end of the Tribulation in Revelation 19.

Second Seal (Revelation 6:3-4)—This is the red horse judgment. The color of the horse appears to indicate blood and death, for the passage says that "it was granted to take peace from the earth, and that men would slay one another; and a great sword was given to him" (verse 4).

Third Seal (Revelation 6:5-6)—In the black horse judgment, the rider comes forth with "a pair of scales in his hand," saying, "A quart of wheat for a denarius, and three quarts of barley for a denarius; and do

not damage the oil and the wine." This indicates a severe famine, which often is the case following military conflicts (as mentioned in the two previous seals). The monetary description indicates that normal purchasing power will be reduced to one-eighth of its former level.

Fourth Seal (Revelation 6:7-8)—The ashen horse judgment is the most severe of the four judgments: "Authority was given to them over a fourth of the earth, to kill with sword and with famine and with pestilence and by the wild beasts of the earth."

Fifth Seal (Revelation 6:9-11)—Evidently 25 percent of the world's population will die during the first week of the Tribulation. When the fifth seal is broken, martyrs of the Tribulation will cry out to God for revenge upon those unbelievers who killed them. They are told that the time for vengeance has not yet come, but it will. The passage mentions that more martyrs are yet to come. Their prayer of vengeance is finally answered in Revelation 16:4-7 during the third bowl judgment.

Sixth Seal (Revelation 6:12-17)—Six things happen: 1) a great earthquake; 2) the sun is blacked out; 3) the moon becomes like blood; 4) the stars fall to the Earth; 5) the sky tears apart like a scroll; and 6) every mountain and island is moved out of place. This will lead many people toward even further rebellion against God. They will pray to the rocks and mountains to "fall on us and hide us from the presence of Him who sits on the throne, and from the wrath of the Lamb."

Seventh Seal (Revelation 8:1)—The seventh seal judgment introduces the next series of seven judgments, known as the trumpet judgments.

The Trumpet Judgments

A trumpet was used in the ancient world to signal a special announcement or the advent of a major event. These trumpet judgments certainly qualify as major events. The judgments are all administered by special angels, and the movement is from heaven to earth, clearly showing that it is God, not nature, that is the origin of these afflictions. Many of these judgments are similar to the ten plagues on Egypt (Exodus 7–11). The seven judgments are as follows:

First Trumpet (Revelation 8:7)—The first trumpet judgment is hail and fire mixed with blood thrown down upon the earth, with the result that "a third of the earth was burned up, and a third of the trees were burned up, and all the green grass was burned up." Many see parallels here with the Old Testament judgments upon Sodom and Gomorrah (Genesis 18:16–19:28) and the sixth plague upon Egypt (Exodus 9:22-26).

Second Trumpet (Revelation 8:8-9)—This judgment involves "something like a great mountain burning with fire" being thrown into the sea so that "a third of the sea became blood, and a third of the creatures which were in the sea and had life, died; and a third of the ships were destroyed." This judgment has similarities with the first plague in Egypt (Exodus 7:16-21).

Third Trumpet (Revelation 8:10-11)—"A great star" falls from heaven, "burning like a torch, and it fell on a third of the rivers and on the springs of waters." The star is named Wormwood (meaning "bitter") and could be an angelic entity since it has a proper name and stars are sometimes associated with angels (Revelation 1:10; see also Job 38:7). Many die from the bitter water.

Fourth Trumpet (Revelation 8:12-13)—In this judgment a third of the sun, moon, and stars are diminished. This parallels the ninth plague in Egypt (Exodus 10:21-23). With this judgment comes an angelic announcement to the earth warning about the three remaining trumpet judgments.

Fifth Trumpet (Revelation 9:1-11)—Here, another star falls to earth from heaven, but this one, possibly Satan himself or a special angel, has the key to the bottomless pit, which he opens to let loose a great swarm of demonic locusts. These special creatures are permitted to torture—but not kill—people for five months. This demonic locust invasion is also spoken of in Joel 2:1-11. This will be a terrible time for unbelievers.

Sixth Trumpet (Revelation 9:13-21)—The sixth trumpet judgment releases four angels who are specially created for this moment

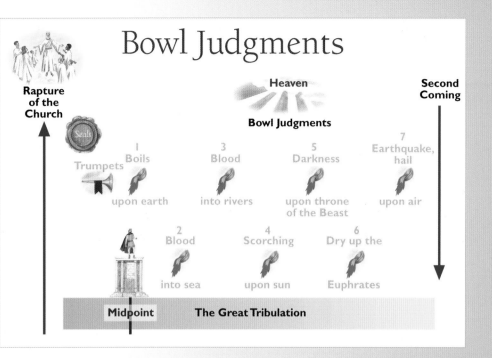

in history. These angels command an angelic host of 200 million demons who go forth as horsemen to inflict death upon a third of the people on earth. (These horsemen are not 200 million Chinese, as has been suggested by some—they are clearly of demonic origin.) They, like the creatures in the previous judgment, come from the bottomless pit and are clearly not human. By this time in history, at least half of the earth's population will have died in only a few years. Even after all these happenings, Scripture reports that people will "not repent of the works of their hands, so as not to worship demons, and the idols."

Seventh Trumpet (Revelation 11:15-19)—The seventh trumpet judgment introduces the seven bowl judgments that follow.

The Bowl or Vial Judgments

These judgments, when compared to the seal and trumpet judgments, appear to be the most intense and severe. It appears that these bowls have been collecting God's wrath, so to speak, for a long time. Now they are filled to the brim and ready to be poured, which will prepare the way for Christ's second coming. The angels who administer these judgments are pictured as turning the bowls upside down to ensure that every last drop of God's wrath goes forth (see

Revelation 15–16). Nothing is held back. Each judgment is specifically directed at an object of God's wrath:

First Bowl (Revelation 16:1-2)—This bowl is poured "on the earth" and aimed specifically at those who have the mark of the Beast. In some measure, it is a fulfillment of Revelation 14:9-11. The judgment is an affliction of grievous, malignant sores upon the human body.

Second Bowl (Revelation 16:3)—This bowl is poured "into the sea," turning the water to blood so that every living thing that was left alive from previous judgments will be killed. The stench and disease that will result from this is unimaginable.

Third Bowl (Revelation 16:4-7)—The third bowl is poured "into the rivers and the springs of waters" so that all remaining fresh water is also turned to blood. This judgment is God's answer to the martyrs' prayer that their deaths be avenged (Revelation 6:10).

Fourth Bowl (Revelation 16:8-9)—This bowl is poured "upon the sun" so that an extraordinary heat goes forth and scorches people with fire. We are told how the people on earth respond: "They blasphemed the name of God...and they did not repent so as to give Him glory."

Fifth Bowl (Revelation 16:10-11)—The next bowl is poured out "on the throne of the beast" so that his whole domain is darkened with a blackout. This is similar to the darkness experienced in Egypt during the ten plagues (Exodus 10:21-23). Apparently this is not a normal darkness but is accompanied by some kind of agony that will cause people to gnaw their tongues because of the pain. Once again the response is to blaspheme "the God of heaven because of their pains and their sores; and they did not repent of their deeds."

Sixth Bowl (Revelation 16:12-15)—This bowl is poured out "on the great river, the Euphrates" so that its flow of water dries up. This prepares the way for the kings of the East to come to the mountains of Israel for the battle of Armageddon. God is clearly baiting the Antichrist and drawing him into His trap, which is set for further and final judgment at the second coming. Joel 3:9-11 and Psalm 2 are parallel passages depicting the gathering of the world's armies for Armageddon.

Seventh Bowl (Revelation 16:17-21)—The last bowl is poured out "upon the air" so that "flashes of lightning and sounds and peals of thunder" announce the greatest earthquake in the history of the world. This judgment apparently takes place in conjunction with the return of Christ and is also reported in Joel 3:14-17, Zechariah 14:4-5, and Matthew 24:29. This worldwide earthquake will cause Jerusalem to be split into three sections, preparing the way for Millennial changes after the second coming. This is also the moment of Babylon's sudden destruction. Further, this global judgment is accompanied by 100-pound hailstones from heaven. Once again the response of unbelievers is to blaspheme God "because of the plague of the hail, because its plague was extremely severe."

The Beast and the harlot in the chart on page 57 signify the governmental system described in Revelation 13, 17, and 18. They represent the religious system that grew out of Babylon—a system so powerful she rides the governmental beast (in other words, controls it) until the midpoint of the Tribulation. Then "the harlot," the false religious system, will be destroyed by the kings of the earth (chapter 17). Then the False Prophet appears and, during the last half of the Tribulation, gets people to worship Satan, who indwells the Antichrist (2 Thessalonians 2:8). In the end, all three entities used to control men—represented by the Beasts and the religious, governmental, and commercial Babylon—will be forever destroyed.

MAKING THE RIGHT DECISION

Those who manage to survive the horrific chaos of the Tribulation as believers will go into the Millennial kingdom. And those who rejected Christ and worshiped the Antichrist will be cast into torment and eventually into the Lake of Fire.

This brings us back to the need for all men to repent of their self-will in the name of Jesus, who alone can both forgive our sins and grant us eternal life. If you do it now, before the seven-year Tribulation begins, you can be among those who are raptured and thus avoid the Tribulation. Our prayer is that if you have not already made this choice, you will do so very soon.

20.
THE CAMPAIGN OF ARMAGEDDON AND CHRIST'S RETURN

Armageddon will be the last great world war of history, and it will take place in Israel in conjunction with the second coming of Christ. The battle or campaign of Armageddon is described in Daniel 11:40-45, Joel 3:9-17, Zechariah 14:1-3, and Revelation 16:14-16. It will occur in the final days of the Tribulation, when the kings of the world will gather together "for the war of the great day of God, the Almighty" in a place known as "Har–Magedon" (Revelation 16:14,16). The site where this will occur is the plain of Esdraelon, around the hill of Megiddo, in northern Israel about 20 miles south-southeast of Haifa.

The term *Armageddon* comes from the Hebrew tongue. *Har* is the word for "mountain" and often appears with the Hebrew definite article *H. Mageddon* is likely the ruins of an ancient city that overlooks the Valley of Esdraelon in northern Israel.

According to the Bible, great armies from the east and the west will gather and assemble on this plain. There will be threats to the power of the Antichrist from the south, and he will move to destroy a revived Babylon in the east before finally turning his forces toward Jerusalem to subdue and destroy it. As he and his armies approach Jerusalem, God will intervene and Jesus Christ will return to rescue His people Israel. The Lord and His angelic army will destroy the armies, capture the Antichrist and the False Prophet, and cast them into the Lake of Fire (Revelation 19:11-21).

In a sense, Armageddon is a battle that never really takes place. That is, it does not take place in accordance with its original human intent. Its human purpose is to gather the armies of the world to execute the Antichrist's "final solution" to the "Jewish problem." This is why Jesus Christ chooses this moment in history for His return to Earth—to thwart the Antichrist's attempted annihilation of the Jews and to destroy the armies of the world, which were gathered for another purpose. It seems only fitting, in light of mankind's bloody legacy, that the return of Christ should be precipitated by a worldwide military conflict against Israel. So it is that history is moving toward Armageddon.

THE EIGHT STAGES OF ARMAGEDDON[7]

The numbers below correspond with the numbers in the chart on page 64:

1. The assembling of the allies of the Antichrist (Psalm 2:1-6; Joel 3:9-11; Revelation 16:12-16).

2. The destruction of Babylon (Isaiah 13–14; Jeremiah 50–51; Zechariah 5:5-11; Revelation 17–18).

3. The fall of Jerusalem (Micah 4:11–5:1; Zechariah 12–14).

4. The armies of the Antichrist at Bozrah (Jeremiah 49:13-14; Micah 2:12).

5. The national regeneration of Israel (Psalm 79:1-13; 80:1-19; Isaiah 64:1-12; Hosea 6:1-13; Joel 2:28-32; Zechariah 12:10; 13:7-9; Romans 11:25-27).

6. The second coming of Jesus Christ (Isaiah 34:1-7; 63:1-3; Micah 2:12-13; Habakkuk 3:3).

7. The battle from Bozrah to the Valley of Jehoshaphat (Jeremiah 49:20-22; Joel 3:12-13; Zechariah 14:12-15).

8. The victory ascent upon the Mount of Olives (Joel 3:14-17; Zechariah 14:3-5; Matthew 24:29-31; Revelation 16:17-21; 19:11-21).

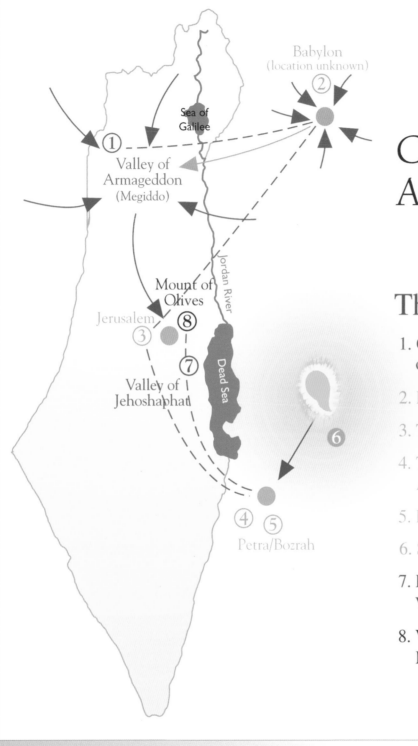

The Campaign of Armageddon

The Eight Stages

1. Gathering of the Armies of the Antichrist

2. Destruction of Babylon

3. The Fall of Jerusalem

4. The Armies of the Antichrist at Bozrah

5. Israel's Regeneration

6. Second Coming of Christ

7. End of Fighting at the Valley of Jehoshaphat

8. Victory Ascent upon the Mount of Olives

21.
THE GLORIOUS APPEARING

The most thrilling event in all of human history is yet to come. It will be that moment in time when our Lord Jesus Christ returns to this earth in power and great glory to set up His kingdom that will last 1000 years. From a prophetic standpoint, it will be the culmination of all prophecy. At least 325 prophecies of Christ's second coming guarantee it will take place, and this event will usher in the most ideal conditions on Earth since the Garden of Eden.

Words seem inadequate to fully describe that magnificent event that will combine all the hopes and dreams of the billions of people who have put their faith in God from Adam and Eve to the end of the Tribulation period. To get a full picture we must turn to several prophecies and put them all together:

EVENTS OF THE GLORIOUS APPEARING

1. It takes place immediately after the Tribulation (Matthew 24:29).

2. Cosmic phenomena will occur in the sun, moon, and stars (Matthew 24:29).

3. The sign of the Son of Man in heaven will be seen by everyone (Matthew 24:30), and Christ will gather His elect (verse 31).

4. Heaven will open and Christ will appear on a white horse (Revelation 19:11).

5. Christ will be followed by the armies of heaven (Revelation 19:14), prepared to judge the ungodly (Jude 14-15).

6. Christ will come in power and great glory (Matthew 24:30).

7. Christ will stand on the Mount of Olives (Zechariah 14:3-5).

8. Unbelievers will mourn, for they are not ready (Matthew 24:30).

9. The Beast (Antichrist) and his armies will confront Christ (Revelation 19:19).

10. Christ casts the Beast and False Prophet into the Lake of Fire (Revelation 19:20).

11. Christ's rejecters will be killed (Revelation 19:21).

12. Satan will be cast into the bottomless pit for 1000 years (Revelation 20:1-3).

13. The Old Testament and Tribulation saints will be resurrected (Matthew 24:31; Revelation 20:4).

14. Christ will judge the nations and establish His kingdom (Matthew 25).

The term "the glorious appearing" (KJV) is not found in the book of Revelation, but in Titus 2:13. There it describes the physical, visible return of Christ to Earth in distinction from that "blessed hope" (Titus 2:13), which is the Rapture of the church, or the coming of Christ for His believers prior to the Tribulation period.

Of all the descriptions of the glorious appearing in the Bible, none is more graphic than that given by the apostle John:

I saw heaven standing open and there before me was a white horse, whose rider is called Faithful and True. With justice he judges and makes war. His eyes are like blazing fire, and on his head are many crowns. He has a name written on him that no one knows but he himself. He is dressed in a robe dipped in blood, and his name is the Word of God. The armies of heaven were following him, riding on white horses and dressed in fine linen, white and clean. Out of his mouth comes a sharp sword with which to strike down the nations. "He will rule them with an iron scepter." He treads the winepress of the fury of the wrath of God Almighty. On his robe and on his thigh he has this name written: King of kings and Lord of lords (Revelation 19:11-16 NIV).

When Christ comes, as the righteous warrior, He will be invincible. He will consume all before Him, all that stand in opposition to Him, and bring every person into subjection. This will be the first clearly righteous war in the history of humankind. The ability of Christ to wage a righteous war is not only seen in His holy nature, but in that His eyes are "like blazing fire," indicating that He will judge according to truth. The best judge on earth cannot know all the facts of a given situation because he or she is limited by human frailty. Jesus Christ is not so limited. He who knows the end from the beginning will be a righteous Judge, for His all-seeing eyes will reveal all truth about every individual and nation.

THE ARMIES OF CHRIST

Note also that Jesus will come with the armies of heaven "following him, riding on white horses and dressed in fine linen, white and clean" (Revelation 19:14 NIV). The armies of heaven consist of the angelic hosts, the Old Testament saints, the church, and the Tribulation saints. What's especially significant is the garb of this army: They are "dressed in fine linen, white and clean." Military men are issued darker-colored uniforms for battle dress—not only for camouflage, but also because light-colored clothes would become soiled immediately. By contrast, the Commander in Chief of the heavenly forces clothes His army in white, a practice unheard of in the history of warfare. Christ will do this because no member of His army will do battle. Not one of us will lift a finger, for the battle will be carried out by the spoken word of our Lord Himself.

The glorious appearing of Christ will not only bring to consummation the enmity of Satan, his Antichrist, the False Prophet, and the millions they deceive, but it will also usher in the Millennial kingdom—the righteous reign of Christ on Earth. Revelation 19:16 tells us that "on his robe and on his thigh he has this name written: King of kings and Lord of lords" (Revelation 19:16 NIV). A warrior goes into battle with his sword on his thigh. Christ's sword will be His spoken word. The word that called the world into being will call every human leader and the world's armies into subjection to Him. Christ Jesus, the living Lord, will be established in that day for what He is in reality—the King above all kings, the Lord above all lords. The prophet Zechariah said it best in 14:9: "The LORD will be king over all the earth; in that day the LORD will be the only one, and His name the only one." Amen!

22.
75-DAY PREPARATION FOR THE MILLENNIUM

Daniel 12:11-12 indicates that there will be a 75-day interval between the second coming of Christ to Earth and the start of the 1000-year Millennial kingdom. How do we derive this conclusion, and what is the purpose of this 75-day period? Let's begin by reading the passage: "From the time that the regular sacrifice is abolished and the abomination of desolation is set up, there will be 1290 days. How blessed is he who keeps waiting and attains to the 1335 days!"

The 75-day time period is derived as follows: First, we know that Jesus the Messiah will return at the end of the seventieth week of Daniel (Daniel 9:24-27). The seventieth week is divided into two halves of 1260 days each (Daniel 9:27). In Daniel 12:6, Daniel asked

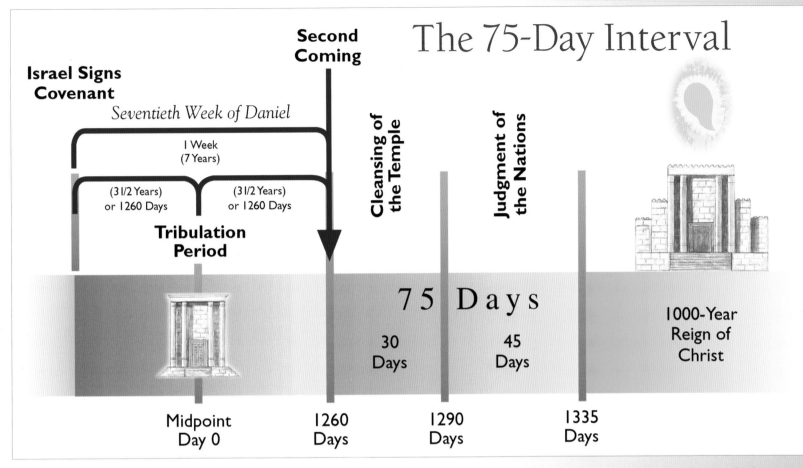

The 75-Day Interval

Second Coming

Israel Signs Covenant

Seventieth Week of Daniel

1 Week (7 Years)

(3 1/2 Years) or 1260 Days

(3 1/2 Years) or 1260 Days

Tribulation Period

Cleansing of the Temple

Judgment of the Nations

75 Days

30 Days

45 Days

1000-Year Reign of Christ

Midpoint Day 0

1260 Days

1290 Days

1335 Days

---

the angel, "How long will it be until the end of these wonders?" The angel replied, "A time, times, and half a time; and as soon as they finish shattering the power of the holy people, all these events will be completed" (Daniel 12:7b). Earlier, in Daniel 12:1-3, the angel set the context of his words as being the second coming of Messiah. Thus we know that "all these events will be completed" (Daniel 12:7) in conjunction with Messiah's coming. Thus, Christ's second coming will occur at the end of the second set of 1260 days.

Next, notice that Daniel 12:11 speaks of something being accomplished at the end of 1290 days—that's 30 days extra beyond the second coming. Since Daniel 12:11 is concerned with the Temple sacrifice and the "abomination of desolation," it is safe to conclude that the first 30-day interval relates to the Temple. We know from Ezekiel 40–48 that the Lord will establish a Temple during the Millennium. Thus the 30-day period will be the time in which the Millennial Temple will be set up and prepared for use.

In Daniel 12:12 we read about those who reach the point of 1335 days. That means we need to include an additional 45 days beyond the 30-day period, giving us a total of 75 days. The angel said that those who make it through that time will be "blessed." This connotes a personal or individual blessing, and it indicates that that particular person is qualified to enter the 1000-year Messianic kingdom. In fact, Matthew 25:34 says, "Then the King will say to those on His right, 'Come, you who are *blessed* of My Father, inherit the kingdom prepared for you from the foundation of the world'" (emphasis added).

Evidently the 75-day interval is a time of preparation for the kingdom. Because so much of the globe will have been destroyed during the judgments of the Tribulation, it is not at all surprising that our Lord will take some time to renovate His creation in preparation for the Millennial kingdom.

23.

FROM THE JUDGMENT INTO THE MILLENNIUM

Very little has been written about who populates the Millennial kingdom, but it is a highly significant subject. Few people will actually be left alive on earth in the transition from the Tribulation to the Millennial kingdom. The low number of people is easy to understand when you consider that possibly half a billion Christians or more will be raptured before the Tribulation, including children under the age of accountability. After the Rapture, over half the world's population will be killed during the seal and trumpet judgments (Revelation 6:8; 9:18), which take place during the first half of the seven-year Tribulation. Many more will be killed during the other plagues or judgments, millions of believers will be martyred by the Antichrist for refusing to worship him or take the mark of the Beast, and then there are the Gentiles who are cast into everlasting punishment (Matthew 25:46) for refusing to receive Christ during the Tribulation. After all that, very few people will remain. How many? Only God Himself knows!

WHO WILL ENTER THE MILLENNIUM?

Those who survive to the end of the Tribulation and aren't cast into punishment by Christ will all be believers. Jesus, in the Olivet Discourse, said, "He that shall endure unto the end, the same shall be saved" (Matthew 24:13 KJV). The word "saved" in the original Greek text translates as "delivered," which means those who endure the frightful events of the Tribulation will be delivered if they survive the judgment of the nations described by Jesus in Matthew 25:31-46.

IDENTIFYING JESUS' "BRETHREN"

At the judgment of the nations, there will be three different groups of people. The unsaved followers of Antichrist who are still alive at the end of the Tribulation are called "goats" (Matthew 25:32-33). The believers who survive are called "sheep" (verses 32-33). The third category is the "brethren" (verse 40 KJV) whom the sheep befriend. Those whom Jesus calls "these brothers of Mine" or "my brethren" (KJV) are the Jews who go into the Millennium as believers. Keep in mind that only believers will be permitted to enter the Millennium.

We know that the children of Israel will be gathered back into their land, in "the time of the end," which has already begun in our lifetime (six million Jews in Israel at this writing and growing). Ezekiel 20:33-38 affirms this. Ezekiel 36–37 describes the vision of "the valley...full of bones" with the bones coming together until they stand up as a living nation. Then the clear identity is given in 37:11 as "the whole house of Israel." And in verses 15-28 Ezekiel predicts the reuniting of Israel and Judah into one nation during the Millennium.

That many Jewish people will receive the Lord is seen in Ezekiel 11:19, when the Lord takes away their "heart of stone" and puts a "new spirit within them....a heart of flesh." This is also seen in Ezekiel 18:31. When will this take place? Right after the Antichrist desecrates the Temple in Jerusalem. The Jews will become so disillusioned that they will turn to their Messiah and flee

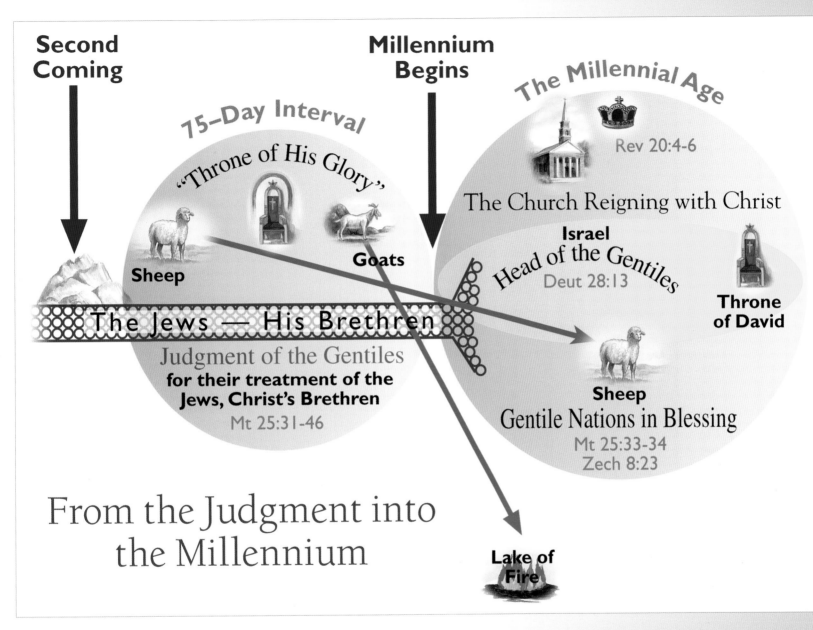

Second Coming

Millennium Begins

75-Day Interval

The Millennial Age

Rev 20:4-6

"Throne of His Glory"

The Church Reigning with Christ

Sheep

Goats

Israel
Head of the Gentiles
Deut 28:13

Throne of David

The Jews — His Brethren

Judgment of the Gentiles
for their treatment of the Jews, Christ's Brethren
Mt 25:31-46

Sheep
Gentile Nations in Blessing
Mt 25:33-34
Zech 8:23

From the Judgment into the Millennium

Lake of Fire

to the wilderness of Petra, where they will be preserved supernaturally. There, God "nourishes them" for the last three-and-one-half years of the Tribulation. These and all the other surviving Jews, which will probably include the 144,000 witnesses of Revelation 7, are believers who our Lord calls "brethren."

Thus we see that only believers will enter the Millennium—Gentile believers and Jewish believers from "the whole house of Israel."

24.
THE MILLENNIUM

The word *Millennium* is a Latin term that means "a thousand years." Revelation 20:1-7 says that Christ will set up a kingdom and reign for 1000 years after His second coming. The Millennium is the capstone of history and a precursor to eternity. During this time Jesus Christ will be the focus of all creation, and He will rule visibly over the entire world in power and great glory. It will be a wonderful time in which righteousness and peace will prevail.

Many Old Testament passages speak of a yet future time of true peace and prosperity for the righteous followers of God under the benevolent physical rule of Jesus Christ on earth. Zechariah 14:9 says, "The LORD will be king over all the earth; in that day the LORD will be the only one, and His name the only one." Then in verses 16-21 we read about what the Millennial kingdom will be like.

Other Old Testament passages on the Millennial kingdom include Psalm 2:6-9; Isaiah 2:2-4; 11:6-9; 65:18-23; Jeremiah 31:12-14,31-37; Ezekiel 34:25-29; 37:1-6; 40–48; Daniel 2:35; 7:13-14; Joel 2:21-27; Amos 9:13-14; Micah 4:1-7; and Zephaniah 3:9-20. These are only a few of the many prophetic passages that describe this kingdom before the first coming of Christ.

The New Testament also speaks of the coming Millennial kingdom in passages such as Matthew 5:1-20; 19:27-30; 26:27-29; Mark 14:25; Luke 22:18; 1 Corinthians 6:9-11; and Revelation 20. Interestingly, it's not until we get to Revelation that we are told the kingdom will last 1000 years.

THE MAJOR FEATURES OF THE MILLENNIUM INCLUDE:

• the binding of Satan at the beginning of the Millennium (Revelation 20:1-3)
• the final restoration of Israel, which will include:
—regeneration (Jeremiah 31:31-34)
—regathering (Deuteronomy 30:1-10; Isaiah 11:11–12:6; Matthew 24:31)
—possession of the land (Ezekiel 20:42-44; 36:28-38)
—re-establishment of the Davidic throne (2 Samuel 7:11-16; 1 Chronicles 17:10-14; Jeremiah 33:17-26)
• the reign of Jesus Christ (Isaiah 2:3-4; 11:2-5)
• the loosing and final rebellion of Satan at the end of the Millennium (Revelation 20:7-10)
• the Great White Throne Judgment and the second resurrection or judgment of the unbelieving dead (Revelation 20:11-15)

The Millennium will be a time in which the Adamic curse will be rolled back, except for death, and in which people will live for 1000 years. Christ will sit on the throne of David and rule the world, bringing peace and righteousness. The Millennium will be a time of great spiritual triumph in which national Israel will fulfill her destiny and Gentiles will partake of tremendous blessings through Jesus Christ and the nation of Israel. The Bible describes the Millennium as a time of righteousness, obedience, holiness, truth, and a fullness of the Holy Spirit as never before.

The Millennium will be a time of tremendous environmental transformation. Isaiah 35:1-2 tells us that the desert will blossom and become productive. There will be abundant rainfall in areas that today are known for their dryness, and there will be plenty of food for animals (Isaiah 30:23-24; 35:7). In addition, the predatory instincts of animals will cease. The distinctions between tame and wild will be erased, as all creatures will live in harmony (Isaiah 11:6-7).

Physical conditions for people will also drastically change for

Key Events of the Millennium

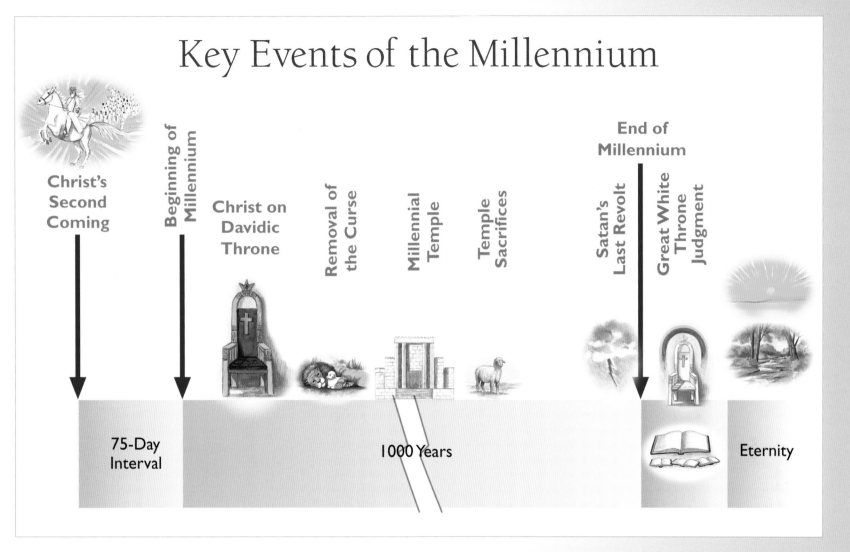

Christ's Second Coming

Beginning of Millennium

Christ on Davidic Throne

Removal of the Curse

Millennial Temple

Temple Sacrifices

End of Millennium

Satan's Last Revolt

Great White Throne Judgment

75-Day Interval

1000 Years

Eternity

the better. People will live much longer and many physical infirmities and health concerns will be eradicated (Isaiah 29:18; 33:24). The absence of sickness and deformity—along with the increased life spans—will minimize the differences between those who still have mortal bodies and those who have resurrected bodies. In the midst of this enhanced environment, people will enjoy prosperity as poverty, injustice, and disease cease (Jeremiah 31:12-14).

Spiritual life in the Millennial kingdom will be unlike anything we've ever experienced. Living daily in the personal and physical presence of Jesus Christ, who will sit on the Davidic throne, will have an enormous impact on the lives of believers. Isaiah said, "The

earth will be full of the knowledge of the LORD as the waters cover the sea" (11:9). The knowledge and worship of Christ will be global and unimpeded. The Millennium will be an era of great spiritual awareness, sensitivity, and activity for both Christians and the restored nation of Israel. For Israel, the New Covenant will be in effect, bringing to fruition the conditions prophesied in passages such as Isaiah 59:20-21; Jeremiah 31:31-34; 32:37-40; Ezekiel 16:60-63; and 37:21-28.

The clearest expression of the spiritual characteristics of the Millennial kingdom is found in the worship and activity in the Millennial Temple. Jesus Christ will be reigning on earth in

Jerusalem and the Millennial Temple will be present and functioning as described in Ezekiel 40–46. Worship in the Millennial Temple will no doubt be of a quality and depth never before seen on earth, as righteous Jews and Gentiles gladly come to Jerusalem to praise the great Savior King (Isaiah 2:2-4; 11:9-10; Ezekiel 20:40-41; 40:1–46:24; Zechariah 14:16).

Unfortunately, even in the midst of such pristine conditions, there will still be human rebellion. Because the complete effects of the Fall will not have been erased, there will be one final revolt against the righteous government of Jesus Christ. This will occur at the end of the Millennium when Satan is briefly released from bondage, but as Scripture says, in the end, he will be judged and punished forever (Revelation 20:7-10).

In a world filled with chaos, despair, corruption, violence, and rampant evil, the certainty of the Millennium offers us assurance that God's prophetic program has not been abandoned. There really will come a day when Christ will rule the world with righteousness and justice. Because of this, Christians today need not have anxiety or fear. Our "blessed hope" is Jesus Christ (Titus 2:13), and we can have confidence that His kingdom will indeed come.

25.
THE GREAT WHITE THRONE JUDGMENT

Written on the table of every man's heart is an intuitive awareness that we will all stand before God to be judged after death and before eternity begins. As our foldout chart titled "Understanding God's Plan for the Ages" reveals, judgment will occur at the end of the Millennial kingdom, after Satan has led his insurrection and failed. Satan, the Beast, and the False Prophet will already have been thrown into the Lake of Fire. On the chart on pages 44–45 you will find this judgment located at the extreme end of the timeline just before the beginning of the ages to come. The last event, then, just before eternity, is the Great White Throne Judgment, described as follows:

I saw a great white throne and Him who sat upon it, from whose presence earth and heaven fled away, and no place was found for them. And I saw the dead, the great and the small, standing before the throne, and books were opened; and another book was opened, which is the book of life; and the dead were judged from the things which were written in the books, according to their deeds. And the sea gave up the dead which were in it, and death and Hades gave up the dead which were in them; and they were judged, every one of them according to their deeds. Then death and Hades were thrown into the lake of fire. This is the second death, the lake of fire. And if anyone's name was not found written in the book of life, he was thrown into the lake of fire (Revelation 20:11-15).

THE IDENTITY OF THE JUDGE

In Acts 17:31 we read that God will judge the world by "that man whom he hath ordained...he hath raised him from the dead" (KJV). The Lord Jesus Christ is the only person who can match this description. John 5:22 confirms Christ's identity as the judge: "The Father judges no one, but has entrusted all judgment to the Son" (NIV). The Judge who sits on the Great White Throne, then, is none other than the Lord Jesus Christ Himself. The very person who was rejected and scorned by the world will ultimately sit in judgment on the world. That is a very sobering thought!

One imposing feature of this judgment is that no individual will be able to hide himself from the Savior's penetrating eye: "There is no creature hidden from His sight, but all things are open and laid bare to the eyes of Him with whom we have to do" (Hebrews 4:13).

THE IDENTITY OF THE JUDGED

Revelation 20:12 identifies those who will be judged at the Great White Throne: "I saw the dead, the great and the small, standing before the throne." It is significant to note that these are "the dead"—dead in trespasses and sins because of their rejection of Jesus Christ, and resurrected in order to appear at this judgment: "The rest of the dead [that is, those who were not raised before the beginning of the 1000 years] did not come to life until the thousand years were completed" (Revelation 20:5).

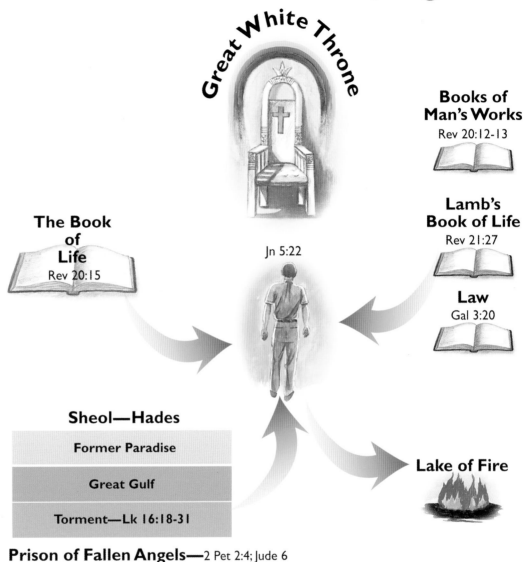

The Great White Throne Judgment

Great White Throne

Jn 5:22

Books of Man's Works
Rev 20:12-13

Lamb's Book of Life
Rev 21:27

Law
Gal 3:20

The Book of Life
Rev 20:15

Sheol—Hades

Former Paradise

Great Gulf

Torment—Lk 16:18-31

Prison of Fallen Angels—2 Pet 2:4; Jude 6

Lake of Fire

What many people do not understand is that all unbelievers are spiritually dead even while they are alive. The apostle Paul said that before a person receives Christ as Savior, he is dead in his trespasses and sins (Ephesians 2:1). And unbelievers go to torment (Luke 16:18-31) when they die because they have no spiritual life in them. They will remain there until judgment day, when they are brought before Christ, whom they have rejected.

Many people hold to the common misconception that at judgment, God will compare their good deeds with their bad ones, and if the good deeds outweigh the bad, then they will make it to heaven. But good works, no matter how many, cannot help us (Titus 3:5). It all comes down to whether we accept or reject Jesus Christ.

The Books Used at Judgment

The Books of Man's Works

Revelation 20:12 says, "And books were opened...and the dead were judged from the things which were written in the books, according to their deeds." Evidently God owns a complete set of books that record every person's deeds, waiting to be recalled on judgment day. These are the books of man's works.

The Books of Life

There are two other books that await every man's encounter with God. Although they are similar, they also bear significant differences.

The New Testament refers to the Book of Life eight different times, and although the Old Testament does not call it by that name, it does allude three times to a book in which names are written. The psalmist speaks of the righteous as having their names written in "the book of the living" (Psalm 69:28 KJV), so we perceive that it is a book in which righteous people have their names written.

Revelation 13:8 tells us about a similar book—"the book of life of the Lamb." "The Lamb" is without doubt the Lord Jesus Christ, for only He is "the Lamb of God who takes away the sin of the world" (John 1:29). Because Christ came into the world to save sinners and to give them eternal life, the Lamb's Book of Life is the book of Jesus Christ in which are entered the names of those who have received His eternal life. (We are inclined to believe that only the believers who have lived since the cross have their names written in this book.)

The major difference between the two books is that the Book of Life seems to contain the names of all living people, whereas the Lamb's Book of Life includes only the names of those who have called upon the Lamb for salvation. A second difference is that the Book of Life is referred to as God the Father's book in Exodus 32:33; it records all those whom God the Creator has made. It is, then, the Book of the Living, much like the records book at the local county government office. On the other hand, the Lamb's Book of Life is referred to as God the Son's book (Revelation 13:8). We may conclude, then, that this book contains the names of all those who have received the new life that the Son provides.

The third and most important difference between these books is that one may have his name blotted out of the Book of Life, but not the Lamb's Book of Life. In Exodus 32:33 God told Moses, "Whoever has sinned against Me, I will blot him out of My book." It is possible, therefore, to have one's name erased from the Book of Life because of sin. The Lamb's Book of Life is different, however. Revelation 3:5 promises, "He who overcomes will thus be clothed in white garments; and I will not erase his name from the book of life."

26.
THE ETERNAL STATE

Revelation 21–22 introduces the eternal future planned by God, and not much is said, but enough is revealed to assure every believer's heart that God has an incredible future in store for those who receive and worship His Son.

THE DESTRUCTION OF THIS EARTH

Three destructions of the earth are described in the Bible, one past and two yet to come. The first destruction came when the Flood covered the earth in the days of Noah, sparing only eight righteous persons (Genesis 6–8). In one of the best-known promises in the Old Testament, God told Noah that He would never again destroy the earth by flood, and sent the rainbow as a sign of this promise.

However, two more destructions are predicted in the Bible. One will come by fire, after which God will restore all things (2 Peter 3:4-14; see also Isaiah 65:17-20). The other destruction is described in Revelation 21:1.

Many Bible scholars say the destruction and restoration in Isaiah 65:17-20 and 2 Peter 3:4-14 are the same as the one in Revelation 21:1. This presents some serious problems. A thorough examination suggests that since death appears in the Isaiah 65 passage, Isaiah was not talking about the eternal order, but the Millennial kingdom. And since 2 Peter 3:10 refers to the Day of the Lord, we are inclined to believe that he meant the second catastrophic event that will come upon the earth, producing a refurbished earth to begin the Millennium. Revelation 20:7-10 describes for us the final insurrection of Satan, when again heaven and earth will be polluted by the rebellion of Satan. Therefore the words of our Lord, "Heaven and earth will pass away, but My words will not pass away" (Matthew 24:35), evidently will be fulfilled when the prophecy of Revelation 21:1 is completed: "Then I saw a new heaven and a new earth; for the first heaven and the first earth passed away, and there is no longer any sea."

THE DESTRUCTION OF HEAVEN

Why will God destroy heaven? Very simply because the atmospheric heavens are filled with evil. Whenever we read about heaven in the Bible, we should keep in mind that there are three heavens: the atmospheric heaven around the earth; the stellar heaven, which contains the great galaxies that we view on a starry night; and the third heaven, or the throne of God (see 2 Corinthians 12:2; Revelation 4–5). Revelation 21:1 in no way indicates that God will destroy the stellar heaven or the place of His throne, but He will destroy the atmospheric heaven, where Satan lives. Ephesians 6:12 indicates that Satan and his emissaries are performing spiritual wickedness "in the heavenly places." After the final rebellion of Satan, God will destroy this earth that is so marred and cursed by Satan's evil, and He will include the atmospheric heaven to guarantee that all semblance of evil has been cleared away.

THE NEW HEAVENS AND THE NEW EARTH

After God does away with this planet as we know it, He will create a new heaven and a new earth. They will be better than anything this world has ever known, including the Garden of Eden. There will be many changes, some of which are listed on the chart on page 76. For example, there will no longer be any seas. Two-thirds of the present earth's surface is covered by water; the remaining one-third includes many large areas rendered worthless because of mountains and deserts. Thus only a small portion of today's earth is inhabitable.

The Eternal State

New Heavens

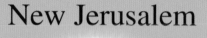

New Jerusalem

New Earth

Lake of Fire

The New Heavens and New Earth

- Satan removed from further influence in history (Rev 20:10)

- No longer any sea (Rev 21:1)

- No longer any death, crying, or pain (Rev 21:4)

- All things made new (Rev 21:1)

- No longer any night (Rev 21:25)

- No longer any unclean, nor those practicing abomination and lying (Rev 21:1)

- No longer any curse (Rev 22:3)

- No longer any sun (Rev 22:5)

- Believers are able to see the Father face to face (Rev 22:4)

The Lake of Fire

- The eternal abode of Satan, the Antichrist, and the False Prophet (Rev 19:20; 20:10)

- The eternal abode of all the human unbelievers throughout history (Rev 20:10)

- It is an eternal lake of fire and brimstone (Rev 20:10)

- All residents will be tormented day and night forever and ever (Rev 20:10)

- It is an eternal, second death (Rev 20:14)

In addition, we are told that "the tabernacle of God is among men, and He will dwell among them" (Revelation 21:3). God's Tabernacle will no longer be in the third heaven, for He will move His headquarters to the new earth and will literally take up His abode in the New Jerusalem. We simply do not have the mental capacity to comprehend the significance of living in an economy where God Himself exists!

Revelation 21:4 adds that God "will wipe every tear from [our] eyes." The wiping away of all tears means that the normal reaction of sorrow will be eliminated. And, "there will no longer be any death." The specter of death, the natural result of sin, will at last be removed.

Then in Revelation 21:5, God says, "Behold, I am making all things new." This is an almost certain indication that God will create for us a dimension that we cannot yet comprehend. He is planning an entirely new way of life for His people.

THE NEW JERUSALEM

The dazzling glory of the new city of Jerusalem that is to come down from heaven is beyond our ability to comprehend. It is pictured in Revelation as the ultimate human habitation, prepared by God. When this city comes to the Earth, it will be filled with people—people in their resurrected bodies who are prepared to dwell with Christ for eternity.

In our mind's eye, gazing at this city with its fantastically beautiful and expensive stones for foundations, its gigantic pearl gates, and its gold streets, we are impressed with the superiority of this city over anything known to us. Today we use concrete and stone for foundations, scarcely the most beautiful materials on Earth, but selected because of their durability, plentiful supply, and low cost. By comparison, the Holy City of God will be so magnificent that we will literally walk on precious metals that today are used only for fine jewelry.

There will be no Temple in the New Jerusalem because "the Lord God the Almighty and the Lamb are its temple" (Revelation 21:22). From the very beginning of the creation of humanity, God has chosen to fellowship with us. He maintained fellowship with Adam and Eve before they sinned. After the Fall, altars were used as a place of sacrifice and for approaching God.

In the days of Moses God established the Tabernacle, and He dwelled in the midst of the people in what is known as the Holy of Holies. Under the reign of Solomon this was transferred to the Temple, but because of Israel's apostasy God departed from the Temple. Then the Lord Jesus Christ came to tabernacle with us and to become the complete and final sacrifice. When He departed, He sent His Holy Spirit to dwell in the bodies of believers.

In the Millennial kingdom a memorial Temple will provide a place for people to worship God because many people will still need to choose between worshiping God or rejecting Him. However, in the eternal order there will no longer be a need for a Temple (or dwelling place of God), for God Himself will be there with His Son and with the Holy Spirit. This will make not only the Holy City one grand and glorious temple or place of worship, but also the eternal Earth.

The many wonders of the eternal state should cause believers to look forward to the future with great anticipation!

27.
THE COVENANTS

God's relationship with man has always been mediated through one or more of the biblical covenants. A *covenant* is a contract between two or more individuals who agree to abide by the terms stated in the covenant. In a similar way, God's covenants state certain promises that He will fulfill. In a covenant, God binds Himself to His people to keep specific promises so that He can demonstrate what kind of God He is. Covenants usually involve intent, promises, and sanctions, and frequently, they are connected to Bible prophecy.

There are three kinds of covenants in the Bible:

- The *Royal Grant* Treaty (unconditional)—a promissory covenant that arose out of a king's desire to reward a loyal servant.

    Examples:
    The Abrahamic Covenant
    The Davidic Covenant

- The *Suzerain-Vassal* Treaty (unconditional)—bound an inferior vassal to a superior suzerain and was binding only on the one who swore.

    Examples:
    Chedorlaomer (Genesis 14)
    Jabesh-Gilead serving Nahash (1 Samuel 11:1)
    The Adamic Covenant
    The Noahic Covenant
    The Mosaic Covenant (Book of Deuteronomy)

Suzerain-Vassal treaties or covenants are unconditional. This is important for Bible prophecy because at stake is whether or not God is obligated to fulfill His promise specifically to the original parties of the covenant. For example, we believe that God must fulfill to Israel as a national entity those promises made through unconditional covenants like the Abrahamic, Davidic,

and Land of Israel. If this is true, then they must be fulfilled literally, and that means many aspects are yet future. Dr. Arnold Fruchtenbaum has said:

> An unconditional covenant can be defined as a sovereign act of God whereby God unconditionally obligates Himself to bring to pass definite promises, blessings, and conditions for the covenanted people. It is a unilateral covenant. This type of covenant is characterized by the formula I will, which declares God's determination to do exactly as He promised. The blessings are secured by the grace of God.[8]

- The *Parity* Treaty—bound two equal parties in a relationship and provided conditions as stipulated by the participants.

    Examples:
    Abraham and Abimelech (Genesis 21:25-32)
    Jacob and Laban (Genesis 31:44-50)
    David and Jonathan (1 Samuel 18:1-4; cf. 2 Samuel 9:1-13)
    Christ and church-age believers, i.e., "friends" (John 15)

In the Bible, we find at least eight covenants between God and people:

- The *Edenic* Covenant (Genesis 1:28-30; 2:15-17)
    This covenant established God's rule and relationship to

mankind. The Edenic Covenant, in conjunction with the Cultural Mandate (Genesis 1:26-28), provides the basis for human responsibility; social, political, and economic duties; and accountability before God. After the fall into sin, God augmented this foundational covenant with other covenants.

- The *Adamic* Covenant (Genesis 3:14-19)

God initiated this covenant because of Adam's sin. This covenant contains the cursed status of man and creation, which man must endure throughout history. The curse will be largely removed during the Millennial reign of Christ (Romans 8:19-23), and finally, death will be eliminated in the eternal state (1 Corinthians 15:53-57; Revelation 21:4; 22:3).

- The *Noahic* Covenant (Genesis 8:20–9:17)

This covenant restates God's authority over man and man's duties as found in the Adamic Covenant (Genesis 9:1), and then it adds new responsibilities, including: 1) animosity between mankind and the animal kingdom (9:2); 2) man could now eat animal flesh for food (9:3); 3) while eating flesh, the blood shall not be consumed, but drained (9:4); 4) human life is so valuable that God requires the death of the one who murders another— capital punishment (9:5-6); 5) and the command, "Be fruitful and multiply, and fill the earth" (Genesis 9:1). The Noahic Covenant is a contract between God and all subsequent humanity, including the entire animal kingdom (9:8-10). In this covenant God promises to never destroy the world again through a flood (9:11). The sign that God will keep His promise is the rainbow set within a cloud (9:12-17). It's possible God chose to use a rainbow because a rainbow surrounds the very throne room of God (Ezekiel 1:28; Revelation 4:3), representing His person and presence. The Noahic Covenant is mentioned specifically in Isaiah 54:9-10.

- The *Abrahamic* Covenant (introduced in Genesis 12:1-3)

The Abrahamic Covenant is the mother of all redemptive covenants. Every blessing experienced by the redeemed, both within Israel and the church, flows from this covenant. While the covenant is first introduced in Genesis 12:1-3, it is made in Genesis 15:1-21, reaffirmed in Genesis 17:1-21, and then renewed with Isaac in Genesis 26:2-5 and Jacob in Genesis 28:10-17. It is a covenant in which God unconditionally obligates Himself to bring to pass definite promises, blessings, and conditions for the covenanted people. The three major provisions of the Abrahamic Covenant are 1) land to Abram and Israel; 2) a seed (including Christ); 3) a worldwide blessing. In all, the Abrahamic Covenant includes over a dozen provisions. Some apply to Abraham; some to Israel, the seed; and some pertain to Gentiles.

- The *Mosaic* Covenant (Exodus 20–23; Deuteronomy)

This covenant was given exclusively and only to the nation of Israel (Psalm 147:19-20) and was fulfilled through the ministry of Jesus Christ during His first advent (Matthew 5:17). It is a conditional covenant that was designed to teach Israel how to please God as His chosen nation. The measuring stick was to be the Law aspect of the covenant. The Law was designed to govern every aspect of Israel's life: the spiritual, moral, social, religious, and civil. The commandments were a "ministry of condemnation" and "of death" (2 Corinthians 3:7-9). The church-age believer is not in any way, shape, or form under the obligations of the Mosaic Law, but under the unconditional law of Christ and the Spirit (Romans 3:21-27; 6:14-15; Galatians 2:16; 3:10,16-18,24-26; 4:21-31; Hebrews 10:11-17). The Mosaic Covenant did not change the provision of the Abrahamic Covenant but was an addendum for a limited time only—until Christ came (Galatians 3:17-19).

- The *Davidic* Covenant (2 Samuel 7:4-17)

This covenant is the foundation upon which the future Millennial kingdom of Christ will be founded. It promises to David 1) posterity in the Davidic house; 2) a throne symbolic of royal authority; 3) a kingdom, or rule on earth; and 4) certainty of fulfillment for the promises to David.

Solomon, whose birth God predicted (2 Samuel 7:12), was not promised a perpetual seed, but only assured that 1) he would build a house for God (2 Samuel 7:13); 2) his kingdom would be established (2 Samuel 7:12); 3) his throne or royal authority would endure forever; and 4) if he sinned, he would be chastised but not deposed. The continuance of Solomon's throne, but not Solomon's seed, shows the accuracy of the prediction. Most of these promises will be

God's Covenants with Israel

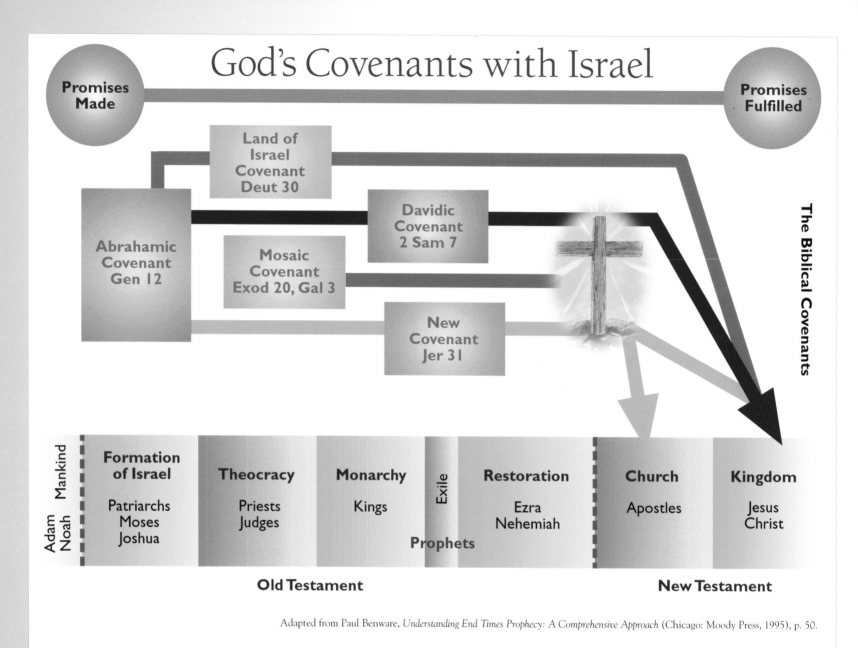

Adapted from Paul Benware, *Understanding End Times Prophecy: A Comprehensive Approach* (Chicago: Moody Press, 1995), p. 50.

fulfilled during the Millennial reign of Christ.

• The *Land of Israel* Covenant (Deuteronomy 30:1-10)

This covenant provides an expansion upon the land promise found in the Abrahamic Covenant (Genesis 12:1-3). In Deuteronomy, after two chapters predicting disobedience and judgment and deportation from the Land, the Lord foretells of ultimate repentance and blessing upon national Israel. The Lord binds

Himself to this ultimate destiny for Israel by establishing a covenant that promises the Land to Israel forever. This covenant unfolds as follows: 1) dispersion for disobedience (Deuteronomy 30:1; see also Deuteronomy 28:63-68; 29:22-28); 2) the future repentance of Israel while in dispersion (Deuteronomy 30:2; see also Deuteronomy 28:63-68); 3) the Messiah will gather the remaining exiles and transport them to the land (Deuteronomy

30:3-6; see also Daniel 12:1; Amos 9:14; Zechariah 2:6; Matthew 24:31); 4) the land will be permanently restored to Israel (Deuteronomy 30:5; see also Isaiah 11:11-12; Jeremiah 23:3-8; Ezekiel 37:21-25); 5) the whole nation of Israel will be converted to their Messiah (Deuteronomy 30:6; see also Hosea 2:14-16; Zechariah 12:10-14; Romans 11:26-27); 6) judgment of those that oppose Israel (Deuteronomy 30:7; see also Isaiah 14:1-2; Joel 3:1-8; Matthew 25:31-46); 7) Israel will experience national blessing and prosperity (Deuteronomy 30:9; see also Amos 9:11-15; Zechariah 14:9-21).

- The *New* Covenant (Jeremiah 31:31-37 and more)

The New Covenant provides for the yet future spiritual regeneration of Israel in preparation for the Millennial kingdom. The New Covenant, as stated here and in other Old Testament passages, is for Israel (Deuteronomy 29:4; 30:6; Isaiah 59:20-21; 61:8-9; Jeremiah 32:37-40; 50:4-5; Ezekiel 11:19-20; 16:60-63; 37:21-28; 34:25-26; 36:24-27; Zechariah 9:11; 12:10; Hebrews 8:1-13; 10:15-18). The New Covenant is applied to the church (Matthew 26:27-28; Luke 22:20; 2 Corinthians 3:6) because it provides the forgiveness of sins and a spiritual dynamic that is not reserved solely for the nation of Israel.

Central to the study of Bible prophecy, then, is how the covenants relate to the Gentiles, Israel, and the church. Because God is all-sovereign and all-powerful, we can have complete confidence that the promises He made in the various covenants will all come to pass.

28.
THE DISPENSATIONS

Dispensationalism views the world and history as a household run by God. In this household-world, God is dispensing or administering affairs according to His own will and in various stages of revelation with the passage of time. These various stages, known as dispensations, can be seen as distinguishably different economies in the outworking of God's plan for the ages. Understanding these differing economies is essential to a proper interpretation of God's revelations within those various economies. It's important to point out up front that the dispensations have nothing to do with how people are saved from their sin.

Dispensationalism is immensely important when it comes to Bible prophecy. The dispensational view of literal interpretation supports a futurist view; that is, that many biblical passages have yet a future fulfillment. The distinction between Israel and the church is important because the church's present distinctiveness in the plan of God provides the theological basis for the pretribulation Rapture, while Israel's Old Testament promises will be literally fulfilled in the future, which requires a detailed and sophisticated understanding of scriptural prophecy.

Perhaps the leading dispensational spokesman today is Dr. Charles Ryrie, formerly of Dallas Theological Seminary. He notes that *The Oxford English Dictionary* defines a theological dispensation as "a stage in a progressive revelation, expressly adopted to the needs of a particular nation or period of time...also, the age or period during which a system has prevailed." The English word *dispensation* translates the Greek noun *oikonomá*, often rendered "administration" in modern translations. The verb *oikonoméô* refers to a manager of a household. "In the New Testament," notes Ryrie, "*dispensation* means to manage or administer the affairs of a household, as, for example, in the Lord's story of the unfaithful steward in Luke 16:1-13."[9]

The Greek word *oikonomá* is a compound of *oikos*, meaning "house," and *nomos*, meaning "law." Taken together, "the central idea in the word *dispensation* is that of managing or administering the affairs of a household."[10]

Ryrie continues:

> The various forms of the word *dispensation* are used in the New Testament twenty times. The verb *oikonoméô* is used in Luke 16:2 where it is translated "to be a steward." The noun *oikonmos* is used ten times (Luke 12:42; 16:1,3,8; Rom. 16:23; 1 Cor. 4:1,2; Gal. 4:2; Titus 1:7; 1 Pet. 4:10), and it is translated "steward" in all instances except "chamberlain" in Romans 16:23. The noun *oikonomá* is used nine times (Luke 16:2,3,4; 1 Cor. 9:17; Eph. 1:10; 3:2,9; Col. 1:25; 1 Tim. 1:4). In these instances it is translated variously ("stewardship," "dispensation," "edifying"). The Authorized Version of Ephesians 3:9 has "fellowship" (*koinonia*), whereas the American Standard Version has "dispensation."[11]

Dr. Ryrie notes the following characteristics of dispensationalism:

- two parties are always involved
- specific responsibilities
- accountability as well as responsibility
- a change may be made at any time unfaithfulness is found in the existing administration
- God is the one to whom men are responsible
- faithfulness is required of the subordinate party
- a stewardship may end at any time
- dispensations are connected with the mysteries of God
- dispensations and ages are connected ideas
- there are at least three dispensations (likely seven)[12]

The definition of a dispensation, according to Ryrie, is "a distinguishable economy in the outworking of God's plan."[13] A description of dispensationalism would include the following:

- distinctive revelation

- testing
- failure
- judgment
- a continuance of certain ordinances valid until then
- an annulment of other regulations until then valid
- a fresh introduction of new principles not before valid
- the progressive revelation of God's plan for history[14]

Many people have believed in dispensations without adhering to the system of theology known as dispensationalism. Dispensationalism combines a view of the dispensations with what Dr. Ryrie calls the three *sine qua nons* (Latin, "that without which") or *essentials* of dispensationalism.[15] These are not a definition or description of dispensationalism; instead, they are basic theological tests that can be applied to an individual to see whether or not he is a dispensationalist. The three are:

- *consistent* literal interpretation
- a distinction between God's plan for Israel and the church
- the glory of God in a multifaceted way is the goal of history

We believe that the theology known today as dispensationalism can be said to at least generally represent what the Bible teaches, especially as it relates to Bible prophecy. To view the Bible dispensationally is to view God's plan for history, including future prophecy, from His perspective.

From the biblical perspective, what are the dispensations or ages in history? There are seven dispensations that can be deduced from God's Word:

- *Innocence* (Genesis 1:28–3:6)—This apparently was the shortest of the dispensations and ended in the fall into sin by the parents of the human race.
- *Conscience* (Genesis 3:7–8:14)—The word *conscience*, used to describe this dispensation, is found in Romans 2:15, which describes the time between the Fall and the Flood.
- *Human Government* (Genesis 8:15–11:9)—After the Flood, God said He would not directly judge men until the second coming; thus, a human agency known as civil government was divinely established to mediate and attempt to restrain the evil of men.
- *Promise* (Genesis 11:10–Exodus 18:27)—This period is domi-

The Dispensations

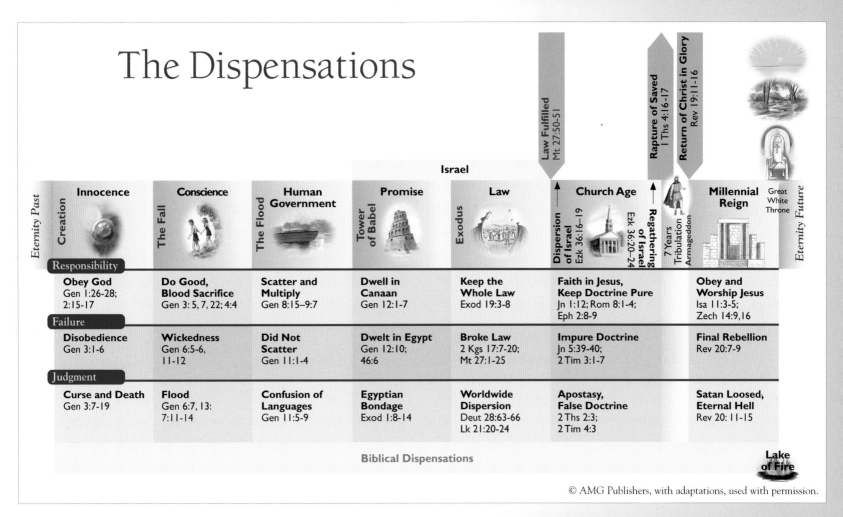

	Innocence	Conscience	Human Government	Promise	Law	Church Age	Millennial Reign	
Responsibility								
	Obey God Gen 1:26-28; 2:15-17	**Do Good, Blood Sacrifice** Gen 3: 5, 7, 22; 4:4	**Scatter and Multiply** Gen 8:15–9:7	**Dwell in Canaan** Gen 12:1-7	**Keep the Whole Law** Exod 19:3-8	**Faith in Jesus, Keep Doctrine Pure** Jn 1:12; Rom 8:1-4; Eph 2:8-9	**Obey and Worship Jesus** Isa 11:3-5; Zech 14:9,16	
Failure								
	Disobedience Gen 3:1-6	**Wickedness** Gen 6:5-6, 11-12	**Did Not Scatter** Gen 11:1-4	**Dwelt in Egypt** Gen 12:10; 46:6	**Broke Law** 2 Kgs 17:7-20; Mt 27:1-25	**Impure Doctrine** Jn 5:39-40; 2 Tim 3:1-7	**Final Rebellion** Rev 20:7-9	
Judgment								
	Curse and Death Gen 3:7-19	**Flood** Gen 6:7, 13; 7:11-14	**Confusion of Languages** Gen 11:5-9	**Egyptian Bondage** Exod 1:8-14	**Worldwide Dispersion** Deut 28:63-66 Lk 21:20-24	**Apostasy, False Doctrine** 2 Ths 2:3; 2 Tim 4:3	**Satan Loosed, Eternal Hell** Rev 20: 11-15	

Biblical Dispensations

Labels on chart: Israel; Law Fulfilled Mt 27:50-51; Rapture of Saved 1 Ths 4:16-17; Return of Christ in Glory Rev 19:11-16; Eternity Past; Creation; The Fall; The Flood; Tower of Babel; Exodus; Dispersion of Israel Ezk 36:16-19; Regathering of Israel Ezk 36:20-24; 7 Years Tribulation Armageddon; Great White Throne; Eternity Future; Lake of Fire

nated by the call of Abram and the promise made to him and his descendants, both physical and spiritual.

- *Law/Israel* (Exodus 19–John 14:30)—Israel was not and never was to be saved by keeping the Law. Instead, the Law stipulated how they, as a redeemed people, were to live. It was to govern every aspect of their lives. But the Law was temporary until the coming of and fulfillment by Christ.
- *Grace/Church* (Acts 2:1–Revelation 19:21)—The rule of life for the church is grace, and through the church, God's grace is extended to everyone worldwide through the gospel.
- *Kingdom* (Revelation 20:1-15)—During Messiah's 1000-year reign in Jerusalem, the promises God made to Israel will be fulfilled to Israel as a nation. The church will also reign and rule

with Christ as His bride. Because Israel will be in her glory, the Gentiles will reap great blessings as well.

Dispensational theology enables us to rightly divide God's Word, which provides a framework for understanding God's plan for history. This is important because when we understand God's purpose for each era of history, we are able to understand God's will for each dispensation. A believer who has a divine perspective on the past, present, and future is able to know what God expects of him in every area of life. In the current church age, the New Testament instructs us in both public and private spheres of life. The dispensationalist, for example, does not live in this age of grace as if he was still under the rule of the Mosaic Law. Instead he understands that he is now under the Law of Christ and awaiting the rapture.

29.
ISRAEL: GOD'S SUPER SIGN OF THE END TIMES

The study of Bible prophecy is divided into three major areas: the nations (Gentiles), Israel, and the church. Of the three, more detail is given concerning God's future plans for His nation Israel than for the nations or the church. When the church takes these prophecies to Israel literally, as we do, then we see a great prophetic agenda that lies ahead for Israel as a people and nation. When the church spiritualizes these promises, as she has done too often in history, then Israel's prophetic uniqueness is subsumed and merged unrealistically into the church. But if we handle Scripture carefully, we can see that God has an amazing and blessed future planned for individual Jews and national Israel. That's why we believe Israel is God's "super sign" of the end times.

God's promises to Abraham and Israel are unconditional and guaranteed through the various subsequent covenants. A definite pattern for Israel's future history was prophesied in Deuteronomy before the Jews set even one foot in the Promised Land (Deuteronomy 4:28-31). The predicted pattern for God's program with Israel was to be as follows: They would enter the land under Joshua, and they would eventually turn away from the Lord and be expelled from the land and scattered among the Gentile nations. From there the Lord would regather the Jewish people during the latter days and they would pass through the Tribulation. Toward the end of the Tribulation they would recognize their Messiah and be regenerated. Christ would then return to earth and rescue Israel from the nations who are gathered at Armageddon to exterminate the Jews. A second regathering of the nation would then occur in preparation for the Millennial reign with Christ, during which time all of Israel's unfulfilled promises will be realized. This pattern is developed by the prophets and reinforced in the New Testament.

As with the church and the nations, God is moving His chosen people—Israel—into place for the future fulfillment of His prophecies relating to the nation. He has already brought the Jewish people back to their ancient land (1948) and has given them Jerusalem (1967). However, the current situation in Israel is one of constant turmoil and crisis, especially in the old city of Jerusalem. Eventually Israel will sign a covenant with the Antichrist, and that will initiate the seven-year Tribulation.

Israel's regathering and the turmoil are specific signs that God's end-time program is on the verge of springing into full gear. In addition, the fact that all three streams of prophecy (the nations, Israel, and the church) are converging for the first time in history constitutes a sign in itself. This is why many students of prophecy believe that we are near the last days. If you want to know where history is headed, simply keep your eye on what God is doing with Israel.

ISRAEL'S DISPERSION

The Latin word *Diaspora* has been coined to refer to Israel's dispersion throughout the Gentile nations. Christ spoke of the current 2000-year dispersion of Israel in His prophecy about the destruction of Jerusalem in A.D. 70 when He said, "They will fall by the edge of the sword, and will be led captive into all the nations; and Jerusalem will be trampled under foot by the Gentiles until the times of the Gentiles are fulfilled" (Luke 21:24). As is usually the case with biblical prophecy, this pronouncement of judgment includes an ultimate hope of restoration. In this statement Christ used the word

Israel: God's Super Sign of the End Times

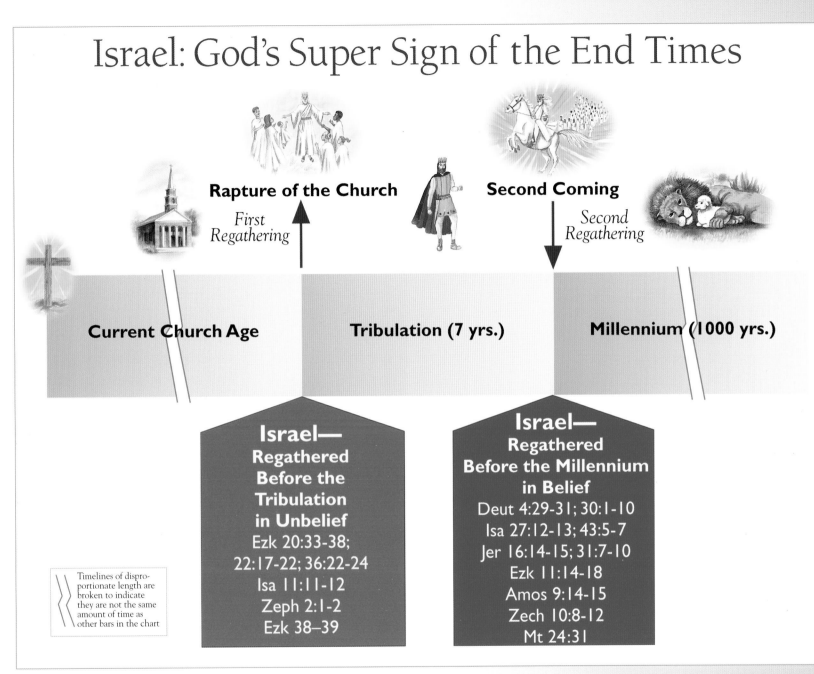

Rapture of the Church

First Regathering

Second Coming

Second Regathering

Current Church Age

Tribulation (7 yrs.)

Millennium (1000 yrs.)

Timelines of disproportionate length are broken to indicate they are not the same amount of time as other bars in the chart

**Israel—
Regathered
Before the
Tribulation
in Unbelief**
Ezk 20:33-38;
22:17-22; 36:22-24
Isa 11:11-12
Zeph 2:1-2
Ezk 38–39

**Israel—
Regathered
Before the Millennium
in Belief**
Deut 4:29-31; 30:1-10
Isa 27:12-13; 43:5-7
Jer 16:14-15; 31:7-10
Ezk 11:14-18
Amos 9:14-15
Zech 10:8-12
Mt 24:31

"until," which means the dispersion will not last forever; eventually it will come to an end.

The threat of dispersion throughout the nations appears as early as the Mosaic Law (Leviticus 26:33; Deuteronomy 4:27; 28:64; 29:28). Nehemiah said, "Remember the word which You commanded Your servant Moses, saying, 'If you are unfaithful I will scatter you among the peoples'" (Nehemiah 1:8). Similar statements appear many times throughout the prophets.

It's important to recognize that the capture of the Northern Kingdom of Israel by the Assyrians in the eighth century B.C. and the captivity to Babylon in the sixth century B.C. did not constitute the worldwide scattering mentioned in Bible prophecy. This did not occur until the nation's rejection of Christ and God's subsequent judgment in A.D. 70.

THE REGATHERING AND CONVERSION OF ISRAEL

There are dozens of biblical passages that predict an end-time regathering of Israel. However, it is a common mistake to lump all of these passages into one fulfillment, especially in relation to the modern state of Israel. Modern Israel is prophetically significant and is fulfilling Bible prophecy. But we need to be careful to distinguish which prophecies are being fulfilled in our day and which ones await future fulfillment. In short, there will be two end-time regatherings: one before the Tribulation and one after.

Hebrew Christian scholar Dr. Arnold Fruchtenbaum explains:

> The re-establishment of the Jewish state in 1948 has not only thrown a wrench in amillennial thinking, but it has also thrown a chink in much of premillennial thinking. Amazingly, some premillennialists have concluded that the present state of Israel has nothing to do with the fulfillment of prophecy. For some reason the present state somehow does not fit their scheme of things, and so the present state becomes merely an accident of history. On what grounds is the present state of Israel so dismissed? The issue that bothers so many premillennialists is the fact that not only have the Jews returned in unbelief with regard to the person of Jesus, but the majority of the ones who have returned are not even Orthodox Jews. In fact the majority are atheists or agnostics. Certainly, then, Israel does not fit in with all those biblical passages dealing with the return. For it is a regenerated nation that the Bible speaks of, and the present state of Israel hardly fits that picture. So on these grounds, the present state is dismissed as not being a fulfillment of prophecy.
>
> However, the real problem is the failure to see that

> *If you want to know where history is headed, simply keep your eye on what God is doing with Israel.*

the prophets spoke of two international returns. First, there was to be a regathering in unbelief in preparation for judgment, namely the judgment of the Tribulation. This was to be followed by a second worldwide regathering in faith in preparation for blessing, namely the blessings of the messianic age. Once it is recognized that the Bible speaks of two such regatherings, it is easy to see how the present state of Israel fits into prophecy.[16]

FIRST WORLDWIDE GATHERING IN UNBELIEF

In 1948 when the modern state of Israel was born, it not only became an important stage-setting development but began an actual fulfillment of specific Bible prophecies about an international regathering of the Jews in unbelief before the judgment of the Tribulation. Such a prediction is found in the following Old Testament passages: Ezekiel 20:33-38; 22:17-22; 36:22-24; 38–39; Isaiah 11:11-12; and Zephaniah 2:1-2 presupposes such a setting.

Zephaniah 1:14-18 provides one of the most colorful descriptions of "the great day of the LORD," which we commonly call the Tribulation period. Zephaniah 2:1-2 says that there will be a worldwide regathering of Israel before the Day of the Lord: "Gather yourselves together, yes, gather, O nation without shame, before the decree takes effect—the day passes like the chaff—before the burning anger of the LORD comes upon you, before the day of the LORD's anger comes upon you."

SECOND WORLDWIDE GATHERING IN BELIEF

Many passages in the Bible speak of Israel's regathering, in belief, at the end of the Tribulation, in conjunction with Christ's second coming and in preparation for the commencement of the Millennium. These references are not being fulfilled by the modern state of Israel. Some of them include Deuteronomy 4:29-31; 30:1-10;

Isaiah 27:12-13; 43:5-7; Jeremiah 16:14-15; 31:7-10; Ezekiel 11:14-18; Amos 9:14-15; Zechariah 10:8-12; and Matthew 24:31.

The fact that the last 50 years have seen a worldwide regathering and reestablishment of the nation of Israel, which is now poised in the very setting required for the revealing of the Antichrist and the start of the Tribulation, is God's grand indicator that all the other areas of world development are prophetically significant. Dr. Walvoord says,

> Of the many peculiar phenomena which characterize the present generation, few events can claim equal significance as far as Biblical prophecy is concerned with that of the return of Israel to their land. It constitutes a preparation for the end of the age, the setting for the coming of the Lord for His church, and the fulfillment of Israel's prophetic destiny.[17]

Israel, God's "super sign" of the end times, is a clear indicator that time is growing shorter with each passing hour. With what we have already seen, we can be assured that God is now preparing the world for the final events leading up to Israel's national regeneration.

30.

DANIEL'S OUTLINE OF THE FUTURE

> It is impossible to understand Bible prophecy without understanding the book of Daniel. Much of the information about the key players and the time sequence of the last days is given in Daniel. What's more, Daniel introduces many facts that the New Testament book of Revelation expands upon.

Daniel contains graphic visions that provide an outline of what God would do from the sixth century B.C., when Daniel lived and wrote, until the coming of Messiah's kingdom in the Millennium. The key prophetic chapters are Daniel 2, 7, 9, 11, and 12. Chapters 2, 7, and 9 also provide outlines for Jewish and Gentile history.

God provided Daniel and the nation of Israel with an outline of their history during the Babylonian captivity in order to give them hope that God would work out His plan for them in the future. In Daniel 2 and 7 we see an overview of the four Gentile kingdoms that would play an important role in world history. The first of the four kingdoms was Babylon, under whose jurisdiction Daniel saw and wrote many of his prophetic visions in the sixth century B.C. The other kingdoms were Medo-Persia, Greece, and Rome. Daniel's prophecy concludes by saying that the Roman Empire would undergo a revival into a ten-nation confederacy right before the coming of Messiah's kingdom. Daniel 2 records these kingdoms from a Gentile perspective while Daniel 7 repeats the overview from God's perspective, which explains why the kingdoms are characterized as beasts.

Here are the specifics of the four kingdoms as revealed in both Daniel 2 and 7:

- *Babylon* (612–539 B.C.)—represented by the head of gold and a lion having the wings of an eagle (2:32; 7:4)
- *Medo-Persia* (538–331 B.C.)—represented by the silver upper body and a bear (2:32; 7:5)
- *Greece* (330–63 B.C.)—represented by the belly and thighs made of bronze and a leopard with four wings and four heads (2:32; 7:6)
- *Rome* (63 B.C.–A.D. 476; Tribulation)—the first phase of

Daniel's Outline of the Future

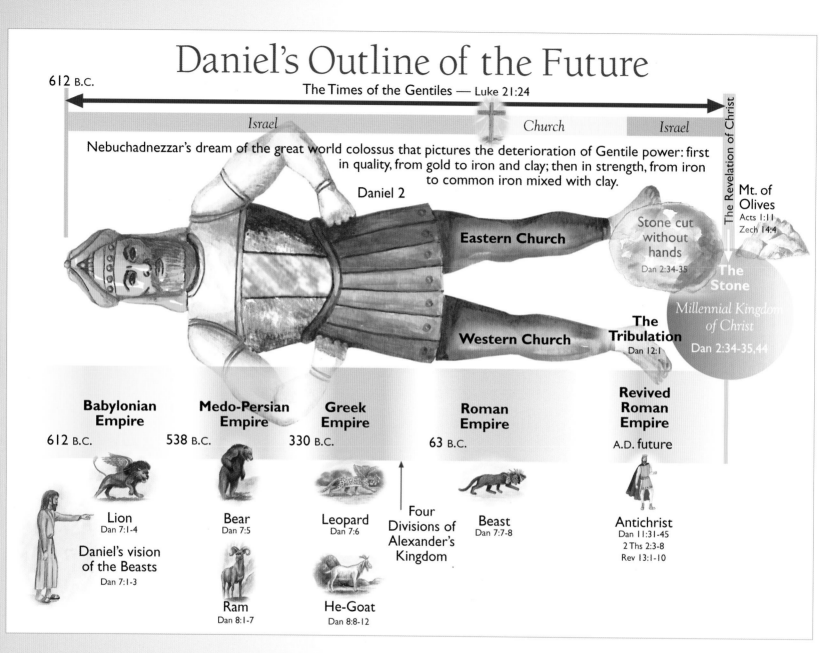

The Times of the Gentiles — Luke 21:24

612 B.C.

Israel | Church | Israel

The Revelation of Christ

Nebuchadnezzar's dream of the great world colossus that pictures the deterioration of Gentile power: first in quality, from gold to iron and clay; then in strength, from iron to common iron mixed with clay.

Daniel 2

Eastern Church

Western Church

Stone cut without hands
Dan 2:34-35

Mt. of Olives
Acts 1:11
Zech 14:4

The Stone

Millennial Kingdom of Christ
Dan 2:34-35,44

The Tribulation
Dan 12:1

Babylonian Empire	Medo-Persian Empire	Greek Empire		Roman Empire	Revived Roman Empire
612 B.C.	538 B.C.	330 B.C.		63 B.C.	A.D. future
Lion Dan 7:1-4	Bear Dan 7:5	Leopard Dan 7:6	Four Divisions of Alexander's Kingdom	Beast Dan 7:7-8	Antichrist Dan 11:31-45 2 Ths 2:3-8 Rev 13:1-10
Daniel's vision of the Beasts Dan 7:1-3	Ram Dan 8:1-7	He-Goat Dan 8:8-12			

---

this kingdom is represented by legs of iron and an unspecified beast with iron teeth and bronze claws (2:33; 7:7). The final phase is described as feet and toes that are a mixture of iron and clay, as well as ten horns or ten kings and "another" (2:41-43; 7:24-25).

The book of Revelation builds upon Daniel's revelation and further develops the final phase of the fourth kingdom that will play

such a significant role during the Tribulation as Antichrist's kingdom. Dr. John Walvoord notes:

The minute description given here of the end time, the fourth beast, and the ten horns followed by the eleventh horn that gained control of three has never been fulfilled in history. Some expositors have attempted to find ten kings of the past and the eleventh king who would arise to somehow fulfill this prophecy, but there is nothing corresponding to this in the history of the Roman Empire. The ten horns do not reign one after the other, but they reign simultaneously. Further, they were not the world empire, but they were the forerunner to the little horn which after subduing three of the ten horns will go on to become a world ruler (v. 23; Rev. 13:7).[18]

Walvoord's words give us a sense for how vital it is that we examine Bible prophecies carefully—in the light of different passages of Scripture—to ensure that we arrive at a proper understanding of those prophecies.

31.
THE 70 WEEKS OF DANIEL

Daniel's "70 weeks" prophecy, given in Daniel 9:24-27, is the framework within which the seven-year Tribulation (or the seventieth week) occurs. The prophecy of the 70 weeks was given to Daniel by God while Daniel was in Babylon (Daniel 9:1; 2 Chronicles 36:21-23; Ezra 1; 6:3-5). In the vision God gave to Daniel, the Lord assured the prophet that He had not forgotten His chosen people. The angel Gabriel told Daniel that God would bring Israel back into their land and would one day set up the Messianic kingdom. What Daniel didn't expect was the revelation that the prophecy would not be fulfilled at the end of the 70-year captivity in Babylon, but at the end of the future 70-week period described in 9:24-27. According to Daniel 9:27, the Antichrist will come to power during the prophetic milestone known as the seventieth week:

He [the Antichrist] will make a firm covenant with the many for one week, but in the middle of the week he will put a stop to sacrifice and grain offering; and on the wing of abominations will come one who makes desolate, even until a complete destruction, one that is decreed, is poured out on the one who makes desolate.

It is this seventieth week, a future seven-year period, that is the Tribulation. This era follows the Rapture of the church and will be a time of unparalleled suffering and turmoil. Many descriptive terms are used in the Bible to describe this time span: Tribulation, Great Tribulation, Day of the Lord, day of wrath, day of distress, day of trouble, Time of Jacob's Trouble, day of darkness and gloom, and wrath of the Lamb.

According to Daniel 9:27, at the beginning of the second half of the seventieth week, the Antichrist will break his covenant with Israel and it will remain broken for three-and-a-half years, or "time, times, and half a time" (Daniel 7:25; 12:7; Revelation 12:14). Since the first 69 weeks (or 69 "sevens") were fulfilled literally, the seventieth "seven," which is yet unfulfilled, must also be fulfilled literally.

EXPLANATION OF DANIEL'S 70 WEEKS OF YEARS

$69 \times 7 \times 360 = 173{,}880$ days
March 5, 444 B.C. + 173,880 = March 30, A.D. 33

Verification

444 B.C. to A.D. 33 = 476 years	
476 years x 365.2421989 days =	173,855 days
+ days between March 5 and March 30 =	25 days
Total =	173,880 days

The 70 Weeks of Daniel

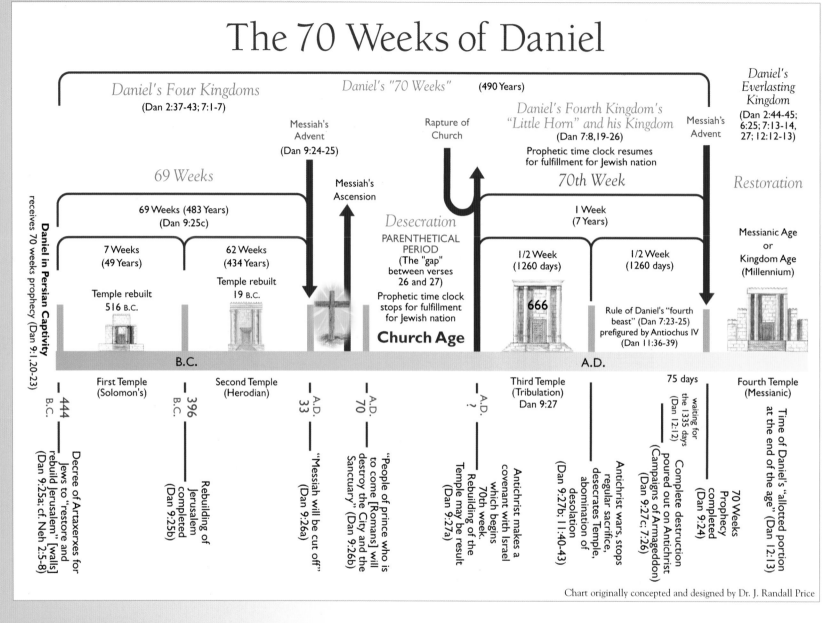

Chart originally concepted and designed by Dr. J. Randall Price

Rationale for 360-Day Years

1/2 week—Daniel 9:27

Time, times, and half a time—Daniel 7:25; 12:7; Revelation 12:14

1260 days—Revelation 11:3; 12:6

42 months—Revelation 11:2; 13:5

Thus: 42 months = 1260 days = time, times, half a time = 1/2 week

Therefore: month = 30 days; year = 360 days[19]

Man's view of government is quite different from God's. Nebuchadnezzar saw government as a beautiful colossus, and God saw it as a series of rapacious beasts. Historically, God's view has proven true; man's view is a delusion.

32.
EZEKIEL 37-39

Ezekiel 37–48 are chapters that are thought to generally follow the sequence that will occur in the future. Chapter 37 speaks of the regathering and regeneration of Israel. Chapters 38–39:20 speak of the Battle of Gog and Magog, and Ezekiel 39:21–48 presents the most detailed account of the Millennium found in Scripture.

EZEKIEL 37

The return of Israel to her land is unique in all of human history. There are ancient peoples who have always occupied their lands, such as the Egyptians. But never have they left their ancient boundaries only to return. Israel is the only nation that has ever been deported from her homeland, remained a distinct people while outside the land, and then returned to her original country.

The Valley of Dry Bones

In Ezekiel 37:1-14 the prophet describes a valley of dry bones. These bones are the remains of a defeated army that was slaughtered and left unburied to decompose into a sun-bleached pile of bones. This prophecy presents the most extreme picture of hopelessness imaginable. But when the Lord is involved, there is always hope. There is no question these "bones" present a clear picture of the depleted nation of Israel. For God instructed the prophet "these bones are the whole house of Israel" (37:11). He then describes the miracle of their regathering as from the "graves" of antiquity. During the twentieth century, that miracle of restoring the Jewish people back into their land was accomplished

when a very few Jews who lived in the land were joined by their brethren from all over the world, to the point where they now number over six million people. This is not a picture of Christian regeneration, but of the restoration and then regeneration of national Israel.

Just as the death and deterioration of a soldier takes place in stages, so will the reverse take place in stages as the pile of dry bones becomes living human beings. This pictures the restoration of national Israel in stages as represented in the chart on this page.

This restoration (37:5-6) is exactly what we have seen take place as the modern state of Israel has been regathered and constituted as a nation again. However, Israel is currently without breath (37:6,8), which refers to the spiritual regeneration of many within the nation (37:9-10). Israel is not spiritually alive to the Lord. This will occur during the Tribulation and will reach its climax by the time of Christ's second coming. Israel will then enter the Millennial kingdom as a regenerate nation (37:10).

Israel and Judah Reunited

Not only will Israel be revived, but this future renewal will remove the internal schism that resulted in the splintering of the

---

RESTORATION STAGES OF ISRAEL IN EZEKIEL 37

Stage	Historical Fulfillment
✡ Scattered bones	Israel in dispersion
✡ Sinews connected to bones	Pre-1948 gathering
✡ Flesh on bone	Israel becomes a nation (present status)
✡ Skin covers body	Israel during the Tribulation
✡ Breath in body	Israel after national conversion

© AMG Publishers, used with permission.

---

nation in 931 B.C. into the two kingdoms of Israel (Northern Kingdom) and Judah (Southern Kingdom) (1 Kings 11:26-40). This aspect of the prophecy is not being fulfilled today but will be fulfilled in conjunction with the national regeneration (37:20-23). This prophecy will be fulfilled when national Israel recognizes that Jesus was and is her promised Messiah.

Davidic Prophecy

The final section of Ezekiel 37 looks forward to the Millennial kingdom and David's role in that kingdom (37:24-28). In the Davidic Covenant, God promised David that "your house and your kingdom shall endure before Me forever; your throne shall be established forever" (2 Samuel 7:16). In the Millennial kingdom, the Lord will rule over the entire globe, and David will be the vice-regent over Israel.

The chapter concludes with God's promise to implement a covenant of peace with Israel—"it will be an everlasting covenant with them" (37:26). The covenant of peace will be commemorated by the Lord's placement of His sanctuary "in their midst forever" (37:26). The sanctuary will be a testimony to the nations that the Lord has sanctified the nation and now dwells in their midst (37:27-28).

EZEKIEL 38–39

Ezekiel then sees a vision of the famous invasion of Gog and Magog (38–39:16). We believe this battle will take place before the seven-year Tribulation, but probably after the Rapture. There will be an interval of days, weeks, months, or years between those two pivotal events. This battle is not to be confused with other end-time battles such as Armageddon.

Gog and Magog Not Armageddon

There are several details in Ezekiel 38–39 that indicate the battle of Gog and Magog, which Arnold Fruchtenbaum associates with Russia, is not the same as the battle of Armageddon. Fruchtenbaum summarizes these differences as follows:

First, in Ezekiel there are definite allies mentioned and they are limited in number while other nations stand in opposition. In the Campaign of Armageddon all nations are allied together against Jerusalem without exception. Secondly, the Ezekiel invasion comes from the north, but the Armageddon invasion comes from the whole earth. Thirdly, the purpose of the Russian [38:6] invasion is to take spoil; the purpose of the Armageddon Campaign is to destroy all the Jews. Fourthly, in the Ezekiel invasion there is a protest against the invasion; in the Armageddon Campaign there is no protest since all the nations are involved. Fifthly, the Ezekiel invasion is destroyed through convulsions of nature; the Armageddon invasion is destroyed by the personal second coming of Jesus Christ. Sixthly, the Ezekiel invasion is destroyed on the mountains of Israel; the Armageddon Campaign is destroyed in the area between Petra and Jerusalem. Seventh, the Russian invasion takes place while Israel is living securely in the land; but the Armageddon Campaign takes place while Israel is in flight and in hiding.[20]

Timing of the Battle of Gog and Magog

One of the major issues that any view of Gog and Magog must address is that seven months are required to bury the dead from the battle (Ezekiel 39:12-14) and seven years are needed to burn the weapons. In the second half of the Tribulation the Jews are fleeing and being persecuted, so they cannot be burying the dead at that time. Also, any view other than that articulated by Fruchtenbaum places at least some of the burning of the weapons beyond the seven-year Tribulation and into the Millennium, or even into the eternal state (which makes no sense). For some, the matter of burning weapons in the Millennium is not an issue but is seen as corresponding with the people beating their swords into plowshares and spears into pruning hooks (Isaiah 2:4; Micah 4:3).

Many interpreters opt for a view that places Ezekiel 38–39 at the end of the Tribulation and in connection with Armageddon, or beginning at the middle of the Tribulation and carrying through to the end. Then there is the view stated by Dr. Fruchtenbaum, which places Ezekiel 38–39 prior to the Tribulation but not necessarily prior to the Rapture. Such a view allows the possibility of a significant lapse of time between the Rapture and beginning of the Tribulation, which comes with the signing of the seven-year covenant between Israel and the Antichrist (Daniel 9:27).

There are several strong supports for this view: First, the nation of Israel today is populated by Jews and other peoples from many nations (38:8,12). Second, the Jews dwell securely (38:11,14), even though not always peacefully. Third, this view allows for the seven years and seven months with no difficulty. Some argue that such a view destroys the doctrine of imminency in relation to the Rapture. This need not be the case. Stating that something must precede the Tribulation is not the same as stating that it must precede the Rapture unless it is further stated that the Rapture begins the Tribulation. However, the act that begins the Tribulation is not the Rapture, but the signing of the seven-year covenant.

> One of the major issues that any view of Gog and Magog must address is that seven months are required to bury the dead from the battle (Ezekiel 39:12-14).

Identity of Participants

We believe that the participants in the battle of Gog and Magog can be identified by tracing the migration of those ancient peoples to their modern-day descendants. Ezekiel says this battle will occur "in the latter years" (38:8) and "in the last days" (38:16). The invasion involves a coalition headed by "Gog of the land of Magog, the prince of Rosh, Meshech and Tubal" (38:2). Magog has been identified as ancient terminology for the area including modern-day Russia, Ukraine, and Kazakhstan. Ezekiel further identifies Magog as coming from "the remote parts of the north" (38:6).

Gog will lead the invasion of Israel, and Ezekiel 38:5-6 adds that other nations will join with Gog—Persia (Iran), Ethiopia or Cush (Sudan), Put (Libya), and Gomer and Beth-togarmah (Turkey). Sheba and Dedan in Ezekiel 38:13 refer to Saudi Arabia. All the allies of Magog are reasonably well identified and they are all presently Muslim. Interestingly, such an alignment of nations is already configured on the world scene today, so such an invasion does not seem like a far-fetched possibility.

The Invasion of Israel

Ezekiel says that God will sovereignly cause this invasion of His people (39:1-2). Yet God will also miraculously deliver Israel from the hands of this overwhelming force. He will use a great earthquake (28:19-20), confusion and infighting among the troops of the invading nations (38:21), disease (38:22), and torrential rain, hailstones, fire, and burning sulfur (38:22). This is something that God does, not the Israel Defense Force, "so that the nations may know Me when I am sanctified through you before their eyes, O Gog" (38:16). Only God will be able to account for Israel's victory over her foes. God further states, "My holy name I will make known in the midst of My people Israel; and I will not let My holy name be profaned anymore. And the nations will know that I am the LORD, the Holy One in Israel" (39:7). Then at the end of Ezekiel 39, we see Israel delivered and restored, and given the calling of being a light to the nations.

33.
EZEKIEL 40–48

The Millennial Temple, discussed in detail in Ezekiel 40:5–43:27, is destined to be perhaps the most beautiful and magnificent building in human history. This will be Israel's final Temple, the focal point of the 1000-year reign of the Messiah. Since the Millennium will be a time in which Israel will be exalted and Christ will rule the world through a theocracy from Jerusalem, it makes sense that worship of Messiah will revolve around a temple. It will be a wondrous time indeed—a time in which the glory of the Lord will return to the Temple (Ezekiel 43:1-5), God will dwell in the midst of His people (37:26-28), and Israel will fulfill her national calling.

This Temple will serve as the center for the priestly rituals and offerings that will provide guidance in the worship of the Messiah. Special sacrifices will be offered on the first month and the first day (45:18-19). The Passover feast is to be observed on the fourteenth day of the first month, and followed by the seven-day Feast of Unleavened Bread (45:21-25).

MILLENNIAL SACRIFICES

The fact that the Millennial Temple includes sacrifices has led many prophecy students to wonder about the purpose of such sacrifices. At least four other Old Testament prophets join Ezekiel in affirming there will be a sacrificial system in the Millennial Temple (Isaiah 56:7; 66:20-23; Jeremiah 33:18; Zechariah 14:16-21; Malachi 3:3-4), making it clear this matter is important enough to merit our attention.

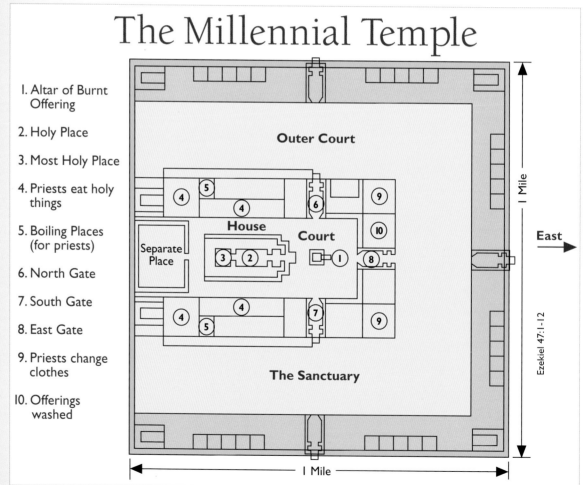

The Millennial Temple

1. Altar of Burnt Offering
2. Holy Place
3. Most Holy Place
4. Priests eat holy things
5. Boiling Places (for priests)
6. North Gate
7. South Gate
8. East Gate
9. Priests change clothes
10. Offerings washed

Outer Court

House

Court

Separate Place

The Sanctuary

1 Mile

East

Ezekiel 47:1-12

1 Mile

If we accept the literal interpretation of a Millennial sacrificial system, then are we contradicting passages such as Hebrews 7:26-27 and 9:26, which teach that Jesus Christ was the perfect and final sacrifice for sin? Premillennial scholars have fully recognized the issues at hand here, and there are at least two legitimate solutions to this question. First, many students and teachers of prophecy have noted that the sacrifices may function as a memorial to the work of Christ. As Dr. Jerry Hullinger says,

> According to this view the sacrifices offered during the earthly reign of Christ will be visible reminders of His work on the cross. Thus, these sacrifices will not have any efficacy except to memorialize Christ's death. The primary support for this argument is the parallel of the Lord's Supper. It is argued that just as the communion table looks back on the cross without besmirching its glory, so millennial sacrifices will do the same.[21]

This reply does not, however, completely resolve all the concerns. Ezekiel says that the sacrifices are *for atonement* rather than a memorial (Ezekiel 45:15,17,20). A second solution, then, is that the sacrifices are for ceremonial purification. Rather than merely functioning as a memorial, Dr. Hullinger suggests "a solution that maintains dispensational distinctives, deals honestly with the text of Ezekiel, and in no way demeans the work Christ did on the cross"[22]:

> ...animal sacrifices during the millennium will serve primarily to remove ceremonial uncleanness and prevent defilement from polluting the temple envisioned by Ezekiel. This will be necessary because the glorious presence of Yahweh will once again be dwelling on earth in the midst of a sinful and unclean people.[23]

Dr. Hullinger concludes by saying:

> Because of God's promise to dwell on earth during the millennium (as stated in the New Covenant), it is neces-

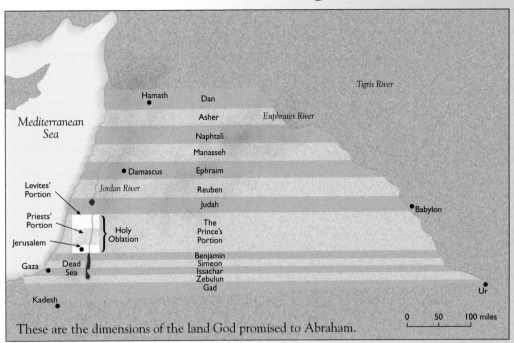

The Division of Land During the Millennium

Hamath
Dan
Asher
Tigris River
Euphrates River
Naphtali
Mediterranean Sea
Manasseh
Ephraim
• Damascus
Levites' Portion
Jordan River
Reuben
Judah
• Babylon
Priests' Portion
The Prince's Portion
Holy Oblation
Jerusalem
Benjamin
Simeon
Issachar
Zebulun
Gad
Gaza
Dead Sea
Ur
Kadesh
0   50   100 miles

These are the dimensions of the land God promised to Abraham.

sary that He protect His presence through sacrifice.... It should further be added that this sacrificial system will be a temporary one in that the millennium (with its partial population of unglorified humanity) will last only one thousand years. During the eternal state all inhabitants of the New Jerusalem will be glorified and will therefore not be a source of contagious impurities to defile the holiness of Yahweh.[24]

The presence and purpose of sacrifices as understood in this way neither diminish the work of Christ nor violate the normal and literal interpretation of Scripture. Although there will be sacrifices, the focus of all worship will remain on the person and work of the Savior. What's more, the sacrifices of the Millennial Temple will not be a return to the Mosaic Law, since the Law has forever been fulfilled and discontinued through Christ (Romans 6:14-15; 7:1-6; 1 Corinthians 9:20-21; 2 Corinthians 3:7-11; Galatians 4:1-7; 5:18; Hebrews 8:13; 10:1-14).

TOPOGRAPHICAL CHANGES IN THE LAND OF ISRAEL

At Christ's second coming, important topographical changes will occur in Jerusalem in order to facilitate the huge Millennial Temple:

> In that day His feet will stand on the Mount of Olives, which is in front of Jerusalem on the east; and the Mount of Olives will be split in its middle from east to west by a very large valley, so that half of the mountain will move toward the north and the other half toward the south (Zechariah 14:4).

In conjunction with a new platform to accommodate the Millennial Temple, Jerusalem and the land around the City of David will be elevated in preparation for Israel's key role during Messiah's rule:

> The Lord will be king over all the earth.... All the land will be changed into a plain from Geba to Rimmon south of Jerusalem; but Jerusalem will rise and remain on its site from Benjamin's Gate as far as the place of the First Gate to the Corner Gate, and from the Tower of Hananel to the king's wine presses. People will live in it, and there will no longer be a curse, for Jerusalem will dwell in security (Zechariah 14:9-11).

Ezekiel 47:13–48:35 describes in further detail the topographical changes that will take place in the land of Israel, which are designed to accompany Israel's new dominance over the nations.

As with all things future, the promise of the Millennial Temple gives us confidence that we can stand boldly for the truth in the dark days in which we currently live, knowing that God's plan cannot be thwarted and will lead to victory for His people. Ezekiel's vision provides hope for both Israel and the church, confirming that our God will stand as the ultimate victor in all history and eternity.

34.
ISRAEL'S TABERNACLE, TEMPLE, AND ARK IN HISTORY AND PROPHECY

> The Tabernacle, Temple, and ark of the covenant play a central role in Israel's spiritual relationship with the Lord. All three taught Israel—and still teach believers today—that you cannot approach God casually. God must be approached in a special way because He is a holy being, and the Tabernacle, Temple, and ark made provision for that.

THE TABERNACLE

The Tabernacle could be viewed as a "mobile Temple"—a transient Temple for a transient people. The Tabernacle was a temporary structure, moving from place to place until the Israelites were settled in the Promised Land and unified politically and spiritually. As a precursor to Solomon's Temple, the Tabernacle served many of the same functions and purposes.

After the nation entered the Promised Land and David became king, God spoke with David about the building of the Temple, which ultimately was built by Solomon. Once the Temple was consecrated, God's visible presence shifted from the Tabernacle to the Temple. "For now I have chosen and consecrated this house that My name may be there forever, and My eyes and My heart will be there perpetually" (2 Chronicles 7:16).

The Tabernacle, Temple, and Ark in History and Prophecy

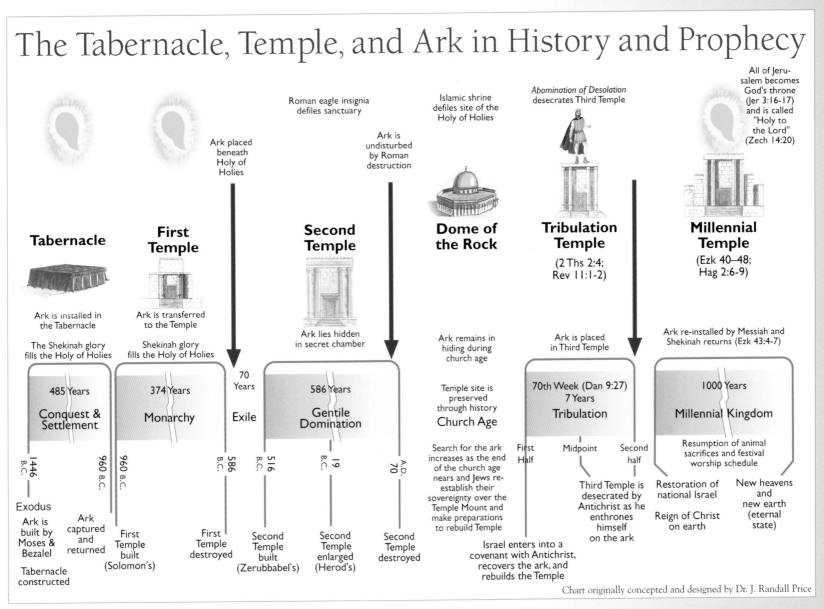

Tabernacle

Ark is installed in the Tabernacle

The Shekinah glory fills the Holy of Holies

| 485 Years |
| Conquest & Settlement |

1446 B.C. — Exodus; Ark is built by Moses & Bezalel; Tabernacle constructed

960 B.C. — Ark captured and returned

First Temple

Ark is transferred to the Temple

Shekinah glory fills the Holy of Holies

| 374 Years |
| Monarchy |

960 B.C. — First Temple built (Solomon's)

586 B.C. — First Temple destroyed

70 Years — Exile

Second Temple

Ark placed beneath Holy of Holies

Roman eagle insignia defiles sanctuary

Ark lies hidden in secret chamber

| 586 Years |
| Gentile Domination |

516 B.C. — Second Temple built (Zerubbabel's)

19 B.C. — Second Temple enlarged (Herod's)

Ark is undisturbed by Roman destruction

A.D. 70 — Second Temple destroyed

Dome of the Rock

Islamic shrine defiles site of the Holy of Holies

Ark remains in hiding during church age

Temple site is preserved through history

Church Age

Search for the ark increases as the end of the church age nears and Jews re-establish their sovereignty over the Temple Mount and make preparations to rebuild Temple

Tribulation Temple

(2 Ths 2:4; Rev 11:1-2)

Abomination of Desolation desecrates Third Temple

Ark is placed in Third Temple

| 70th Week (Dan 9:27) 7 Years |
| Tribulation |

First Half — Midpoint — Second half

Israel enters into a covenant with Antichrist, recovers the ark, and rebuilds the Temple

Third Temple is desecrated by Antichrist as he enthrones himself on the ark

Millennial Temple

(Ezk 40–48; Hag 2:6-9)

All of Jerusalem becomes God's throne (Jer 3:16-17) and is called "Holy to the Lord" (Zech 14:20)

Ark re-installed by Messiah and Shekinah returns (Ezk 43:4-7)

| 1000 Years |
| Millennial Kingdom |

Resumption of animal sacrifices and festival worship schedule

Restoration of national Israel

Reign of Christ on earth

New heavens and new earth (eternal state)

Chart originally concepted and designed by Dr. J. Randall Price

THE TEMPLE

The English word *temple* is derived from the Latin term *templum*, which is a translation of the Hebrew noun *hekal*, meaning "big house." In the Bible, "temple" almost always refers to the Jerusalem Temple. The Bible, at times, also speaks of a heavenly Temple. Isaiah was caught up to heaven and describes a scene that could well be the heavenly Temple (Isaiah 6). John, having been caught up into heaven, specifically speaks of a heavenly Temple from where God oversees the judgments of the Tribulation and sends forth His angels at His command (Revelation 7:15; 11:19; 14:15,17; 15:5-6,8; 16:1,17). The heavenly Temple, in some sense, serves as the model for the various earthly dwellings of God (that is, the Tabernacle, Temple, and spiritual Temple—the church).

The Bible speaks of four Temples in Jerusalem. The first two, Solomon's and Herod's, have already been built and destroyed. The final two, the Tribulation Temple and the Millennial Temple, have yet to be built and are described in great detail in biblical prophecy.

In the eternal state there will be no Temple because the new heavens and new earth are not polluted with sin, and God, who is holy, will be able to dwell openly with man.

Solomon's Temple

The First Temple, also known as Solomon's Temple, was constructed by King Solomon. Although it had been David's desire to build the Temple, God did not permit this because David was a man of war rather than peace (1 Kings 5:3; 2 Samuel 7:1-13).

The purpose of the Temple was to provide a permanent home for the ark of the covenant and for the worship of the Lord, and we can read detailed accounts of the Temple's construction in 1 Kings 5–8 and 2 Chronicles 2:1-18. This Temple, following the dimensions of the Tabernacle, was about 3500 square feet and built on a ten-foot-high platform with ten steps leading to the entrance. The first and smallest room of the Temple was a porch leading into the main room, or the Holy Place. The Holy Place housed the magnificent seven-branched *menorah* or candelabra, the table of showbread, the golden altar of incense, ten tables (five on the north side and five on the south), ten lamps on lampstands, and numerous implements used in the priestly service.

The Holy of Holies, the third and final room, was the most significant. It was closed off by a fabric veil. Access to this room was forbidden to all except the high priest, who entered only once a year at Yom Kippur, the high holy Day of Atonement. In this room was the ark of the covenant, which was covered with gold.

The destruction of Jerusalem by King Nebuchadnezzar and the Babylonians proceeded in stages, beginning in 605 B.C. In 586 B.C., in the final stage of destruction, the Babylonian army destroyed Jerusalem and burned the Temple to the ground (2 Kings 25:8-9; 2 Chronicles 36:18-19).

Zerubbabel's and Herod's Temple

Israel's captivity in Babylon lasted 70 years. A remnant of about 50,000 people returned to Israel in 538 B.C. under the leadership of Zerubbabel. The Persian king Cyrus, as prophesied by Isaiah, had given permission for the Temple to be rebuilt (Isaiah 44:28).

The book of Ezra describes Israel's efforts to rebuild the Temple.

The foundation for the Second Temple followed the Solomonic outline (Ezra 3:7-10). The Temple vessels and utensils were returned from Babylon, an altar was constructed, sacrifices began to be offered, and the observance of the biblical festivals was restored (Ezra 3:1-5). Further progress, however, met with opposition from nearby Samaritan residents, and construction was not resumed for another 15 years. The work was finally completed in 515 B.C. after a decree from the Persian king Darius not only permitted the rebuilding but prescribed local taxes that required even the Samaritans to help finance the construction (Ezra 6:1-15).

The Second Temple was a modest edifice when compared with Solomon's Temple. However, it was greatly enlarged and remodeled under Herod the Great, beginning in 20 B.C. Herod doubled the height of the original Second Temple and made the building significantly wider. It is believed that Herod's improvements enabled the Second Temple to exceed in beauty and greatness Solomon's earlier Temple. In fact, it was regarded as one of the marvels of the ancient world.

An insurrection against Rome by Jewish Zealots in A.D. 66 led to a prolonged period of fighting between Israel and Rome. Rome, fed up with the Jewish people's constant resistance, decided to crush all opposition. By A.D. 70 only Jerusalem and the outpost of Masada remained defiant. A siege against the city finally led to its defeat. And on the ninth day of the Jewish month of Av in A.D. 70, the city and the Temple were burned (as Daniel had prophesied).

When the building burned, it is said that the gold on the walls melted and ran into the seams between the stones. In an attempt to recover the gold, the Roman soldiers tore apart the stone walls, fulfilling Jesus' prediction that not one stone of the Temple would be left upon another (Matthew 24:2).

The Tribulation Temple

The fact that there will be a third Jewish Temple in Jerusalem at least by the midpoint of the seven-year Tribulation period is supported by at least four scriptural references:

- *Daniel 9:27:* This passage predicts a future time-period of seven years, during which the Antichrist defiles Israel's Temple at the halfway point. In order for this to happen, there must be a Temple in Jerusalem.

- *Matthew 24:15-16:* In this passage, Jesus mentions "the abomination of desolation…standing in the holy place," which speaks of the same event described in Daniel 9:27. "The holy place" is a reference to the most sacred room within Israel's Temple. In order for this to happen, there has to be a third Temple.

- *2 Thessalonians 2:3-4:* Here we see "the abomination of desolation" described as the event in which Antichrist "takes his seat in the temple of God." Again, this requires a future third Temple, for this prophecy has not yet been fulfilled.

- *Revelation 11:1-2:* Because this portion of the book of Revelation takes place during the Tribulation, the Temple

mentioned here must be Israel's third Temple.

This Temple is also called Antichrist's Temple because he will defile it by setting up his image in the Holy of Holies. This blasphemous act is known in the Bible as "the abomination of desolation" (Daniel 9:27; 11:31; 12:11; Matthew 24:15; Mark 13:14; 2 Thessalonians 2:4; Revelation 13:15).

The Millennial Temple

As explained on pages 94–96, in Ezekiel 40–48 we read about a fourth Temple, or the Millennial Temple that will serve as the center of the world's worship of Jesus Christ. This Temple will stand all through Christ's 1000-year reign.

35.
ELIJAH AND JOHN THE BAPTIST IN HISTORY AND PROPHECY

Elijah is often remembered as one of the only two individuals who were translated to heaven without dying (Enoch was the other). Yet that's not the last we see of Elijah. We read a prophecy about him in Malachi 4:5-6, which says, "Behold, I am going to send you Elijah the prophet before the coming of the great and terrible day of the LORD. He will restore the hearts of the fathers to their children and the hearts of the children to their fathers, so that I will not come and smite the land with a curse." This teaches us that Elijah will play a key role in the conversion of the nation of Israel during the Tribulation. It is likely that Elijah will be one of the two witnesses mentioned in Revelation 11:3.

There are some who teach that John the Baptist was the fulfillment of the prophecy about Elijah in Malachi 4:5-6. However, as we'll see in a moment, that is not the case. First we need to look at Isaiah 40:3-4, which clearly points to John the Baptist: "A voice is calling, 'Clear the way for the LORD in the wilderness; make smooth in the desert a highway for our God. Let every valley be lifted up, and every mountain and hill be made low; and let the rough ground become a plain, and the rugged terrain a broad valley.'" This passage predicted that John the Baptist would precede Jesus and prepare the way for His first coming (see Matthew 3:1-6). A parallel passage is Malachi 3:1, which says, "'Behold, I am going to send My messenger, and he will clear the way before Me. And the LORD, whom you

Elijah and John the Baptist in History and Prophecy

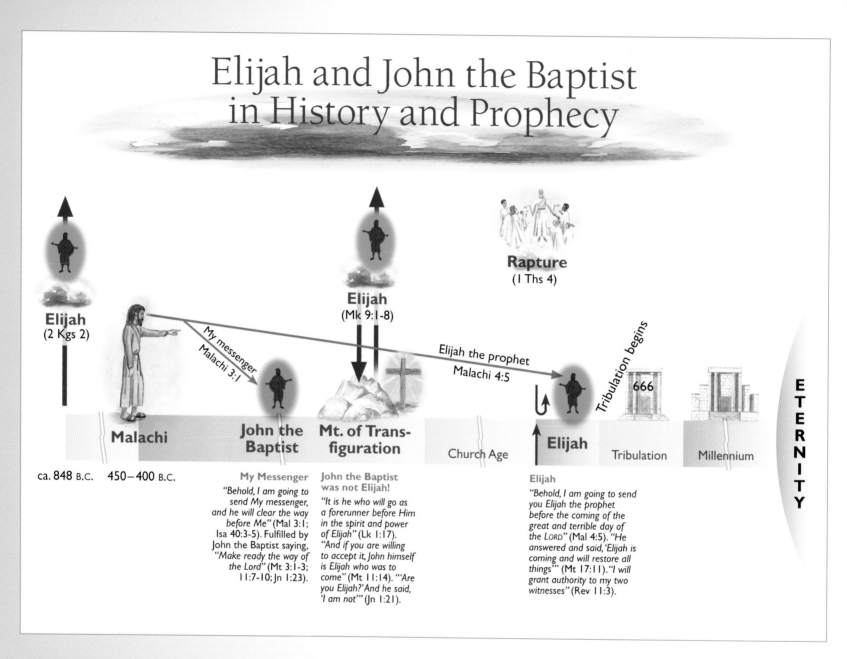

Elijah
(2 Kgs 2)

Rapture
(1 Ths 4)

Elijah
(Mk 9:1-8)

My messenger
Malachi 3:1

Elijah the prophet
Malachi 4:5

Malachi

John the Baptist

Mt. of Trans-figuration

Church Age

Elijah

666

Tribulation begins

Tribulation

Millennium

E T E R N I T Y

ca. 848 B.C.   450–400 B.C.

My Messenger

"Behold, I am going to send My messenger, and he will clear the way before Me" (Mal 3:1; Isa 40:3-5). Fulfilled by John the Baptist saying, *"Make ready the way of the Lord"* (Mt 3:1-3; 11:7-10; Jn 1:23).

John the Baptist was not Elijah!

"It is he who will go as a forerunner before Him in the spirit and power of Elijah" (Lk 1:17). *"And if you are willing to accept it, John himself is Elijah who was to come"* (Mt 11:14). *"'Are you Elijah?' And he said, 'I am not'"* (Jn 1:21).

Elijah

"Behold, I am going to send you Elijah the prophet before the coming of the great and terrible day of the LORD" (Mal 4:5). *"He answered and said, 'Elijah is coming and will restore all things'"* (Mt 17:11). *"I will grant authority to my two witnesses"* (Rev 11:3).

---

seek, will suddenly come to His temple; and the messenger of the covenant, in whom you delight, behold, He is coming,' says the LORD of hosts."

So, John the Baptist fulfilled Isaiah 40:3-4 and Malachi 3:1, and he was "a forerunner" who would come "in the spirit and power of Elijah" (Luke 1:17). Christ told His disciples concerning John the Baptist that "if you are willing to accept it, John himself is Elijah

who was to come" (Matthew 11:14). But Israel did not accept Jesus as their Messiah at His first coming, and therefore the kingdom did not arrive. In fact, when John the Baptist was asked directly, "Are you Elijah?" he clearly said, "I am not" (John 1:21). Thus, John the Baptist was not Elijah, and Elijah is still to come.

As Malachi 4:5-6 says, Elijah will come "before...the great and terrible day of the LORD" for the purpose of restoring "the hearts of the fathers to their children and the hearts of the children to their fathers." Elijah will most likely be one of the two witnesses mentioned in Revelation 11:3. These two witnesses will proclaim the gospel for a period of 1260 days during the Tribulation. Revelation 11:6 says they will "have the power to shut up the sky, so that rain will not fall during the days of their prophesying." Elijah also kept rain from falling during his ministry before he was taken up to heaven in the fiery chariot (1 Kings 17:1; 18:41-45).

We think these two witnesses will probably be Moses and Elijah (or perhaps Enoch and Elijah). Both Moses and Elijah were at the Transfiguration, which anticipates the second coming of Jesus Christ (Matthew 17:3). Like the prophets of the Old Testament, these two witnesses will be able to perform miracles and will be protected by God against harm until their mission is complete. At the end of the first half of the Tribulation, God will remove their special protection so that the Antichrist will then kill them and their bodies will be left in the streets of Jerusalem for three-and-a-half days, after which God will resurrect them and rapture them to heaven. After they have ascended to heaven, a great earthquake will destroy a tenth of Jerusalem, killing 7000 people.

The two witnesses will be clothed in sackcloth (Revelation 11:3), which is symbolic of the fact that they are prophets of doom (see Isaiah 37:1-2; Daniel 9:3). While Jerusalem is not mentioned by name as the city of their ministry, Revelation 11:8 says that their dead bodies will lie "in the street of the great city which mystically is called Sodom and Egypt, where also their Lord was crucified." The reference to the crucifixion clearly places the location as Jerusalem. The reference to Sodom and Egypt implies that during this time there will be licentious behavior and persecution of the Jews in the city.

36.
THE FEASTS OF ISRAEL IN PROPHECY

It seems evident that the seven annual feasts of Israel as listed in Leviticus 23 have prophetic significance. This is true, but are they fulfilled in relation to Israel or the church? We believe the evidence supports that these feasts are fulfilled in history and prophecy in relation to Israel alone.

The seven annual feasts are as follows:

SPRING
- Passover (Leviticus 23:5)
- Unleavened Bread (Leviticus 23:6)
- First Fruits (Leviticus 23:10-11)
- Weeks or Pentecost (Leviticus 23:15-17)

FALL
- Trumpets (Leviticus 23:24)
- Day of Atonement (Leviticus 23:27)
- Tabernacles (Leviticus 23:39-43)

There is a prophetic aspect to Israel's feast cycle. Christ fulfilled the four feasts in the spring cycle at the exact times they were celebrated on Israel's annual calendar. It appears certain, then, that events related to His second coming will fulfill the three fall feasts (we'll explain why in a moment). What's more, they will be fulfilled in relation to God's plan for Israel and not the church, for the feasts relate to Israel and Israel alone. While it's true that the fulfillment of Israel's feasts relate to salvation for *all* mankind, the precise prophetic significance and fulfillment relate exclusively to the nation of Israel.

Many premillennialists tend to see at least one of Israel's feasts fulfilled by the church—the Feast of Pentecost, which is usually seen as fulfilled by the church at her birth in Acts 2. This creates a problem because it does not fit with maintaining a consistent distinction between God's plan for Israel and His plan for the church. The errant notion that the church fulfills the Feast of Pentecost gives a basis to the perspective that the church will fulfill the Feast of Trumpets at the Rapture. If this were true, then it would also follow that the Rapture would have to occur on the day in which that feast is celebrated. However, we do not think that the church fulfills any of Israel's feasts. Israel's feasts have been and will continue to be fulfilled in relation to Israel.

The seven feasts were divinely revealed to the Hebrew nation as yearly reminders of God's promises in the Abrahamic Covenant—promises that He said He would fulfill. These feasts can be fulfilled by and to Israel alone. Thus, the typology of the feasts can relate to the Jewish nation only.[25]

This does not mean that the church is not built upon the sacrificial work of Christ on the cross. That is the basis for the forgiveness of sin in any dispensation. However, it does mean that the seven feasts of Israel do serve as a specific typological prophecy picturing God's plan of redemption for His people Israel. It is important to understand that the Feast of Pentecost was not fulfilled by or for the church. Dr. Terry Hulbert wrote:

> The fourth feast did not foreshadow a church composed of sin-prone Jewish and Gentile believers pictured by two loaves of unleavened bread. This point is important, for if the church had fulfilled this feast, it could also fulfill the last three as the Amillennarian claims. However, the church is not revealed in the typology of any of the feasts, being related to them in the same way it is related to unconditional covenants made to Israel. It benefits from God's fulfillments to that nation, but is distinct from it.[26]

If we are going to consistently apply the literal method of interpretation, then we cannot see any of Israel's feasts being fulfilled by God's program for the church. Why? Because these feasts are given in Leviticus 23 to Israel as part of her law. The church has been given the Lord's Table as the feast we are to celebrate "from now on *until* the kingdom of God comes" (Luke 22:18, emphasis added). If we see any

of the feasts as being fulfilled by the church, then we are practicing the same kind of "replacement theology" that is espoused by those who see the church as completely replacing Israel in God's plan. But nowhere in the New Testament do we see evidence of the church fulfilling any of Israel's feasts. Because Israel's feasts are fulfilled only by Israel and not by the church, then Rosh Hashanah or the Feast of Trumpets *cannot* be a foreshadowing of the Rapture of the church. Israel's fifth feast does not give any insight into the day of the year on which the Rapture will occur.

Dr. Hulbert's summary of the purpose for the fulfillment of Israel's feasts makes the best sense within the framework of a *consistent* literal hermeneutic:

> When God fulfilled the first four feasts He had provided everything necessary for Israel to enter into literal kingdom blessing—redemption, separation, resurrection, and the presence of the Holy Spirit. Israel's rejection of these, however, made necessary a national change of heart before the kingdom could be established. Foreknowing this, God included the Feast of Trumpets and Day of Atonement in the annual cycle. Thus, the Feast of Trumpets predicted God's alerting of the nation for the impending event which would bring about repentance. The Feast of the Day of Atonement predicted not the death of Christ, which had already been typified in the Passover, but the new reaction of Israel to the Redeemer's death. This change will take place when the believing Remnant repents during the Tribulation period. The event which fulfills this sixth feast is identified as God's intervention to save Israel from destruction as Gentile armies attack Jerusalem.[27]

Dr. Hulbert goes on to say this:

> Israel as a nation officially rejected in turn each spiritual provision offered by God and made available through the fulfillment of the first four feasts. The paschal lamb of God pointed out by John the Baptist was rejected as an imposter. The resurrection of Christ, as it answered to the Feast of Firstfruits, was suppressed in its proclamation by

The Feasts of Israel in Prophecy

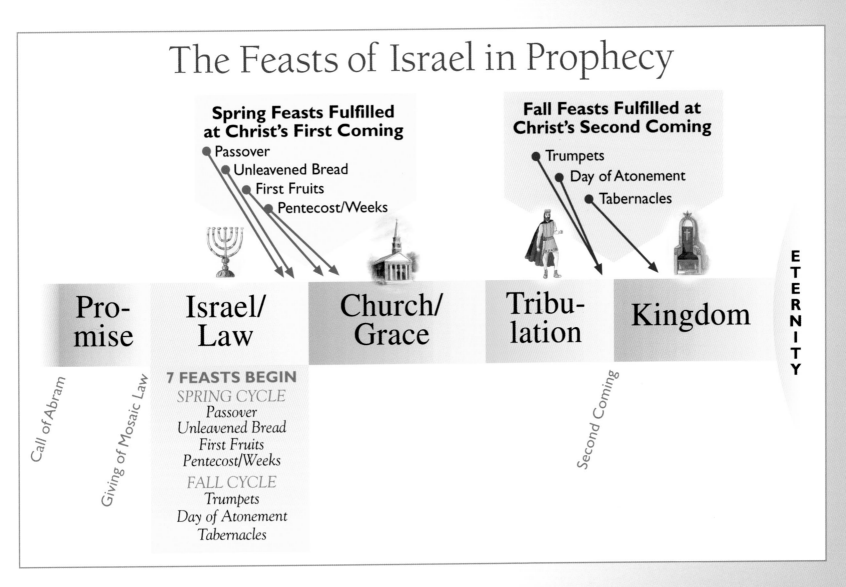

Spring Feasts Fulfilled at Christ's First Coming
- Passover
- Unleavened Bread
- First Fruits
- Pentecost/Weeks

Fall Feasts Fulfilled at Christ's Second Coming
- Trumpets
- Day of Atonement
- Tabernacles

Pro-mise	Israel/ Law	Church/ Grace	Tribu-lation	Kingdom	E T E R N I T Y

Call of Abram

Giving of Mosaic Law

Second Coming

7 FEASTS BEGIN
SPRING CYCLE
Passover
Unleavened Bread
First Fruits
Pentecost/Weeks
FALL CYCLE
Trumpets
Day of Atonement
Tabernacles

the bribe money paid to the sentries…. Finally, the coming of the Spirit was rejected at Pentecost as the Jews taunted the apostles with charges of drunkenness.

By the time of the close of Acts chapter 2, God had done all He could do for Israel until they repented as a nation. Thus, the significance of Peter's second sermon in Acts 3 was that it reemphasized the condition of millennial blessing already laid down in the Old Testament, but as yet unfulfilled….

Of the utmost importance here is the fact that with the shedding of the blood of Christ to take away sin, and with the coming of the Spirit to empower the life of the redeemed, all of the spiritual requirements for the millennial kingdom had been met as far as God was concerned. But God's provision could not be operative until man appropriated it. This point cannot be overemphasized, for it is not only the reason for the delay in the fulfillment of the final three feasts, it is the basis for understanding the relationship of the church to the feasts.[28]

The three fall feasts await fulfillment in events that will take place at the second coming of Christ and in the Millennium. The Feast of Trumpets will take place at the second coming, as Matthew 24:31 indicates: "He will send forth His angels with a great trumpet and they will gather together His elect from the four winds, from one end of the sky to the other." The Day of Atonement will be applied to the nation of Israel when the people realize that Jesus was their long-awaited Messiah all along (Zechariah 12:20; Romans 11:25-27). And the Feast of Tabernacles will be fulfilled by the Millennial kingdom when the Jewish nation will dwell with their God in the land of Israel for 1000 years.

37.
BABYLON IN HISTORY AND PROPHECY

Someday I (Tim) would like to write a book titled *The Tale of Two Cities*, and in it discuss the history and future of the two most influential cities in the world—Jerusalem and Babylon. Jerusalem, mentioned over 300 times in the Bible, is "the city of peace" where God sacrificed His Son for the sins of the world. It is there He revealed Himself to Abraham, Melchizedek, kings, prophets, and holy men through whom He gave a holy book to His followers. In that book He gave them instructions on how they should live, care for their families, run their country, and enjoy unprecedented freedom and blessing.

Satan chose Babylon, the second most-mentioned city in the Bible, from which to launch his ancient diabolical attack on mankind. There he lied to humanity about God, creation, sin, salvation, moral values, culture, and eternity. His primary objective was to get people to worship and serve him. It is there that he introduced idolatrous religions, both polytheistic and naturalistic, based on the theory of evolution. These false religious systems are the source of all idolatry in the world today. Satan sought to get man to fulfill his hunger for God through idols that could be seen and touched. Through these religions, Satan taught that humanity, not God, is "the measure of all things"—man is the center of his universe. Therefore, anything people want to do is okay. There are no rights and wrongs, nor a hereafter. So eat, drink, and be merry, for tomorrow we die.

Satan's many forms of idolatry, all of which had their origin in Babylon, spread quickly through the ancient world. In the midst of that idolatry, God raised up Abraham, and through him the nation of Israel—the torchbearers of His truth to the world. It was at Jerusalem and through Israel that God revealed His plan to send His only begotten Son into the world to be the divine sacrifice for the sins of all humankind. However, Israel did not remain true to God. The nation eventually got to the point where the Babylonish worship of the pagan religions supplanted the worship of Jehovah. The idolatry got so bad that God sent judgment on His chosen people by allowing King Nebuchadnezzar to take them captive into Babylon.

It's ironic, isn't it, that God would cause the children of Israel to be conquered by Babylon and taken captive to the very citadel of all idolatry. But in the book of Daniel, we can see how God revealed Himself to be the one true God in the midst of pagan Babylon. For example, in Daniel chapter 2 He confounded the best "wise men, astrologers, necromancers, and soothsayers" and permitted only

Babylon in History and Prophecy

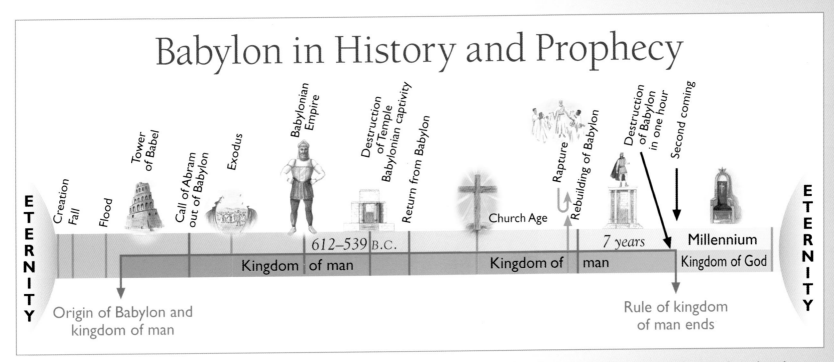

Daniel to recall and interpret the king's vision. Thus all of Babylon could not help but realize that God alone is able to reveal history in advance, which is what prophecy really is. What's more, Israel seemed to get the message, for the captivity cured them from ever again worshiping idols as a nation.

History reveals that Babylon, under the rule of Rome, declined until it was abandoned about two centuries after Christ. The city of Babylon remained hidden beneath the sands of time for 1700 years, but recently it has begun to rise again. Watch for Babylon to become a dominant force in the world religiously, commercially, and governmentally, for Revelation 17–18 predicts the destruction of that city and, in order for it to be the city described in those prophecies, it must be rebuilt on a grand scale as in the days of Nebuchadnezzar.

Now, there are some people who say the Babylon in Revelation 17–18 is a different city, such as Rome or New York. Yet those of us who believe we should take Scripture literally whenever possible are inclined to believe that the city of Babylon will be rebuilt. Admittedly there are good Bible teachers who do not hold that position, but the weight of Bible prophecy convincingly requires the literal rebuilding of Babylon. The main reason for believing that

Babylon must be rebuilt relates to some prophecies about her destruction that have yet to be fulfilled:

1. Isaiah 13–14 and Jeremiah 50–51 describe the destruction of Babylon as being at the time of "the day of the LORD." A careful reading of these four chapters reveals that the prophecies concerning the destruction of Babylon in the Old Testament use the law of double reference; that is, they refer to the overthrow of Babylon in the seventieth year of Israel's captivity, and they mention the destruction of the city in the Day of the Lord, or the Tribulation.

2. The ruins of ancient Babylon have been proven to be used to build other cities. But Jeremiah 51:26 says, "'No rock will be taken from you for a cornerstone, nor any stone for a foundation, for you will be desolate forever,' declares the LORD" (NIV). If ancient Babylon's stones have been used in surrounding towns and villages, then God's prophecy in Jeremiah 51:26 is wrong. However, we know that God is never wrong when it comes to prophecy. Clearly, Jeremiah 51:26 is speaking about a future, rebuilt Babylon that, upon its destruction, will be left desolate to the point that

its stones will remain untouched.

In addition, Isaiah 13:20 says that the ruins of Babylon were never to be inhabited: "She will never be inhabited or lived in through all generations; no Arab will pitch his tent there, no shepherd will rest his flocks there" (NIV). The fact is, Babylon has grown over the past 100 years and now houses over 250,000 people. Obviously, Isaiah 13:20 awaits a future fulfillment. According to Revelation 17–18, that powerful city will be destroyed "in a single day," just before Christ comes to set up His Millennial kingdom on this earth. At that time, it will remain forever desolate.

38.
THE VARIOUS VIEWS OF THE RAPTURE

Everyone who takes the Bible literally believes in the physical second coming of Jesus. Almost as many believe in a Rapture of the church to the Father's house according to Jesus' promise in John 14:1-3. These events are so clearly taught in the Bible it is all but impossible to deny them. There is, however, a divergence of opinion as to the exact timing of the Rapture. There is no one verse that teaches specifically that Jesus will come before the Tribulation, during it, or at the end. The timing of that event is a matter of deduction based on a careful study of all the Bible passages on the Lord's return. What's unfortunate is that there has been some bitter disagreement over the timing of the Rapture—a most regrettable circumstance, since all these teachers (whatever their interpretations) love the Lord and long for His return.

THE FOUR VIEWS

1. *The Pre-Tribulation View*—Christ comes in fulfillment of His own promise in Revelation 3:10 to keep His church from "the hour of temptation, which shall come upon all the world, to try them that dwell upon the earth" (KJV). This is the prevailing view and the one held by the authors of this book.

2. *The Partial Rapture View*—Christ will only rapture those "that look for him" (Hebrews 9:28 KJV), causing some Christians to enter the Tribulation but be raptured at another time during that traumatic period in one of the subsequent raptures. This view is not popular today for many reasons, including the fact that it is not supported by other Rapture teachings in the Scriptures.

3. *The Mid-Tribulational View*—Christ raptures His church in the middle of the Tribulation, with the rapture of the two witnesses in Revelation 11 serving as an illustration of it. One problem with this view is that the two witnesses are Jews who have come to minister to Jews in Jerusalem, and are not members of the church. People who hold this view skip over the fact that Revelation 4:1-3 has John (a member of the church) being taken up to heaven as an illustration of the Rapture of the church.

4. *The Post-Tribulation View*—This view is second in popularity after the pre-Trib position. Christ will come at the end of the Tribulation, which means the church will go through the Tribulation and be raptured just before the glorious appearing. Thus those who are raptured zip right up to the sky then right back down. This leaves no time to visit the Father's house, no time for the judgment seat of Christ, and no time for the Marriage Supper of the Lamb. One important fact post-Trib advocates forget is Jesus' promise to "keep" believers from that time of trial (Revelation 3:10). This promise would be broken if Christ came for His church after an overwhelming majority of its members had been martyred.

WHY THE RAPTURE MUST BE PRETRIBULATIONAL

Will the Lord come back for His church before, in the middle, or at the end of the Tribulation? When properly understood, the Scriptures are quite clear on this subject. We believe they teach that the Rapture will occur before the Tribulation begins. Here are some reasons why:

1. The Lord Himself promised to deliver us.

A clear promise guaranteeing the church's rapture before the Tribulation is found in Revelation 3:10: "Since you have kept my command to endure patiently, *I will also keep you from the hour of trial that is going to come upon the whole world* to test those who live on the earth" (NIV, emphasis added). Though this promise appears in a letter written to the church at Philadelphia, we can be certain it refers to members of the universal church throughout the ages: 1) the passage refers to a future event; 2) the church of Philadelphia has long since been destroyed and disbanded; 3) this was a letter to all the churches; and 4) this promise will not be fulfilled until a time of trial that comes upon the whole world—not just the church at Philadelphia.

In addition, the word "from" (Greek, *ek*) in Revelation 3:10 literally means "out of," which is how it's rendered many other times in the Bible. God is saying, "I will keep you out of the wrath to come."

2. Only the pre-Trib view preserves imminency.

Imminency is the word used to refer to the doctrine that Christ could come at any moment to call His bride to be with Him in His Father's house. That is why Scripture has so many admonitions to watch, be ready, and to look for Him to come at any moment. The other three views destroy that immediate, at-any-time coming. In fact, those views have Christians looking not for *Christ* to come at any time, but rather for the Antichrist and the Tribulation.

3. The church is to be delivered from the wrath to come.

The promise in 1 Thessalonians 1:10 ("Jesus…rescues us from the wrath to come") was given by the Holy Spirit through the apostle Paul to a young church planted on his second missionary journey. He had only three weeks to ground this church in the Word of God before being driven out of town. Many of his teachings during that brief period evidently pertained to Bible prophecy and end-time events, for this letter—one of the first books of the New Testament to be written—emphasizes the second coming, the imminent return of Christ, the Rapture, the Tribulation, and other end-time subjects. Paul apparently considered these topics essential for new converts.

Paul mentions the second coming in every chapter, so there is no doubt about the main subject of his letter. After complimenting his readers on their faith and testimony, he commends them for turning "to God from idols to serve a living and true God, and to wait for His Son from heaven, whom He raised from the dead, that is *Jesus, who rescues us from the wrath to come*" (1 Thessalonians 1:9-10, emphasis added).

The context of that passage is the Rapture, for Christians are not waiting for the glorious appearing. Paul tells these people in 2 Thessalonians 2:1-12 that the latter will not occur until Antichrist (or "that lawless one") is revealed (verse 8). No, the Christians in Thessalonica were awaiting the coming of Christ for His church—that is, the Rapture. They already knew the Tribulation (or "wrath to come") would follow the Rapture, and that God had promised to rescue them from the wrath to come.

4. Christians are not appointed to wrath.

According to 1 Thessalonians 5:9, "God hath not appointed us to wrath, but to obtain salvation by our Lord Jesus Christ" (KJV). This passage, which follows the strongest passage on the Rapture in the Bible (in 1 Thessalonians 4) must be considered in the light of its context.

After teaching about the Rapture, Paul takes his readers to "times and...seasons" (KJV) of "the day of the Lord" (1 Thessalonians 5:1-2). Some suggest this refers to the single day on which Christ returns to this earth to set up His kingdom, but that is not consistent with the Bible's other uses of the phrase "the day of the Lord." Sometimes this phrase does refer to the glorious appearing, but on other occasions it encompasses the Rapture, the Tribulation, and the glorious appearing.

For our purposes here, 1 Thessalonians 5:9 (KJV) makes it clear that God has not "appointed us to wrath" (the Tribulation) but to "obtain salvation," or deliverance from it. Since so many saints will be martyred during the Tribulation, there will be few (if any) alive at the glorious appearing of Christ. This promise cannot mean, then, that He will deliver believers *during* the time of wrath, for the saints who live through the Tribulation will *not* be delivered; in fact, most will be martyred. To be delivered out of it, the church will have to be raptured before it begins.

Since the Tribulation is *especially* the time of God's wrath, and since Christians are not appointed to wrath, then it follows that the church will be raptured *before* the Tribulation. In short, the Rapture occurs before the Tribulation, while the glorious appearing occurs after it.

5. The church is absent in Revelation 4–18.

The church is mentioned 17 times in the first three chapters of Revelation, but after John (a member of the church) is called up to heaven at the beginning of chapter 4, he looks down on the events of the Tribulation, and the church is not mentioned or seen again until chapter 19, when she returns to the earth with her Bridegroom at His glorious appearing. Why? The answer is obvious: *She isn't in the Tribulation.* She is raptured to be with her Lord before it begins!

There are many other reasons for believing that the Rapture occurs

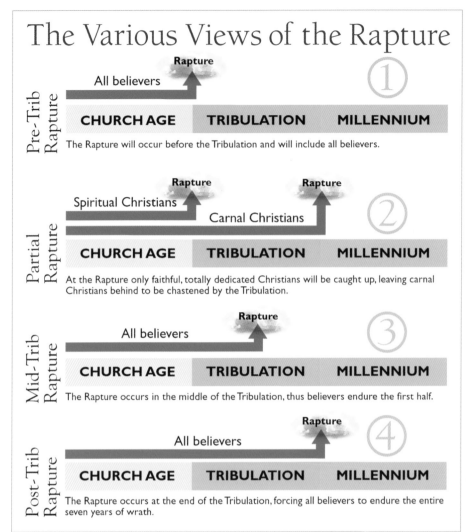

The Various Views of the Rapture

Pre-Trib Rapture ①
Rapture — All believers
CHURCH AGE | TRIBULATION | MILLENNIUM
The Rapture will occur before the Tribulation and will include all believers.

Partial Rapture ②
Rapture — Spiritual Christians | Rapture — Carnal Christians
CHURCH AGE | TRIBULATION | MILLENNIUM
At the Rapture only faithful, totally dedicated Christians will be caught up, leaving carnal Christians behind to be chastened by the Tribulation.

Mid-Trib Rapture ③
Rapture — All believers
CHURCH AGE | TRIBULATION | MILLENNIUM
The Rapture occurs in the middle of the Tribulation, thus believers endure the first half.

Post-Trib Rapture ④
Rapture — All believers
CHURCH AGE | TRIBULATION | MILLENNIUM
The Rapture occurs at the end of the Tribulation, forcing all believers to endure the entire seven years of wrath.

prior to the Tribulation; these are found in the *Tim LaHaye Prophecy Study Bible* (Chattanooga, TN: AMG Publishers, 2000), pp. 1479-82.

The pre-Trib position does not have answers for all the questions regarding the Lord's coming for His church. Since there is no one verse or passage that gives all the details of the Lord's coming in a neat little package, it is necessary to consider all the second-coming scriptures together. Our conclusion is that the pre-Trib Rapture fits the biblical model better than any of the other views. It fits well with all that the Bible teaches about the end times, and it is a commonsense view that brings comfort to the hearts of believers, which is one of the main purposes for teaching end-times prophecy (1 Thessalonians 4:18).

39.
VARIOUS RAPTURES IN HISTORY AND PROPHECY

Up to now, we have looked a lot at what the Bible says about the Rapture of the church. But there are other rapture events documented in the Bible, too. By definition, we use the term *rapture* to refer to those times when God takes a person to the next life apart from experiencing the curse of death. With that in mind, we would like to survey some of the other rapture events chronicled in Scripture.

OLD TESTAMENT RAPTURES

Enoch

Enoch was the first person ever raptured and taken to be with the Lord. Genesis 5:24 says this about Enoch's translation to heaven: "Enoch walked with God: and he was not; for God *took* him" (KJV, emphasis added). What does it mean that Enoch "was not; for God took him"? Enoch was translated, without dying, and went directly to be with the Lord. Enoch was raptured, to use the language of 1 Thessalonians 4:17, or he was received, to use the language of John 14:3. That Enoch was raptured or translated to heaven is clear when compared with the dismal refrain "and he died" that accompanies the legacy of the other patriarchs mentioned in Genesis 5.

Enoch's rapture is confirmed by the divinely inspired New Testament commentary found in Hebrews 11:5, which says, "By faith Enoch was *taken up* so that he would not see death; and he was not found because God *took* him *up*; for he obtained the witness that before his being *taken up* he was pleasing to God" (emphasis added). The New Testament word for "taken up" conveys the idea of being removed from one place and taken to another. So, Genesis 5:24 and the three phrases in Hebrews 11:5 affirm the idea of translation to heaven.

Elijah

Like Enoch, Elijah was translated to heaven without dying. Second Kings 2:1 says he was taken "by a whirlwind to heaven."

Later, we see Elijah at Christ's transfiguration (Matthew 17:3). And according to Malachi 4:5, Elijah will make some kind of appearance during the Tribulation.

Isaiah

In Isaiah chapter 6, we see Isaiah in God's throne room. While this was not a rapture like that experienced by Enoch and Elijah (for Isaiah did not avoid death), still, a rapture of sorts may have been involved here.

A PATTERN FOR THE FUTURE

First Corinthians 10:11, speaking of some Old Testament events, says, "Now these things happened to them as an example, and they were written for our instruction." The word "example" is from the Greek word *tupos*, which means "form, figure, or pattern." The English word *type* is developed from the Greek word, and the word *typology* refers to Old Testament patterns that illustrate doctrine—usually New Testament doctrine. It is wrong to teach a doctrine from a type itself. Types serve only to illustrate a doctrine that is taught clearly in the biblical text.

The Old Testament raptures, though they don't teach about the New Testament truth of the Rapture of the church, do provide us with Old Testament types, patterns, or illustrations of the Rapture. Thus, Enoch and Elijah stand as types of the Rapture of the church.

Various Raptures in History and Prophecy

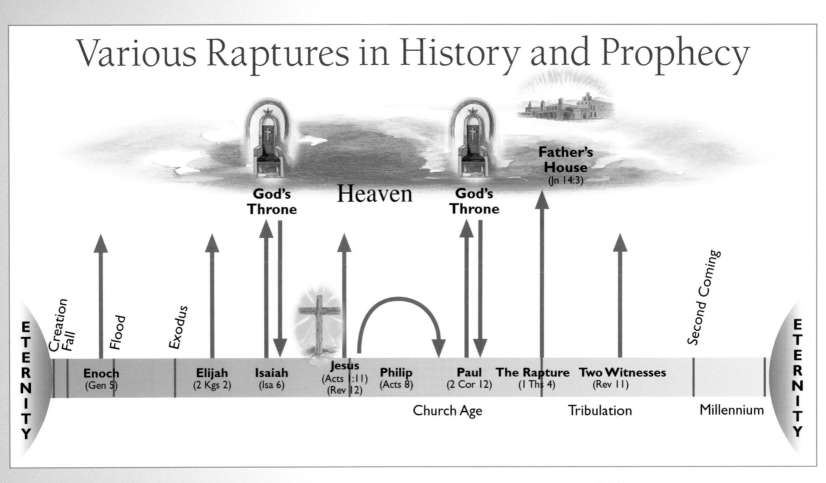

NEW TESTAMENT RAPTURES

Other than the Rapture of the church, there are other examples of raptures in the New Testament. These do not teach about the Rapture of the church, but they do serve to strengthen our understanding that a rapture involves the translation of someone from one point to another.

Jesus Christ

In Revelation 12:5, Christ is called the "male child" who "was caught up to God and to His throne." This picture looks back to Christ's ascension in Acts 1:8-11, where Christ ascended to heaven in a cloud. Because Revelation 12:5 uses the term "caught up" (or "rapture"), this means that Christ's ascension in Acts 1:11 is viewed as a rapture—a trip from earth to heaven.

Philip

Philip was "snatched…away" by the Spirit of the Lord after he preached the gospel to an Ethiopian eunuch and "found himself at Azotus" (Acts 8:39-40), which is located in the Gaza Strip in modern-day Israel. Philip was not taken to heaven but was physically transported by the Lord.

Paul

The apostle Paul mentions that he was "caught up [raptured] to the third heaven" and received "visions and revelations of the Lord" (2 Corinthians 12:1-4). Paul's heavenly trip reminds us of Isaiah's throne-room commission (Isaiah 6:1-13). Perhaps a rapture was involved in this incident. Paul, via rapture, received a commission, message, and revelation that became the foundation for the unique purpose for the church during this age, "which in other generations was not made known to the sons of men, as it has now been revealed to His holy apostles and prophets in the Spirit" (Ephesians 3:5).

The Two Witnesses

Reminiscent of Elijah, the two witnesses in Revelation 11 are summoned "into heaven in the cloud" (verse 12). The divinely commissioned and protected messengers serve as ambassadors for our Lord to the Jewish nation during the first half of the Tribulation. In a similar way, the "male child" in Revelation 12:5 is said to be "caught up [raptured] to God and to His throne."

The Bible provides us with seven instances of the rapture of individuals throughout history. This provides a strong support that a group—the church—will be raptured in the future, as 1 Thessalonians 4 teaches. Some opponents of the Rapture seek to suggest that the worldwide disappearance of millions would be too odd to consider as a realistic possibility. Such is not the case if the Bible is the criterion for establishing possibilities. After all, if God can take one person directly to heaven—as He did with Enoch or Elijah—who's to say He can't take millions at one moment in time?

40.
THE TWO PHASES OF HIS ONE COMING

Some Bible teachers see the second coming in two phases. The Rapture of the church is the first phase and Christ's glorious coming in power to the earth is the second. Other fine teachers contend the coming of Christ in the air for His church is a special event all in itself, which obviously is the second coming. Actually, there is only one second coming. The appearance of Christ in the air to rapture His church is a separate event that precedes the seven-year Tribulation period, and the second coming will occur at the end of the Tribulation, after which the Lord appears gloriously on the earth.

There is no doubt that there are two separate phases of our

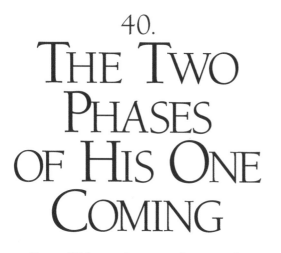

Rapture Passages

John 14:1-3	1 Thessalonians 1:10	Hebrews 9:28
Romans 8:19	1 Thessalonians 2:19	James 5:7-9
1 Corinthians 1:7-8	1 Thessalonians 4:13-18	1 Peter 1:7,13
1 Corinthians 15:51-53	1 Thessalonians 5:9,23	1 Peter 5:4
1 Corinthians 16:22	2 Thessalonians 2:1	1 John 2:28–3:2
Philippians 3:20-21	1 Timothy 6:14	Jude 1:21
Philippians 4:5	2 Timothy 4:1,8	Revelation 2:25
Colossians 3:4	Titus 2:13	

Second Coming Passages

Daniel 2:44-45	Mark 13:14-27	1 Peter 4:12-13
Daniel 7:9-14	Mark 14:62	2 Peter 3:1-14
Daniel 12:1-3	Luke 21:25-28	Jude 1:14-15
Zechariah 12:10	Acts 1:9-11	Revelation 1:7
Zechariah 14:1-15	Acts 3:19-21	Revelation 19:11–20:6
Matthew 13:41	1 Thessalonians 3:13	Revelation 22:7,12,20
Matthew 24:15-31	2 Thessalonians 1:6-10	
Matthew 26:64	2 Thessalonians 2:8	

Lord's coming because so many Bible passages refer to one or both events, as shown in the chart on this page.

As you study the specific details in these passages you will find they describe two different events. One has believers going up to the

The 15 Differences Between the Rapture and the Glorious Appearing

Rapture / Blessed Hope	Glorious Appearing
1. Christ comes in the air for His own	1. Christ comes with His own to earth
2. Rapture of all Christians	2. No one raptured
3. Christians taken to the Father's house	3. Resurrected saints do not see Father's house
4. No judgment on earth	4. Christ judges inhabitants of earth
5. Church taken to heaven	5. Christ sets up His kingdom on earth
6. Imminent—could happen any moment	6. Cannot occur for at least 7 years
7. No signs	7. Many signs for Christ's physical coming
8. For believers only	8. Affects all humanity
9. Time of joy	9. Time of mourning
10. Before the "day of wrath" (Tribulation)	10. Immediately after Tribulation (Matthew 24)
11. No mention of Satan	11. Satan bound in abyss for 1000 years
12. The judgment seat of Christ	12. No time or place for judgment seat
13. Marriage of the Lamb	13. His bride descends with Him
14. Only His own see Him	14. Every eye will see Him
15. Tribulation begins	15. 1000-year kingdom of Christ begins

Father's house and the other has Christ coming to the earth. The chart here shows 15 differences between the Rapture and the glorious appearing.

When examining Scripture, the honest seeker after truth must face the fact that there are at least 15 differences between the two phases of Christ's coming that cannot be reconciled. This alone makes it impossible for them to be the same event. One is a secret coming, the other is public for all to see. One will cause the participants to rejoice, and the other will cause people to mourn.

What's more, many Scripture passages show Christ's coming (the Rapture) could take place at any moment. That's not true about the glorious appearing, for the "man of sin" (Antichrist) must come first (1 Thessalonians 2:8-10), then the earth must endure seven years of tribulation before Christ comes in power and great glory. Thus Christ cannot return at any moment to set up His great kingdom—at least, not until those prerequisites have been met. By contrast, we find a number of passages that admonish the church to "watch," "wait," and "look" for Christ's appearing. The only way those passages can be fulfilled is for Christ to suddenly snatch (or rapture) His church up to be with Himself. Then at the end of the Tribulation, He will come in all His glory to triumph over Satan and set up His Millennial kingdom.

41.
THE RAPTURE: COMPARING JOHN 14 AND 1 THESSALONIANS 4

We believe that John 14:1-3 speaks of Christ's return at the Rapture for His church. However, many who do not believe that the Rapture will occur before the Tribulation say this passage refers to Christ coming to receive a believer. Let's take a closer look at the passage and see what it says.

CHRIST COMING AT DEATH

Many who deny a pre-Trib Rapture teach that John 14:1-3 speaks of Christ coming to believers at death. Yet the majority of ancient and modern Bible interpreters view this text as a future second coming passage. That's because the plain meaning of the passage, taken in context, demands such an understanding.

In John 14:3, Christ tells His disciples, "I will come again, and receive you to Myself." That expression is never used of death anywhere in the whole Bible. Those holding the "coming at death" view do so simply because they declare it to be so, without substantiation. By contrast, passages that speak of the coming of Christ are consistently found in the context of His second advent (Matthew 24:27,30,37,39,42-44,46; 25:31; John 21:23; Acts 1:9-11; 1 Thessalonians 4:15; 2 Thessalonians 1:10; 2:1,8; etc.).

The Bible never speaks of the Lord coming to a believer at death. Instead, we read, for example, that Lazarus was "carried away by the angels to Abraham's bosom" (Luke 16:22). Stephen the martyr saw "the heavens opened up and the Son of Man *standing at the right hand of God*" (Acts 7:56, emphasis added). Jesus didn't come for Stephen; He was at God's right hand. The Lord doesn't come to a believer at death; rather, the believer goes to be with the Lord. For a believer to be absent from the body means he is "at home with the Lord" (2 Corinthians 5:8).

CHRIST COMING AT THE RAPTURE

Further study of John 14:3 reveals that our Lord's coming again is not only a future coming, but a coming for the church at the Rapture. The coming again is the counterpart of the going away—visibly Jesus ascends (Acts 1:9-11), visibly He returns. Note also that the language in John 14:1-3 speaks of Christ coming from heaven to Earth to take His own back to the Father's house. This passage, taken literally, indicates that the believer is going to go to heaven at the time of Christ's coming for Him. It cannot be talking about Christ's second advent, because in that event, Christ comes *with* His saints, who are already in heaven, not *for* His saints, as stated as John 14:1-3. What we have here is Christ's revelation of a new mystery: that the church will be raptured and taken to the Father's house.

SOME SIGNIFICANT PARALLELS

Many Bible scholars note that our Lord's statement in John 14:1-3 parallels the words in another New Testament passage—1 Thessalonians 4:13-18. It was the late Mennonite commentator, J. B. Smith,[29] who demonstrated just how similar these two passages are.

Dr. Smith made word-for-word comparisons between a Rapture passage (1 Thessalonians 4:13-18) and a clear second coming text (Revelation 19:11-21) and found no significant parallels. "Hence it is impossible that one sentence or even one phrase can be alike in the two lists," observes Dr. Smith. "And finally, not one word in the two lists is used in the same relation or connection."[30] He goes on to conclude that "it would be difficult if not impossible to find elsewhere any two important passages of Scripture that are so diverse in the words employed and so opposite in their implications....We believe...the words of these two passages...describe different events."[31]

When we compare John 14:1-3 and 1 Thessalonians 4:13-18, we see amazing parallels. That John 14:1-3 is a Rapture reference is supported by the progression of the words and thoughts of Paul's more extensive Rapture teaching in 1 Thessalonians 4:13-18.

Dr. Smith notes the following as a result of this comparison:

> The words or phrases are almost an exact parallel. They follow one another in both passages in exactly the same order. Only the righteous are dealt with in each case. There is not a single irregularity in the progression of words from first to last. Either column takes the believer from the troubles of earth to the glories of heaven.[32]

It appears obvious, then, that Jesus' teaching in John 14:1-3

COMPARING JESUS' AND PAUL'S WORDS ON THE RAPTURE

John 14:1-3		1 Thessalonians 4:13-18	
trouble	v. 1	sorrow	v. 13
believe	v. 1	believe	v. 14
God, me	v. 1	Jesus, God	v. 14
told you	v. 2	say to you	v. 15
come again	v. 3	coming of the Lord	v. 15
receive you	v. 3	caught up	v. 17
to myself	v. 3	to meet the Lord	v. 17
be where I am	v. 3	ever be with the Lord	v. 17

© AMG Publishers, used with permission.

and Paul's revelation in 1 Thessalonians 4:13-18 speak of the same event. Dr. Smith concludes, "It is but consistent to interpret each passage as dealing with the same event—the Rapture of the church."[33] How else does one explain the progression of eight specific words/phrases in exactly the same order, in two different passages, by two different spokesmen? It is clear that these passages refer to a single future event: the Rapture of the church.

42.
THE HOLY SPIRIT AND THE RAPTURE

One of the most compelling yet often misunderstood arguments for a pre-Trib Rapture relates to the Holy Spirit's role in the Tribulation period. Most people who hold to the pre-Trib position believe that 2 Thessalonians 2:6-7 teaches that the Holy Spirit works as a restrainer of evil in the world through the agency of the church. Thus when the church is raptured before the Tribulation, the Holy Spirit's restraining influence will be removed as well. If this interpretation is correct, then it is a strong argument in favor of the pre-Trib Rapture view. This view does not advocate that the Holy Spirit will stop ministering altogether, as some people assume.

Second Thessalonians 2:1-12 mentions a man of lawlessness who is held back until a later time. Since "the lawless one" (the Beast or Antichrist) cannot be revealed until the restrainer (the Holy Spirit) is taken away (2:7-8), the Tribulation cannot occur until the church is removed from Earth. Of all the views on the timing of the Rapture, only the pre-Trib position harmonizes with Scripture when we understand that the restrainer is referring to the Holy Spirit.

The use of unusual grammar in the passage helps us to understand it better. In verse six "the restrainer" is in the neuter gender (*to katéchon*), while in verse seven "the restrainer" is masculine (*o katechôn*). The significance of this grammar, and how it relates to the Holy Spirit and the Rapture, is explained by Dr. Robert Thomas:

> To one familiar with the Lord Jesus' Upper Room Discourse, as Paul undoubtedly was, fluctuation between neuter and masculine recalls how the Holy Spirit is spoken of. Either gender is appropriate, depending on whether the speaker (or writer) thinks of natural agreement (masc. because of the Spirit's personality) or grammatical (neuter because of the noun *pneuma*; see John 14:26; 15:26; 16:13,14)....This identification of the restrainer with deep roots in church history...is most appealing. The special presence of the Spirit as the indweller of saints will terminate abruptly at the *parousia* as it began abruptly at Pentecost. Once the body of Christ has been caught away to heaven, the Spirit's ministry will revert back to what he did for believers during the OT period.... His function of restraining evil through the body of Christ (John 16:7-11; 1 John 4:4) will cease similarly to the way he terminated his striving in the days of Noah (Gen. 6:3). At that point the reins will be removed from lawlessness and the Satanically inspired rebellion will begin. It appears that *to katechon* ("what is holding back") was well known at Thessalonica as a title for the Holy Spirit on whom the readers had come to depend in their personal attempts to combat lawlessness (1 Thess. 1:6; 4:8; 5:19; 2 Thess. 2:13).[34]

Dr. Gerald Stanton cites six reasons why this passage should be understood to refer to the Holy Spirit's restraining ministry through the church:

1. By mere elimination, the Holy Spirit must be the restrainer. All other possibilities fall short of meeting the requirements of one who is to hold in check the forces of evil until the manifestation of Antichrist....

The Church: A Spiritual Temple

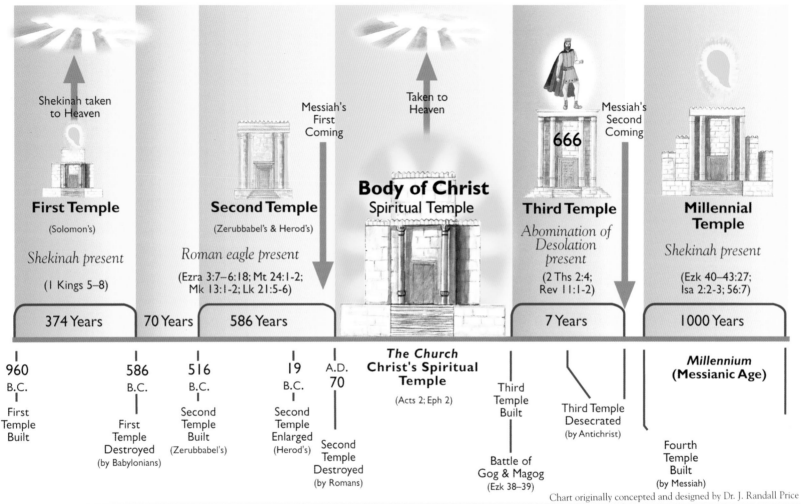

Shekinah taken to Heaven

First Temple

(Solomon's)

Shekinah present

(1 Kings 5–8)

Messiah's First Coming

Second Temple

(Zerubbabel's & Herod's)

Roman eagle present

(Ezra 3:7–6:18; Mt 24:1-2; Mk 13:1-2; Lk 21:5-6)

Taken to Heaven

Body of Christ
Spiritual Temple

Messiah's Second Coming

666

Third Temple

Abomination of Desolation present

(2 Ths 2:4; Rev 11:1-2)

Millennial Temple

Shekinah present

(Ezk 40–43:27; Isa 2:2-3; 56:7)

| 374 Years | 70 Years | 586 Years | | 7 Years | 1000 Years |

960 B.C. — First Temple Built

586 B.C. — First Temple Destroyed (by Babylonians)

516 B.C. — Second Temple Built (Zerubbabel's)

19 B.C. — Second Temple Enlarged (Herod's)

A.D. 70 — Second Temple Destroyed (by Romans)

The Church Christ's Spiritual Temple

(Acts 2; Eph 2)

Third Temple Built

Battle of Gog & Magog (Ezk 38–39)

Third Temple Desecrated (by Antichrist)

Millennium **(Messianic Age)**

Fourth Temple Built (by Messiah)

Chart originally concepted and designed by Dr. J. Randall Price

---

2. The Wicked One is a personality and his operations include the realm of the spiritual. The restrainer must likewise be a personality and of a spiritual order, to resist the wiles of the Devil and to hold Antichrist in check until the time of his revealing....

3. To achieve all that is to be accomplished, the restrainer must be a member of the Godhead. He must be stronger than the Man of Sin, and stronger than Satan....

4. This present age is in a particular sense the "dispensation

of the Spirit," for He works in a way uncommon to other ages as an abiding Presence within the children of God....

5. The work of the Spirit since His advent has included the restraint of evil. The Spirit is God's righteous Agent for the age, and there are many reasons to be grateful for His restraining hand upon this world's iniquity. None but the Lawful One could restrain this world's iniquity....

6. It is not difficult to establish that although the Spirit was not resident on earth during Old Testament days, what-

ever restraint was exerted was by the Spirit....(Isa. 59:19)...The wickedness of Noah's day and the fact that life went on as usual in blindness to impending destruction is used of the Spirit in vivid portrayal of careless and wicked men upon whom Tribulation judgment shall fall....

In light of this Scriptural parallel, it is exceedingly significant that in the days immediately preceding the destruction of the flood, the restraining work of the Spirit is emphasized....[35]

The church began on the Day of Pentecost with a visitation of the Holy Spirit, as recorded in Acts 2. The church will end at the Rapture with the translation of the living saints and the resurrection of those who have died in Christ (1 Thessalonians 4:13-18). Until then, God is gathering out from the Gentiles a people for His name (Acts 15:14) and combining them with the elect remnant of Israel (Romans 11:5) into one new body called the church (Ephesians 2:11–3:13). This great task is being accomplished by a unique ministry of the Holy Spirit only during the church age—a ministry called the baptism of the Holy Spirit. Paul taught in 1 Corinthians 12:13, "By one Spirit were we all [Jewish and Gentile believers] baptized into one body, whether Jews or Greeks, whether slaves or free, and we were all made to drink of one Spirit." This work of the Holy Spirit is only for the church. Therefore, it is not surprising that at this time, the man of lawlessness is restrained as a result of the Holy Spirit indwelling church-age believers—the Holy Spirit is acting as a restrainer through the church. Dr. John Walvoord explains,

We search the prophetic Scriptures in vain for any reference to baptism of the Spirit except in regard to the church, the body of Christ (1 Cor. 12:13). While, therefore, the Spirit continues a ministry in the world in the tribulation, there is no longer a corporate body of believers knit into one living organism. There is rather a return to national distinctions and fulfillment of national promises in preparation for the millennium.[36]

Those who do not hold to the pre-Trib view of the Rapture often mischaracterize the pre-Trib view of the Holy Spirit in the Tribulation. They often say that pre-Trib advocates do not believe that the Holy Spirit will be present on earth during the Tribulation. This is not correct, however. We who hold to the pre-Trib Rapture view believe that the Holy Spirit *will* be present and active during the Tribulation. However, the Holy Spirit will not be carrying out His present unique ministry related to the church since, during the Tribulation, all members of that body will be in heaven. Also, pre-Trib supporters say that the Holy Spirit *will* be present in His trans-dispensational ministry of bringing the elect of the Tribulation to faith in Christ, even though they will not be part of the body of Christ, the church. The Holy Spirit will also aid Tribulation believers as they endeavor to live holy lives for the Lord. And, the Holy Spirit will also seal and protect the 144,000 Jewish witnesses for the great evangelistic ministry described in Revelation 7 and 14 and the two witnesses of Revelation chapter 11.

Even though pretribulationists believe that many unique aspects of the current work of the Holy Spirit will cease at the Rapture, it is not correct to say that they believe the Holy Spirit will not be present on earth during the Tribulation.

43.
SETTING THE STAGE

We believe that God is now setting the stage for the next era of history, which is known as the Tribulation. There are signs around us that give evidence of this. However, we must be careful about how we view these signs. A careful look at the signs shows that they relate to Israel and not the church. For example, one major indicator that we are likely near the beginning of the Tribulation is the fact that Israel has been restored as a nation after almost 2000 years of being scattered without a homeland.

We need to keep in mind that the Rapture is a signless event. There are no signs mentioned in the Bible that will indicate the Rapture is near. That's because the Rapture is imminent; it could happen at any moment. It is impossible for an imminent event to have signs. Because the New Testament says the Rapture is an event that could occur at any moment (1 Corinthians 1:7; 16:22; Philippians 3:20; 4:5; 1 Thessalonians 1:10; Titus 2:13; Hebrews 9:28; James 5:7-9; 1 Peter 1:13; Jude 21; Revelation 3:11; 22:7,12,17,20), it cannot be related to any signs at all. Thus the signs that reveal we are nearing the last days must have to do with the Tribulation—a time in which God will work through Israel, not the church.

Now, even though the signs of the end times have to do with Israel, we can see that these signs are drawing nearer to fulfillment during the present church age. So while Bible prophecy is not being *fulfilled* in our day, it is still possible for us to track "general trends" that set the stage for the coming Tribulation, especially since it follows the Rapture. Just as many people set their clothes out the night before they wear them the following day, so in the same sense is God preparing the world for the certain fulfillment of prophecy in a future time.

Dr. John Walvoord explains:

> But if there are no signs for the Rapture itself, what are the legitimate grounds for believ-

ing that the Rapture could be especially near of this generation?

The answer is not found in any prophetic events predicted before the Rapture but in understanding the events that will follow the Rapture. Just as history was prepared for Christ's first coming, in a similar way history is preparing for the events leading up to His Second Coming.... If this is the case, it leads to the inevitable conclusion that the Rapture may be excitingly near.[37]

The Bible provides detailed prophecies about the seven-year Tribulation. In fact, Revelation 4–19 gives a clear, sequential outline

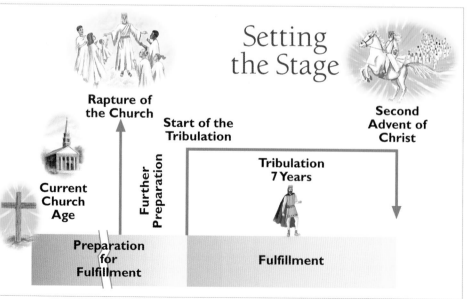

Setting the Stage

Rapture of the Church

Start of the Tribulation

Second Advent of Christ

Current Church Age

Further Preparation

Tribulation 7 Years

Preparation for Fulfillment

Fulfillment

of the major players and events. Using Revelation as a framework, a Bible student is able to harmonize the hundreds of other biblical passages that speak of the seven-year Tribulation and come up with a clear picture of what is next for planet Earth. Another way of looking at this is to see the future time period as casting shadows of expectation into our own day so that current events are providing us with discernible signs of the end times.

44.
THE SIGNS OF CHRIST'S RETURN

Through the ages, "date setters," "sign spotters," and false prophets have brought disrepute to the study of prophecy by speculating on the timing of Christ's return. Their wrong guesses have deceived and disillusioned many. But this is no reason to avoid the legitimate study of prophetic signs that show the approximate time of the Lord's return. After all, when the disciples asked Jesus, "What will be the sign of Your coming, and of the end of the age?" (Matthew 24:3), He did not rebuke them. Instead, Jesus answered their questions and provided us with one of the best outlines of end-times prophecies in the Bible. While it is true that no man knows the day or the hour of Christ's return, Jesus Himself took the time to explain the signs that would indicate His return was near. What's more, as we examine each of the signs depicted on page 120, we can say we believe that our generation has more signs to indicate that Christ *could* come in our lifetime than any generation before us. That does not mean He will, but it certainly means He could. Examine the signs, and see if you agree.

ISRAEL: THE SUPER SIGN

The first and most important sign, the regathering of the Jews in Israel after nearly 2000 years of wandering around the world, is so highly significant that we have devoted one whole chart on that subject alone (see page 85). That this could happen after so many centuries of dispersion is a miracle in itself. No nation in history has been able to maintain its national identity after being uprooted from its homeland for more than 300 years—or at best, 500 years. Israel is the lone exception. The fact that six million Jews are living in Israel today is a testimony to the faithfulness of our God, who always keeps His word. He promised so many times to regather that nation into their national homeland that if He had failed to do so, He would have destroyed the faithfulness of

His prophetic Word, particularly the promises stated in Ezekiel 36 and 37.

THE RISE OF RUSSIA

The rise of Russia to become a world superpower militarily from 1950 to 1995 and beyond is a fulfillment of prophecy. For millennia, Russia was a backward nation that seldom looked outside itself. The Bolshevik Revolution of 1917 launched this nation toward superpower status. Even though the Soviet Union itself is no more, mother Russia is still a formidable threat to world peace with her outlandish investment in military hardware and her allies, particularly among the hostile Arab Muslim nations.

The future of Russia is clear: Her lifelong hostility toward the Jews will finally lead to her undoing, for God will destroy all her military might on the mountains of Israel. This supernatural destruction will be for the purpose of exalting and honoring God among the nations.

CAPITAL AND LABOR CONFLICTS

The greatest fear of Wall Street bankers and stockbrokers is a financial meltdown that would see a repeat of the Great Depression of the 1930s. We have lived through the recession of 1973, the financial glitch in 1997, and the fear of a technology meltdown as we entered the year 2000. The reason people are so fearful about the possibility of economic collapse is because of our world's dependence on material possessions rather than on the God who controls all things.

This greed-based problem will surface in the last days, showing a great conflict between the rich and poor, or "the haves and the have-nots." All the strikes and unrest we see in the various parts of the work world are not just a disruption to society, they are a fulfillment of prophecy for the last days. By themselves they might not seem like much, but together with all these other signs of the end of the age, they add weight to the mounting evidence that Jesus' coming could be soon.

INCREASE IN TRAVEL AND KNOWLEDGE

Probably the third most significant sign is that which was given to the prophet Daniel immediately after he was told to "shut up the words, and seal the book even to the time of the end" (Daniel 12:4 KJV). Then he added, "Many shall run to and fro and knowledge shall be increased" (KJV). Most prophecy scholars regard this as the

Signs of the Times

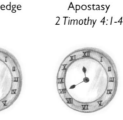

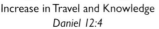

Israel 1948
Ezekiel 37

Rise of Russia
Ezekiel 38–39

Capital and Labor Conflict
James 5:1-6

Increase in Travel and Knowledge
Daniel 12:4

Apostasy
2 Timothy 4:1-4

Occultism
2 Timothy 4:3-4

Scoffers
2 Timothy 3:1-5

Moral Breakdown
2 Peter 3:1-12

One-World Church
Revelation 17

One-World Government
Daniel 2

obvious—an increase in travel and knowledge at the end of the age.

Never in the history of the world have there been more means of transport than today. And the speed of travel is increasing all the time. What made that possible? An increase in knowledge! All this speed would not be possible were it not for mankind's incredible increase in knowledge.

ONE-WORLD GOVERNMENT

For most of this century, many world leaders have advocated that a one-world government is the only way to assure world peace. We have seen expressions of this in the attempt to start the League of Nations in 1919 right after World War I and the creation of the United Nations in 1947. Today the United Nations is trying to secure more governmental power over the sovereignty of independent nations. While we do not know the exact events that will lead us to the one-world government predicted in the Bible, we do know that in the last days, there will be a world government led by ten kings or heads of regions (Daniel 2:40-43; 7:23-24). The Bible also predicts that this world government will control the commerce of the world—probably through a one-world currency. There will be a one-world commercial system and a one-world religion established and controlled by the one-world government, or the man who leads it.

We see all of this described in Daniel chapters 2, 7–8; Matthew 24:15-22; 2 Thessalonians 2:8; and Revelation chapters 13, 17–18. These are not the only passages that mention the one-world governmental system, but they are sufficient to get you started.

MANY OTHER SIGNS

Space does not permit that we detail the other six clocks on the chart—apostasy, occultism, scoffers, the moral breakdown of society, the one-world church, and more.

Thus we placed only 11 signs on the chart. Some prophecy teachers suggest there are 20 signs today, and one of our friends has a list of 36 signs. We have tried to remain reasonable in our selection of the most obvious signs, and, as stated previously, we do not know if Christ will come in our generation, but we have more reason to believe His return is near than any generation before us.

45.
THE RESURRECTIONS AND JUDGMENTS OF SCRIPTURE

In spite of popular belief to the contrary, God will judge His creation. He will also renew the creation and resurrect all mankind, some to everlasting life and the rest to eternal death (John 5:29). Let's look first at the biblical teaching on the resurrections.

RESURRECTIONS

The concept of future bodily resurrection is found throughout the Bible. It is important to note that in the Bible, the word *resurrection* is used solely to refer to the raising up of the physical body. There is no such thing as a spiritual resurrection. When the Bible speaks of the spiritual newness or a new believer in Christ Jesus, the Bible uses the imagery of a new birth (John 3:3; Ephesians 2:5), not of a resurrection. When the New Testament speaks of a believer having been "raised up" with Christ (Ephesians 2:6; Colossians 3:1-2), it speaks of one's position in Christ at the right hand of the Father, not a resurrection.

The resurrections in Scripture fall into two categories: the first resurrection, or the resurrection of life; and the second resurrection, or the resurrection of judgment (John 5:28-29). The first resurrection includes the redeemed of all the ages. The timing of the resurrection of these individuals varies, depending upon whether they are an Old Testament saint (Jew or Gentile), a Christian living before or at the time of the Rapture, or a Christian martyred during the Tribulation. All of these people will take part in the "resurrection of life" (John 5:29). The "resurrection of judgment" will include the unredeemed of all the ages who will be raised at the end of the Millennium, judged before the Great White Throne, and cast into the Lake of Fire.

The multiple resurrections will take place in this sequence:
1. The resurrection of Jesus Christ as the first fruit of many to be raised (Romans 6:9; 1 Corinthians 15:23; Colossians 1:18; Revelation 1:18)
2. The resurrection of the redeemed at Christ's coming (Daniel 12:2; Luke 14:14; John 5:29; 1 Thessalonians 4:16; Revelation 20:4,6)
    a. Resurrection of the church at the Rapture
    b. Resurrection of Old Testament believers at

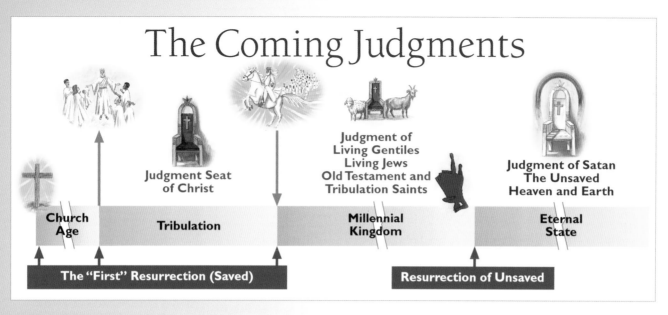

The Coming Judgments

Judgment Seat of Christ

Judgment of Living Gentiles Living Jews Old Testament and Tribulation Saints

Judgment of Satan The Unsaved Heaven and Earth

Church Age | Tribulation | Millennial Kingdom | Eternal State

The "First" Resurrection (Saved)

Resurrection of Unsaved

---

the second coming (Jews and Gentiles)

   c. Resurrection of all martyred Tribulation saints at the second coming (Jews and Gentiles)

   d. Resurrection of all Millennial believers after the Millennium

3. The resurrection of the unredeemed (Revelation 20:11-14)

JUDGMENTS

There are several times of judgment in the future, each with a specific purpose, end, and constituency. To speak of a single all-encompassing judgment day is incorrect. There are different judgments for the sins and works of believers, Old Testament saints, Tribulation saints, Jews living at the end of the Tribulation, Gentiles living at the end of the Tribulation, Satan and the fallen angels, and unredeemed people.

Christ's death on the cross was a past event where God placed upon Jesus the sin of all who would become believers. Christ paid for our sins substitutionarily through His death (John 5:24; Romans 8:1-4; 10:4). All who bring their sin to Christ at the cross will not have to face the future judgments (except the judgment seat of Christ) because Christ has legally paid our debt of sin in full.

Bema is the transliteration of a Greek word used in the New

Testament as a technical term to distinguish the judgment of rewards for believers from the final judgment of unbelievers, which is known as the Great White Throne Judgment in Revelation 20:11-15. In the Roman world of New Testament times there was a raised platform in the city square or at the coliseums where a dignitary would sit to hear civil matters or hand out rewards (usually a wreath) for competitive accomplishments. These platforms were known as *bema*. Paul told the Corinthian believers, "We must all appear before the judgment seat [*bema*] of Christ, so that each one may be recompensed for his deeds in the body, according to what he has done, whether good or bad" (2 Corinthians 5:10). First Corinthians 3:11-16; 4:1-5; 9:24-27 provide extensive details about the basis on which believers will be evaluated at the *bema* judgment.

At the Rapture the church will be removed from the earth and will be taken by Christ (John 14:1-3) to remain with Him throughout the Tribulation (Revelation 19:1-10). The *bema* judgment will take place in heaven while the Tribulation is taking place on earth so that the church may be adorned as Christ's bride when she descends with Him at the second coming (Revelation 19:1-10). That the *bema* evaluation of the entire church takes place after the Rapture but before the second coming is seen in Revelation 19:7-8, which tell us that "His bride has made herself ready. It was given to her to clothe herself in fine linen, bright and clean; for the fine linen is the righteous acts of the saints." Since the church is pictured as being clothed in fine linen, she must have gone through her evaluation or *bema* judgment by the time of the second coming.

Next, the Tribulation is said to be a time in which God will make Israel "pass under the rod" in order to "purge from you the rebels" (Ezekiel 20:37-38). Thus, the Tribulation is a time of judgment upon the nation of Israel, which will result in the death of two-thirds of the nation (Zechariah 13:8-9), so that of those who are left "all Israel will be saved" (Romans 11:26) by coming to faith in Jesus as their Messiah. The Tribulation will also be a time of judgment upon unbelieving Gentiles who have rejected Christ as their Savior (Deuteronomy 30:7; Revelation 3:10).

At the end of the Tribulation will come the judgment of the nations. This will be a time, according to Matthew 25:31-46, when all unbelievers will be put to death in preparation for the Millennial kingdom. Only believers will populate the kingdom at its beginning, and the judgment of the nations will ensure that all unbelievers are removed before the kingdom commences.

The final judgment of history is known as the Great White Throne Judgment, and will involve the judgment of all unbelievers throughout history (Revelation 20:11-15). The Bible does not specifically state who sits on the throne, but it is probably Jesus Christ Himself, as in Revelation 3:21. This judgment is the "resurrection of judgment" spoken of in John 5:29 (as opposed to the "resurrection of life"). The people who experience this judgment will be those who rejected Jesus Christ during their lifetimes. Because of their rejection of Christ's substitutionary work, God will judge them on the basis of their own works, which will fail to measure up to God's holy standard. In this judgment their works are judged to show that the punishment is deserved, and after this judgment, these people will be thrown into the Lake of Fire for eternity.

Though we often hear people speak of a single "judgment day," this is not biblically accurate, for there are several future judgments in God's prophetic plan. These judgments will occur at various times between the Rapture and the end of the Millennium, and they are certain and no one will escape them. They will make manifest God's justice and righteousness to the entire world and will silence all who have scoffed at or denied God.

46.
REVELATION 19–22

Revelation 19–22 covers, in consecutive order, three major eras of the future: the end of the Tribulation, the Millennial kingdom, and the eternal state. These chapters provide a clear chronology of these three time periods, and Revelation 21–22 is virtually the only scripture we have that describes the eternal state.

REVELATION 19

Heavenly Praise

John begins Revelation 19 with an exposition of God's worthiness to rule, as recognized in heaven by both the angelic and human realms (19:1-7). This is set against the backdrop of what has just happened on earth. Chapters 17–18 describe the judgment of the great harlot, Babylon, and thus the heavenly court recognizes God's right to rule because He has justly judged "the great harlot who was corrupting the earth with her immorality, and He has avenged the blood of His bond-servants on her" (19:2). The heavenly court does not think that one acknowledgment is enough, so they praise God "a second time" (19:3) for his great earthly victory. The battle that began with the fall of Satan (Isaiah 14:12-23; Ezekiel 28:11-19) has been historically decided in favor of the Triune God, which is certainly reason enough for heavenly praise. History is a demonstration of God's right to rule as worked out through the second person of the Trinity—Jesus Christ (Romans 11:36).

The Bride of Christ

In Revelation 19:7 we read that the bride of Christ (the church) has prepared herself for her marriage to the Groom (Jesus Christ). How does she do this? Through the judgment seat of Christ, which is explained in other passages (Romans 14:10; 1 Corinthians 3:10-15; 2 Corinthians 5:10) but demonstrated in Revelation (19:7-8). The bride makes herself ready, with a fine linen garment, "bright and clean," that is given to her (19:8). It is said that the fine linen is "the righteous acts of the saints" (19:8). At this point, the Lamb (Jesus Christ) takes the bride for His wife (19:7), but the Marriage Supper of the Lamb does not commence until after the second coming of Christ, during the first part of the Millennium, when all believers throughout the ages will be present to enter into the festivities (Matthew 8:11; Mark 14:25; Luke 13:29; 14:12-15).

The Second Coming of Jesus Christ

The apostle John opens this section of Revelation with a phrase that he will repeat nine more times through chapter 21. That phrase is "and I saw" (19:11,17,19; 20:1,4,11,12; 21:1-2). This supports the notion that John is witnessing and recording real historical events as they will happen. This also bolsters the clear intent of the passage that these events will take place in the sequence in which they are presented in Revelation, thus supporting the premillennial view of Christ's return because He returns in chapter 19 and then, after His advent, He reigns for 1000 years in chapter 20.

Revelation 19:11-16 presents Christ as He has never before appeared in history. He is in battle dress for the purpose of judging His enemies, who have been proven in history to be unjust rebels against the Triune God. Christ returns riding a white horse, with an intent to judge, as depicted by His flaming eyes and a robe dipped in blood (19:12-13). He destroys His enemies with a mere word (19:12,15). The same One who spoke creation into existence (Genesis 1–2) will speak the word of judgmental destruction. Christ's bride follows close behind Him on white horses (19:14). And judgment must precede the establishment of His righteous kingdom (the Millennium of Revelation 20), for evil cannot be allowed to exist in a righteous kingdom.

Armageddon

Next John saw the conclusion of the campaign of Armageddon (19:17-18). An angel "standing in the sun" will call "to all the birds which fly in midheaven, 'Come, assemble for the great supper of God'" (19:17). God's judgment will impact all His enemies regardless of their status (19:18). We who have often witnessed inequities in our human judicial system can be confident that God will administer complete and righteous justice.

The Beast and False Prophet

Next (19:19-21), John sees the Beast (Antichrist) and the False Prophet, who are captured and thrown into the Lake of Fire, which the Bible says "burns with brimstone" (19:20). After the battle is won, the outlaws are gathered up and sentenced. The Bible says that the Lake of Fire was created for the devil and his angels (Matthew 25:41), and the first two who will occupy it will be the Antichrist and the False Prophet. But why are they thrown into the Lake of Fire, while the dragon (Satan) is placed into the bottomless pit for 1000 years (20:1-3)? The answer is that the Antichrist's and False Prophet's roles in history are finished. The Lake of Fire is where the non-elect go after they have been judged and sentenced. Satan still has one last act at the end of the Millennium, so he is bound in the bottomless pit to await a final but temporary release (Revelation 20:7-10). After the Antichrist and the False Prophet are thrown alive into the Lake of Fire (19:20), the remainder of mankind is then "killed with the sword which came from the mouth of Him who sat on the horse" (19:21). This paves the way for the establishment of God's kingdom upon earth.

Revelation 20
Satan Bound

What will perhaps be the greatest arrest of a felon in the history of the world is what John sees next (20:1-3). Satan is taken by an angel and bound for 1000 years in the abyss "so that he would not deceive the nations any longer until the thousand years were completed" (20:3). The abyss is in Hades or Sheol, which is popularly

Revelation 19–22

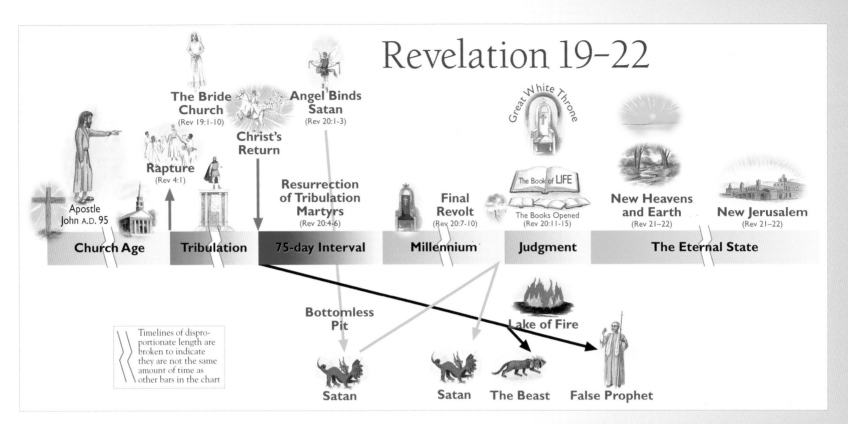

The Bride Church (Rev 19:1-10)

Angel Binds Satan (Rev 20:1-3)

Christ's Return

Rapture (Rev 4:1)

Resurrection of Tribulation Martyrs (Rev 20:4-6)

Great White Throne

Apostle John A.D. 95

Final Revolt (Rev 20:7-10)

The Book of LIFE
The Books Opened (Rev 20:11-15)

New Heavens and Earth (Rev 21–22)

New Jerusalem (Rev 21–22)

Church Age	Tribulation	75-day Interval	Millennium	Judgment	The Eternal State

Timelines of disproportionate length are broken to indicate they are not the same amount of time as other bars in the chart

Bottomless Pit

Lake of Fire

Satan   **Satan**   **The Beast**   **False Prophet**

---

known in our days as hell. Putting Satan into the abyss will be like arresting a criminal and keeping him in a county jail while he awaits his trial. After a criminal is convicted of his crime, he is then sent to the state or federal penitentiary to serve out his sentence. He is not returned to the county jail that held him while he awaited his trial. We know from the story of the rich man and Lazarus (see Luke 16:19-31) that Hades or Sheol is a lot like the Lake of Fire, even though they are two different locations—just as the county jail and penitentiary are different though similar. Note that the passage says that Satan "must be released for a short time" (20:3). Why? So that he can call all unbelievers to himself at the end of the Millennium (20:7-10) in his final attempt to battle God. But he will fail, and his followers will be identified and judged.

RESURRECTION OF THE SAINTS

In Revelation 20:4-6 John sees the resurrection of the Tribulation saints. We know from Daniel 12:2 that all the Old Testament saints will also be raised at this time. Church-age believ-ers will already have been resurrected at the Rapture of the church before the seven-year Tribulation (1 Corinthians 15:51-58; 1 Thessalonians 4:13-18). The saints of the ages will then be able to join one another in the long-awaited kingdom. What a time that will be, when we "recline at the table with Abraham, Isaac and Jacob in the kingdom of heaven" (Matthew 8:11)! In contrast to the condemnation of Satan and his followers, believers "who had been beheaded because of their testimony of Jesus and because of the word of God" (20:4) get to spend eternity with Jesus, starting with the 1000-year kingdom.

Some people try to argue that there is a single resurrection that will occur only at the end of all history. Usually they quote John 5:28-29: "Do not marvel at this; for an hour is coming, in which all who are in the tombs will hear His voice, and will come forth; those who did the good deeds to a resurrection of life, those who commit-ted the evil deeds to a resurrection of judgment." While this passage is a statement about the fact of the resurrection in general, it does not contradict other passages that provide greater detail concerning the different resurrections. Revelation 20:5 calls the resurrection of the Tribulation saints "the first resurrection." The "rest of the dead"—that is, all the unbelievers—"did not come to life until the thousand years were completed." Scripture makes it clear that unbelievers and believers will be resurrected at different times.

The "first resurrection," by the way, is a qualitative distinction, rather than indicating a mere chronological sequence. There are multiple first resurrections: Christ's resurrection after His death, the Rapture of the church, the resurrection of Tribulation saints and Old Testament believers after the second coming, and presumably the resurrection of mortal believers at the end of the Millennium. Yet there will be only one "second resurrection" of all the unbelievers who are collected in Sheol or Hades throughout history to be judged at the end of history (20:5). So, there will be multiple resurrection events throughout history, and we can be certain that every human being will be raised from the dead at some point in order to be made fit for eternity—whether to dwell in the new Jerusalem or the Lake of Fire.

> The same One who spoke creation into existence (Genesis 1–2) will speak the word of judgmental destruction.

SATAN'S RELEASE

In a sense, Revelation 20:7-10 describes the "second coming" of Satan. Instead of coming from the Father's right hand, as will our Lord Jesus Christ, Satan will be released from his prison in the bowels of the earth (20:7). If it proves nothing else, Satan's imprisonment clearly demonstrates that spending time in prison does not rehabilitate. At the end of his 1000-year term, he will be just as evil as he has ever been. The same is true with people: Prison does not bring true reform; only a changed heart will lead to a changed life.

Why will Satan be released from the abyss? He "will come out to deceive the nations which are in the four corners of the earth…to gather them together for the war" (20:8). Satan and his followers will come up on "the broad plain of the earth and surround the camp of the saints and the beloved city" (20:9), which is Jerusalem. And

how does God deal with this final revolt of history? He will dispense of it in a moment, by calling fire to come down from heaven and devour them (20:9). Then Satan will be cast into the Lake of Fire, his eternal abode, and join his two cohorts in crime, the Antichrist and False Prophet (20:10). The text adds, "They will be tormented day and night forever and ever" (20:10). This is one of the many clear statements that teach that punishment in the Lake of Fire is eternal and will never come to an end.

THE GREAT WHITE THRONE JUDGMENT

John next sees "a great white throne and Him who sat upon it, from whose presence earth and heaven fled away, and no place was found for them" (20:11). This is the final judgment for all unbelievers, where John sees "the dead, the great and the small, standing before the throne" (20:12). Every individual who has rejected the free offer of salvation through Christ will now have to stand before God and give an account of their sins. No one will be exempt.

On what basis will these unbelievers be judged? "According to their deeds" (20:12). And by what standard will their deeds be measured? God's own standard of righteousness. Scripture teaches that "all our righteous deeds are like a filthy garment" (Isaiah 64:6). If that is the value of the very best we can offer to God, can you imagine what God thinks of our evil deeds? There is no hope for anyone to pass God's judgment apart from Christ. We are told that these unbelievers will all be "thrown into the lake of fire" (20:15) along with the other three who are already there.

REVELATION 21–22

The final two chapters of Revelation conclude with John's report of what he saw in the blessed state believers will experience throughout all eternity. Believers in Christ have a wonderful destiny ahead of them; the best is yet to come!

A New Heaven and New Earth

In eternity, the apostle John sees "a new heaven and a new earth; for the first heaven and the first earth passed away" (21:1). Peter also provides more detail, saying that the present universe "will pass away with a roar and the elements will be destroyed with intense heat, and the earth and its works will be burned up" (2 Peter 3:10). God will then replace our present universe with "new heavens and a new earth, in which righteousness dwells" (2 Peter 3:13).

As indicated in the accompanying list, there are great contrasts between the present universe and the new one God will provide at the start of eternity. For example, on the new earth, "There is no longer any sea" (Revelation 21:1). What does that mean? Throughout the Bible, the sea represents the potential for evil (Genesis 1:6-10,21; Daniel 7:2-3; Ephesians 4:14; Revelation 13:1; 17:15). How so? The sea, in biblical imagery, is a picture of dangerous instability because it is shapeless and formless. Water assumes the shape of its container and thus it can be manipulated and influenced in negative ways. Thus the sea is a symbol of fallen humanity, which is without the Word of God and is therefore vulnerable to satanic influences. That there will no longer be any sea on the new earth means there will no longer be any potential for evil. And there will no longer be the potential for anyone to fall anew into sin, for it has been forever removed from God's new creation.

Descent of the New Jerusalem

John then goes on to describe the new Jerusalem in Revelation 21:2–22:5. Of all the great cities in the history of the world, only Jerusalem will have a presence in eternity. The new Jerusalem, prebuilt in heaven, will come "down out of heaven from God, made ready as a bride adorned for her husband" (21:2). This city will be the most amazing one in all of history! Most amazing of all is that in this city, which will be free of evil, it will be possible for God, who is holy, to dwell with mankind: "Behold, the tabernacle of God is among men, and He will dwell among them, and they will be His people, and God Himself will be among them" (21:3).

What will this new Jerusalem be like? John provides us with a description:

The New Jerusalem Described

- There is no longer any sea (21:1)
- All things will have been made new (21:1)
- God the Father will dwell among His people (21:3)
- No longer any death, crying, or pain (21:4)
- All believers will inherit the blessings of the new Jerusalem (21:7)
- The new Jerusalem will have a brilliance like a very costly stone as clear as jasper (21:11)
- The city has a great and high wall, with 12 gates guarded by an angel at each one (21:12)
- The names of the 12 tribes of Israel will appear on the gates (21:12)
- There are three gates on each of the four sides of the city (21:13)
- The wall of the city has 12 foundation stones, and on them are the names of the 12 apostles of the Lamb (21:14)
- The city is a cube measuring 1500 miles wide, 1500 miles long, and 1500 miles high (21:15-17); possibly a mountain
- The wall is made out of jasper (21:18)
- The city will be pure gold, like clear glass (21:18)
- The foundation stones of the city wall are made from the following precious stones: jasper, sapphire, chalcedony, emerald, sardonyx, sardius, chrysolite, beryl, topaz, chrysoprase, jacinth, and amethyst (21:19-20)
- The 12 gates are 12 pearls; each one of the gates is a single pearl (21:21)
- There is no Temple in the city, for the Lord God the Almighty and the Lamb are its Temple (21:22)
- No sun or moon, for the glory of God will illumine the city, and its lamp is the Lamb (21:23)
- The nations will walk by the light of God's glory (21:24)
- The kings of the earth will bring their glory into the city (21:24)
- No longer any night, only day (21:25)
- No longer anyone unclean, nor anyone who practices abomination and lying (21:27)
- The "river of the water of life," clear as crystal, will come from

the throne of God and of the Lamb in the middle of the city's street (22:1-2)

- On either side of the river will stand the tree of life, bearing 12 kinds of fruit, yielding its fruit every month; and the leaves of the tree will be for the healing of the nations (22:2)
- No longer any curse (22:3)
- The throne of God and of the Lamb shall be in the city (22:3)
- Believers are now able to see the Father's face, and His name will be on their foreheads (22:4)
- No longer any sun, because the Lord God will illumine the city, and the people will reign forever and ever (22:5)

What a great and glorious future awaits all believers in Christ!

And we know only a small fraction of what God has in store for the future—"things which eye has not seen and ear has not heard, and which have not entered the heart of man, all that God has prepared for those who love Him" (1 Corinthians 2:9).

Revelation 22 then closes with general remarks of conclusion and comfort for believers. In keeping with God's gracious character, it is only fitting that this final book of the Bible closes with one last invitation for the lost to trust Christ: "The Spirit and the bride say, 'Come.' And let the one who hears say, 'Come.' And let the one who is thirsty come; let the one who wishes take the water of life without cost" (Revelation 22:17).

47.
THE VARIOUS VIEWS OF THE MILLENNIUM

There are three views of the Millennium, which is mentioned six times in Revelation 20:1-7. The three views are premillennialism, amillennialism, and postmillennialism.

PREMILLENNIALISM

Premillennialism teaches that the second coming of Christ to the earth and the establishment of His kingdom will take place before the 1000-year kingdom of Revelation 20:1-7. The English term is made up of the following Latin elements: *pre* means "before," *mille* means "thousand," and *annus* means "years" in relation to Christ's second coming. Thus, *premillennialism* means that Christ will return to earth "before the thousand years."

Dispensational premillennialism holds that there will be a future, literal 1000-year reign of Jesus Christ upon the earth following the Rapture, Tribulation, and second coming. There are several forms of premillennialism, which differ as to how the Rapture relates to the

Tribulation (see pretribulationism, midtribulationism, posttribulationism, partial Rapture views in the chart on page 108), but all teach that the Millennium is 1000 literal years and follows Christ's second advent.

There are many references in the Old Testament that speak about the Millennium in terms of the time of Israel's end-time restoration to the land in blessing. However, it is not until Revelation 20 that the length of Messiah's earthly reign is specified.

Premillennialism, or *chiliasm* as it was known in the early church, was the earliest of the three Millennial systems to arise. Premillennialism fell out of favor during the Middle Ages, but was revived by the Puritans in the seventeenth century. It is the viewpoint of a majority of those who are conservative in their approach to biblical interpretation.

AMILLENNIALISM

Amillennialism teaches that there will be no literal, future 1000-year reign of Christ on earth. However, most proponents say that a spiritual form of the kingdom is now present. The English term is made up of the following elements: *a* is from the Greek and means "no." *Mille* and *annus* are Latin and mean "thousand" and "years" respectively. Thus, *amillennialism* means "no 1000 years."

Amillennialism teaches that from the ascension of Christ in the first century until His second coming (no Rapture), both good and evil will increase in the world as God's kingdom parallels Satan's kingdom. Even though amillennialists believe that Satan is currently bound, they teach that evil will increase. When Jesus Christ returns, the end of the world will occur with a general resurrection and general judgment of all people. The view is essentially a spiritualization of the kingdom prophecies.

The amillennialism viewpoint was not present in the earliest church—at least there is no record of its existence. It appears to have risen as a result of opposition to premillennial literalism. Amillennialism came to dominate the church when the great church fathers and theologian Augustine (354-430) and Jerome (c. 345-419) abandoned premillennialism in favor of amillennialism. It is no exaggeration to say that among the church's leadership, amillennialism has been the most widely held view for much of the church's history, including the greater part of Protestant Reformers during the fifteenth and sixteenth centuries.

POSTMILLENNIALISM

Postmillennialism teaches that Christ's kingdom is now being extended throughout the world through the preaching of the gospel and that a majority of people will be converted to Christ, resulting in a consequent Christianization of the current world's society. The English term is made up of the following Latin elements: *post* means "after," *mille* means "thousand," and *annus* means "years" in relation to the second coming of Christ. Thus, *postmillennialism* means that Christ will return to earth "after the thousand years."

Postmillennialism teaches that the current age is the Millennium, which is not necessarily a literal 1000 years. Postmillennialists

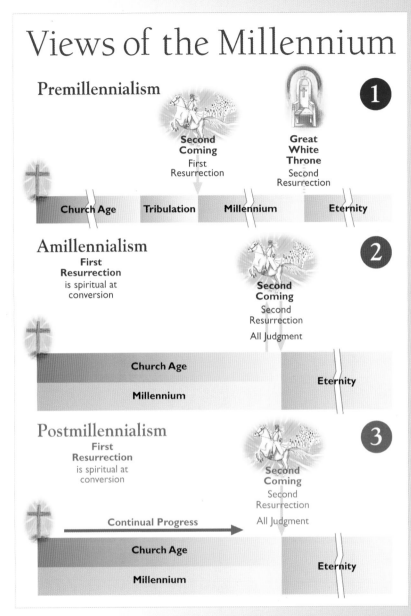

Views of the Millennium

Premillennialism

Second Coming — First Resurrection

Great White Throne — Second Resurrection

Church Age | Tribulation | Millennium | Eternity

Amillennialism

First Resurrection is spiritual at conversion

Second Coming — Second Resurrection — All Judgment

Church Age

Millennium

Eternity

Postmillennialism

First Resurrection is spiritual at conversion

Continual Progress

Second Coming — Second Resurrection — All Judgment

Church Age

Millennium

Eternity

believe that through spiritual means there will be progressive growth of righteousness, prosperity, and development in every sphere of life as a growing majority of Christians eventually subdue the world for Christ. Then, after Christianity has dominated the world for a long time (the church's glorious reign of victory), Christ will return. At such time, there will be a general resurrection, the destruction of this present creation, and the entry into the eternal state. Postmillennialism differs from premillennialism and amillennialism in that it is optimistic that this victory will be realized without the need for a cataclysmic return of Christ to impose righteousness. Rather, victory will result from the faithful application of means available during our present age.

Postmillennialism did not really develop into a distinct system of eschatology until after the Reformation. Prior to that time, there were some strains of thought that later were included in the theological mix of modern postmillennialism. Postmillennialism, then, was the last major Millennial position to develop.

John Walvoord notes that there are two principal types of post-millennialism:

> Stemming from [Daniel] Whitby [1638-1726], these groups provided two types of postmillennialism which have persisted to the twentieth century: 1) a Biblical type…finding its material in the Scriptures and its power in God; 2) the evolutionary or liberal theological type which bases its proof on confidence in man to achieve progress through natural means. These two widely separated systems of belief have one thing in common, the idea of ultimate progress and solution of present difficulties.[38]

Postmillennialism was the dominant view of the Millennium in America during much of the nineteenth century, but became virtually extinct up until the 1960s. The last 25 years have witnessed an upsurge in postmillennialism in some conservative arenas through the Christian Reconstruction movement.

Premillennialism is the only view that anyone can hold to if they interpret the text of Revelation 20 in a literal or normal way. It's important to observe that Christ returns in Revelation 19 and then sets up His Millennial kingdom in Revelation 20. Any normal reading of the words and phrases makes it clear that the events of Revelation 19 precede and prepare the way for the events of Revelation 20. Thus, the second coming of Christ precedes the 1000-year Millennium, which means the Bible teaches the premillennial view.

48.
WHERE THE DEAD ARE NOW

One question many people ask is, "Where are the dead?" All through the ages, people have longed to know the answer—particularly right after the death of a loved one. As a child I (Tim) asked that question after the death of my father. Hundreds of times at funerals I have been asked that question. Man is born with an eternal consciousness, so that he knows intuitively there is life after death.

No one but Jesus Christ has ever given a credible answer to that question—no religion, no educator, no one. That's because no one knows where or how the afterlife will unfold. No one, that is, except Jesus Christ. He has given us the most definitive teaching on that subject, and the chart on page 132 is based on that teaching. Before we examine what Jesus said, let's look at what the Bible as a whole says about death.

In the 39 books of the Old Testament, the world of the dead is called "Sheol" 65 times. That word may be translated to mean "the grave," "hell," or "death." Sheol must not be confused with "the pit" or the Lake of Fire, for it is the place of all those who have departed this life, *both* believers and unbelievers. The New Testament word for this world of the dead is "Hades" (which appears 42 times). It is important to note that Sheol and Hades are not really hell, as the King James Version of the Bible translates those words. The Hebrew word *Sheol* and the Greek word *Hades* both refer to the same temporary place, whereas hell is a permanent abode of punishment that lasts forever.

"Tartarus," a word that appears only once in the entire Bible (2 Peter 2:4), is defined by Bible scholars as "the deepest abyss of Hades." Admittedly, we don't know much about that deep abyss, except that, as part of Hades, it too is probably temporary.

"Gehenna" is the New Testament word for the permanent place of the dead, used by Jesus Christ himself 11 times. James also used the word (James 3:6). Of Hebrew origin from the words *valley* and *Hinnom, Gehenna* refers to the Valley of Hinnom, just outside Jerusalem, where the refuse of the city was dumped. It was characteristic of this valley that a fire was continually burning there. Many see this as a perfect characterization of hell—a place where "the fire is not quenched" (Mark 9:48), otherwise known as the Lake of Fire (Revelation 20:14).

The King James version of the Bible translates all of these words—Sheol, Hades, Gehenna, Tartarus—the same: "hell." This leads readers to assume that they refer to the same place when actually they do not. Several modern Bible versions have clearly distinguished the differences. The New American Standard Bible, for instance, calls the temporary places "Sheol" or "Hades," and the final place of the dead "hell."

A Description of Sheol-Hades

In order to provide a more complete picture of Sheol-Hades, we've listed some verses that describe this place:

Proverbs 9:18   A place where the dead exist
Psalm 86:13   A place for the soul
Psalm 9:17   A place for the wicked and those who forget God
Genesis 44:29   A godly Jacob expected to go there
Psalm 88:3   David expected to go there
Psalm 89:48   All men will go to Sheol

It seems apparent that Sheol is a place where both the righteous and the wicked go immediately after death. It is a specific place and seems to be the dwelling place of the soul. Psalm 49:15 says, "God will redeem my soul from the power of Sheol,"

which indicates that the righteous expected one day to be released from Sheol.

The most complete description of Sheol-Hades in the Bible comes from Jesus Christ Himself in Luke 16:19-31, where we read the account about the two men who die and end up in Hades. It is important to note that this story is not a parable, but the record of what actually happened. Characters in parables are not given definite names; rather, they are identified as "a certain man," "a man," "a householder," and so on. This story uses real names— Abraham and Lazarus. Both Lazarus and the rich man went to Hades, but not to the same part. The chart on page 132 clarifies our Lord's account of what happened and can serve as a basic guide to some of the future events discussed in this book.

Three Compartments in Hades

It appears from Luke 16:19-31 that Hades is composed of three compartments: Abraham's Bosom, the Great Gulf Fixed, and the Place of Torment.

The most desirable compartment in Hades, picturesquely called "Abraham's Bosom" or "Paradise," is a place of comfort. In verse 25, Abraham says of Lazarus, "Now is he comforted." This would be the Paradise of the Old Testament, to which the souls of the righteous dead went immediately after death. We can rightly assume that, like Lazarus, they were carried by angels to this place of comfort. It is also a place of companionship for Lazarus, for he has the joy of fellowship with Abraham. Though he had been treated poorly on earth, he now holds an enviable position by the side of Abraham. This, of course, indicates the wonderful possibility of fellowship with all the other saints of God who have gone on before us: Elijah, Moses, David, and millions of others.

Very few details are given about the second compartment, the Great Gulf Fixed, but we know that it is an impassable gulf over which men may look and converse but not cross. God designed it so that "those who want to go from here to you cannot, nor can anyone cross over from there to us" (verse 26 NIV). Evidently there is a chasm that separates the believers and unbelievers in the next life. Once a person dies, he is confined to one side or the other—comfort or

Where the Dead Are Now

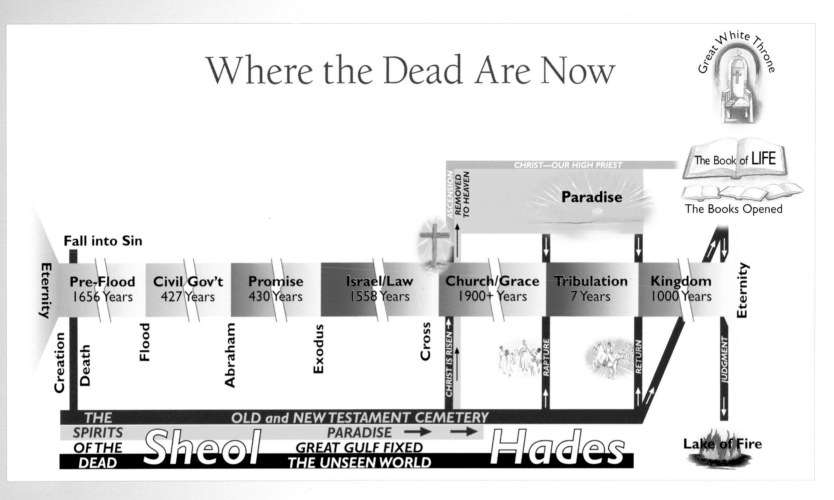

torment. (Some Bible teachers also believe that this Great Gulf Fixed has no bottom to it, and that it could well be the bottomless pit of Revelation 20:3 into which the devil is cast at the glorious appearing of the Lord Jesus Christ.)

More details are given by Jesus about the Place of Torment than the other two compartments. Jesus was clearly interested in warning men about this place in order to keep them from going there. The rich man called Hades a *place* of torment, indicating that it is a real place, not merely a state of existence, as some would like to believe. Verse 22 tells us that "the rich man also died and was buried," and verse 23 begins, "In Hades he lifted up his eyes, being in torment." There seems to be no intermediary state; the unbeliever goes immediately to the Place of Torment. Verse 23 also suggests that the rich man is conscious of what he missed, for it states, "He lifted up his

eyes...and saw Abraham far away and Lazarus in his bosom." This indicates that one of the horrible tortures of Hades will be that its victims will be able to look across the Great Gulf Fixed and view the comforts and blessings of the believers who are being comforted. The unbeliever will constantly be reminded of what he missed due to his rejection of God.

ESCAPE FROM SHEOL-HADES

One of the victories wrought by the death, burial, and resurrection of Jesus Christ is that the church-age believer does not have to go to Sheol-Hades. Psalm 16:10, as quoted by Peter in Acts 2:25-31, establishes the fact that Jesus Christ is not in Sheol-Hades today. Whereas the location of Hades is spoken of as "down," we know from Acts 1:9 the Lord Jesus was "taken up...toward heaven." Later, in 2 Corinthians 5:8, Paul tells us, "We are confident, I say, and willing rather to be absent from the body, and to be present with the Lord" (KJV). In other words, ever since the resurrection, the believer at death has gone not to Sheol-Hades, but to be "present with the Lord," who dwells in heaven. In fact, the Lord Jesus is presently "standing at the right hand of God" (Acts 7:55). Consequently, when a present-day believer (or any Christian during the church age) dies, he no longer goes to Sheol-Hades, but his soul proceeds immediately to heaven to be with his Savior Jesus Christ.

One question naturally confronts us: When did this change take place? We know that the Lord Jesus went to Paradise, for in Luke 23:43 he told the thief on the cross who cried out for salvation, "Today you shall be with Me in Paradise." Therefore, we know that Jesus went directly from the cross into the Paradise section of Sheol-Hades. What's more, Ephesians 4:8-10 reveals that Paradise is no longer located in Hades, but was taken by Christ up into heaven. This indicates that the believer now goes to heaven, where he is joined with the Old and New Testament saints. That means the Paradise section of Hades is an empty compartment. It is also very possible that in this transition the Lord Jesus snatched the keys of Hades and death from the hand of Satan, for we see in Revelation 1:18 that He now holds them.

This leads to yet another question: Why were the Old Testament saints sent to the Place of Comfort or Paradise in the first place? Why couldn't Daniel, David, Abraham, and all the other great men and women of God go directly to heaven? After all, they believed in God while they lived on the earth. The answer is found in the inadequacy of the covering for their sins. In the Old Testament, sins were temporarily covered by the blood of a lamb. But an animal's blood was not sufficient to permanently cleanse their sins (Hebrews 9:9-10). Animal sacrifice was an exercise of obedience in which people trusted by faith that God would someday provide a permanent cleansing from sin through the sacrifice of His Son.

When our Lord cried from the cross, "It is finished!" (John 19:30), He was saying that the final sacrifice for man's sin was paid. God in human flesh could accomplish what no animal sacrifice could ever do: atone for the sins of the whole world. After releasing His soul, Jesus descended into Hades and led all the Old Testament believers, held captive until sin was finally atoned for, up into heaven, where they are presently with Him.

NO LIMBO OR PURGATORY

The soulish state should not be confused with the much-popularized Purgatory or Limbo, which we do not find in God's Word. Purgatory is said to be a place where men go to do penance or suffer for the sins they have committed in this world in order to purify them for a better afterlife. The startling difference between the biblical teaching on the present state of the dead and this false teaching is that there is no indication whatsoever in the Bible that those in the torment section of Sheol-Hades or those in heaven will ever be anywhere but where they are for all eternity. We have already learned that those who are in the Place of Torment can never bridge the Great Gulf Fixed and enter Paradise. On the contrary, all those who are presently in torment will eventually be cast into the Lake of Fire because they have not accepted Jesus Christ and because their names are not written in the Book of Life (Revelation 20:12-15). The suggestion that those in torment today will be granted a later opportunity to be saved contradicts Isaiah 38:18, which says, "For the grave [Sheol] cannot praise thee, death cannot celebrate thee: they that go down into the pit cannot hope for thy truth" (KJV). The Place of Torment is strictly a place of suffering and is void of the teaching of truth. Therefore, those who enter that place cannot hope for escape.

THE WAY TO PARADISE

A man winds up in Hades not because he is rich or poor, or because he is a murderer, a whoremonger, or a thief. A man is sent to Hades because he is an unbeliever—someone who has never accepted Jesus Christ as his Savior. According to John 3:18, "He who believes in Him is not judged; he who does not believe is judged already, because he has not believed in the name of the only begotten Son of God."

Note that both those who go to Paradise and those who end up in Hades are sinners. The latter die in their sins, while those who reside in Paradise were forgiven of their sins sometime during their life. Jesus Himself gave us clear directions on how to obtain admittance to this glorious place when He said, "I am the way, and the truth, and the life; no one comes to the Father but through Me" (John 14:6). Only by Jesus Christ, then, can we gain access to the Father, who is in heaven (where Paradise is now located). The Bible says that all men deserve to go to hell (Romans 3:23; 6:23), and only through faith in the Lord Jesus Christ and His finished work on the cross can we escape Hades and hell. John 1:12 says, "As many as received Him, to them He gave the right to become children of God, even to those who believe in His name."

To activate the eternal effects of God's forgiveness of sins through the death of His Son, a person must call on the name of the Lord and be saved (Romans 10:13). There is no other way—and no second chance.

49.
HISTORY'S END, ETERNITY'S BEGINNING

The end of history as we know it will come with a flurry of the most incredible events ever confronted by mankind. After that, we will enter eternity, which is beyond human imagination. The apostle Paul said of eternity, "Eye hath not seen, nor ear heard, neither have entered into the heart of man, the things which God hath prepared for them that love Him" (1 Corinthians 2:9 KJV). That was written before God gave the apostle John a small preview of eternity in the book of Revelation. The things we do know about the future are so appealing they should motivate anyone to prepare for eternity immediately by personally receiving Christ as their Lord and Savior.

Many of the 18 events listed below are mentioned or described in the last four chapters of the Bible. Most of them are mentioned in the Bible by the Hebrew prophets, the apostles, or the Lord Himself, and we have dealt with many of them in the preceding pages. Below are some additional details about these future events:

1. *The Marriage of the Lamb* (Revelation 19:7-10)

This event occurs in heaven at the conclusion of the Tribulation just before Jesus descends to earth to establish His kingdom.

2. *The Glorious Appearing of Christ* (Revelation 19:11-18)

This magnificent event culminates the entire prophetic plan of God, first seen by Enoch, "the seventh from Adam" (Jude 14-15), and last revealed to the apostle John. According to Jesus, the glorious appearing will happen "immediately after the tribulation" (Matthew 24:29).

3. *The Battle of Armageddon* (Revelation 14:14-20; 16:16)

This conflict should be called, as in the ASV Bible, "the war of the great day of God almighty." It should not be envisioned as a single battle; rather, it is a brief war that includes several battles.

4. *The World's Greatest Earthquake* (Revelation 16:18)

Just before God establishes His kingdom on this earth, an enormous earthquake will occur that will sink the islands of the seas and flatten the entire surface of today's world.

5. *The Judgment of the Nations* (Matthew 25:31-46)

This is also called the judgment of the sheep and goats, when Jesus separates believers from unbelievers at the end of the Tribulation. The sheep are believers and go into the Millennial kingdom; and the goats are those who have endured the Tribulation and are still unsaved, so they are taken to "everlasting punishment."

6. *Antichrist and False Prophet Cast into the Lake of Fire* (Revelation 19:20-21)

In judgment for their evil deeds during the Tribulation, these two men are cast immediately into the Lake of Fire. No indication is given that they are judged as all other men are—probably because they will receive the most severe punishment imaginable for committing the worst sin known to man: deceiving other souls about God and the way to God. They will probably be willing accomplices in deceiving more people and damning more souls during that seven-year period than any two men in history.

7. *Satan Bound 1000 Years* (Revelation 20:1-3)

The world's master deceiver will be bound in the bottomless pit so he cannot deceive men about God during the Millennial kingdom. No one knows where the bottomless pit is located; some suggest it is at the bottom of the Great Gulf Fixed, which is mentioned in Jesus' description of Hades in Luke 16.

8. *Resurrection of All Believers* (Revelation 20:4)

The Rapture occurs prior to the Tribulation as the first phase of the resurrection that takes all believers up to the Father's house. Some suggest that because the Old Testament saints died in anticipation of Christ's death on the cross they will be included as well. If so, the only believers left to be included after the Rapture will be all those who receive Jesus as their Lord during the Tribulation. These Tribulation saints are both Jew and Gentile.

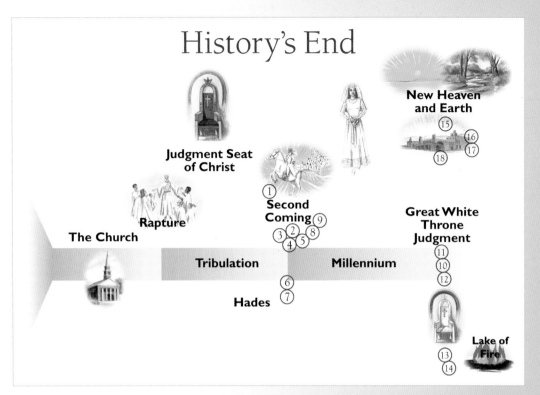

History's End

New Heaven and Earth

Judgment Seat of Christ

Second Coming

Great White Throne Judgment

Rapture

The Church

Tribulation

Millennium

Hades

Lake of Fire

9. *Christ Establishes His Millennial Kingdom* (Revelation 20:1-6)

Many Old Testament prophecies about the kingdom of God on earth will be fulfilled at this point. However, they are not included in this scripture. The only things described here are the location, duration, and the fact that Satan will be bound.

10. *Satan Released One Last Time* (Revelation 20:7-9)

That God will release Satan after the 1000-year kingdom to deceive men may seem a mystery at first, but it will give people who are born during the Millennium an opportunity to either rebel against God or receive Him and worship Him (see Isaiah 65).

11. *The Final Rebellion* (Revelation 20:7-9)

The fact that a large multitude will choose to follow Satan is evidence that the population during the Millennium will be huge. It will be a "youth movement," so to speak, for Isaiah 65:20 indicates only believers will live past their hundredth birthday. If everyone who chooses to follow Satan is under 100 and "the number of them is like the sand of the seashore" (verse 8), then you can imagine the even greater number of believers there will be in that kingdom.

12. *Satan Cast into the Lake of Fire* (Revelation 20:10)

After the rebellion is extinguished by God, Satan will be thrown alive into the Lake of Fire. By this time, the Antichrist and False Prophet will already have been there for 1000 years, proving that hell is clearly a place of suffering for eternity.

13. *The Great White Throne Judgment* (Revelation 20:11-15)

Only the unsaved will face this judgment. No believer from any age will be there. The purpose of this judgment will be for unbelievers to acknowledge Jesus as Lord and to receive the degree of punishment they have earned by their rejection of Christ and the deeds of their life.

14. *The Acknowledgment That Jesus Christ Is Lord* (Philippians 2:9-11)

It is probable that at this point in time, right after the Great White Throne Judgment, unbelievers will have to bend their knee and "confess that Jesus Christ is Lord, to the glory of God the Father" (verse 11). Had they been willing to acknowledge that Jesus is Lord during their lifetime, they would have escaped this judgment and the eternity in hell that results from it.

15. *The New Heaven and New Earth* (Revelation 21:1)

While we are not given many details about the new heaven and earth, we do understand that this world will be replaced by a new earth that more resembles the Garden of Eden than anything we know today.

16. *The Holy City Comes to Earth* (Revelation 21:2-8)

The incredible house that Jesus is building will descend to become the capitol of the new earth. A 1500-mile cube, it will be large enough to accommodate all the people who have ever lived on planet earth. It will probably be centered on the site of modern Jerusalem, from which Jesus Christ will rule this world in righteousness.

17. *Heaven Described* (Revelation 21:8-27)

The future home of all believers will be a beautiful walled city where the streets are gold (compared to our gravel, blacktop, and cement streets today) and the 12 gates to the city are huge, beautiful pearls. The foundation stones of the walls will be adorned with every kind of precious stone.

18. *Christ's Last Call to Mankind* (Revelation 22:6-20)

After promising to make His ultimate coming "suddenly," the Savior says, "The Spirit and the bride say, 'Come.' And let the one who hears say, 'Come.' And let the one who is thirsty come; let the one who wishes take the water of life without cost" (verse 17). This is the last call by Him who died for all mankind, to appeal to them to receive Him personally by faith. Any thirsty soul who wants God in his or her life and his or her sins forgiven through Jesus Christ can "take the water of life without cost." Salvation is a free gift of God, received by faith. Have you received that gift?

50.
WHAT IS YOUR CHOICE?

It should be obvious by now that God loves mankind and has a wonderful plan for the future of those who receive Jesus as Savior. It is called heaven, and it is eternal. We have seen in this book a constant battle, from the days of Adam and Eve to the end of the Millennium, between God and Satan for the souls of men. That God truly loves man should be clear not only because of His wonder-

ful plan for the future, but because He was willing to send His only begotten Son into the world to die on the cross for our sins. Had He not done so, no one would ever know redemption from their sins and enjoy the blessings of heaven.

The problem has been this: When Adam and Eve chose to disobey God, sin entered into the human race, and since then has been passed on to all mankind. Sin created a chasm between God and man that could not be bridged until His divine and holy Son Jesus identified

with the human race by becoming one of us through the virgin birth. This made it possible for a holy God to not only identify with us but become the sacrifice for our sins. His bodily resurrection was God's way of proving to all mankind that He accepted His Son's sacrifice for all humanity.

Since the cross it has been possible for man to come back to God by stepping out on faith and receiving Christ personally. Just like the decision a person makes to walk out on a bridge to cross a chasm, the choice to receive Christ is an individual matter. When it comes to receiving Christ, every person must make his or her own decision.

Those who choose to accept Christ will enter heaven. Those who do not choose Him will die in their sins, be judged, and then sent to the eternal Lake of Fire.

It is no exaggeration, then, to say that the choice you make about trusting Jesus Christ is the most important decision you will ever make on this Earth. Have you personally trusted Jesus to forgive your sin and provide eternal life? If you haven't, then we invite you to express your trust in Christ with the following prayer:

"Dear God, thank You for sending Your Son Jesus to die on the cross for my sins. I confess I am a sinner, and I ask You for Your forgiveness. Today I want to trust Jesus as my Lord and Savior. I give my life and future to You. In Jesus' name I pray, Amen."

Don't miss this great offer of eternal salvation—believe on the Lord Jesus Christ today!

Chart Index

SUBJECT INDEX

NOTES

1. David L. Cooper, *The World's Greatest Library Graphically Illustrated* (Los Angeles: Biblical Research Society, 1942), p. 7.

2. Ibid.

3. Clarence Larkin, *Dispensational Truth* (Philadelphia: Clarence Larkin Est., 1920), p. 6.

4. Kenneth S. Wuest, *Prophetic Light in the Present Darkness* (Grand Rapids: Eerdmans, 1955), pp. 39-40.

5. Gary Cohen, *Understanding Revelation* (Chicago: Moody Press, 1978), pp. 53-54.

6. J. Dwight Pentecost, *Things to Come* (Grand Rapids: Zondervan, 1958), p. 149.

7. The eight stages of Armageddon are adapted from Arnold G. Fruchtenbaum, *Footsteps of the Messiah: A Study of the Sequence of Prophetic Events* (Tustin, CA: Ariel Ministries Press, 1982), pp. 216-54.

8. Arnold G. Fruchtenbaum, *Israelology: The Missing Link in Systematic Theology* (Tustin, CA: Ariel Ministries Press, 1993), p. 570.

9. Charles C. Ryrie, *Dispensationalism* (Chicago: Moody Press, 1995), pp. 25-26.

10. Ibid., p. 25.

11. Ibid., pp. 25-26.

12. Ibid., pp. 26-27.

13. Ibid., p. 28.

14. Ibid., pp. 29-31.

15. Ibid., p. 41.

16. Arnold G. Fruchtenbaum, *Footsteps of the Messiah*, p. 65.

17. John F. Walvoord, *Israel in Prophecy* (Grand Rapids: Zondervan, 1964), p. 26.

18. John F. Walvoord, *The Prophecy Knowledge Handbook* (Wheaton, IL: Scripture Press Publishing, Inc., 1990), p. 233.

19. Harold Hoebner, *Chronological Aspects of the Life of Christ* (Grand Rapids: Zondervan, 1977), p. 139.

20. Arnold G. Fruchtenbaum, *Footsteps of the Messiah*, pp. 78-79.

21. Jerry M. Hullinger, "The Problem of Animal Sacrifices in Ezekiel 40–48," *Bibliotheca Sacra* 152 (July-September 1995), p. 280.

22. Ibid., p. 281.

23. Ibid.

24. Ibid., p. 289.

25. Terry C. Hulbert, "The Eschatological Significance of Israel's Annual Feasts," Th.D. dissertation from Dallas Theological Seminary, 1965, p. 2.

26. Ibid., p. 1.

27. Ibid., pp. 2-3.

28. Ibid., pp. 115-16.

29. J. B. Smith, *A Revelation of Jesus Christ: A Commentary on the Book of Revelation* (Scottdale, PA: Herald Press, 1961), pp. 311-13.

30. Ibid., p. 312.

31. Ibid.

32. Ibid., pp. 312-13.

33. Ibid., p. 313.

34. Robert L. Thomas, "2 Thessalonians" in the *Expositor's Bible Commentary*, vol. 11, ed. Frank E. Gaebelein (Grand Rapids: Zondervan, 1978), pp. 324-25.

35. Gerald B. Stanton, *Kept from the Hour*, 4th ed. (Miami Springs, FL: Schoettle Publishing Company, 1991), pp. 99-102.

36. John F. Walvoord, *The Holy Spirit* (Grand Rapids: Zondervan, 1958), p. 231.

37. John F. Walvoord, *Armageddon, Oil, and the Middle East Crisis*, rev. ed. (Grand Rapids: Zondervan, 1990), p. 217.

38. John F. Walvoord, *The Millennial Kingdom* (Findlay, OH: Dunham Publishing Company, 1959), p. 27.

OTHER PROPHECY BOOKS BY TIM LAHAYE

Are We Living in the End Times? (Tyndale House)
Rapture Under Attack (Multnomah)
Revelation Unveiled (Zondervan)
The Tim LaHaye Prophecy Study Bible (AMG Publishers)
Understanding Bible Prophecy for Yourself (Harvest House)

Prophetic Novels Coauthored with Jerry B. Jenkins

The Left Behind® Series
Left Behind
Tribulation Force
Nicolae
Soul Harvest
Apollyon
Assassins
The Indwelling
The Mark
Desecration
(five additional books to come)

Left Behind: The Kids®
18 books as of September 2001, with 18 more to come

OTHER PROPHECY BOOKS BY THOMAS ICE

Fast Facts on Bible Prophecy (Harvest House)
The Great Tribulation, Past or Future? (Kregel)
The Return: Understanding Christ's Second Coming and the End Times (Kregel)
The Tim LaHaye Prophecy Study Bible (Associate Editor, AMG Publishers)

ABOUT THE PRE-TRIB RESEARCH CENTER

In 1991, Dr. Tim LaHaye became concerned about the growing number of Bible teachers and Christians who were attacking the pretribulational view of the Rapture as well as the literal interpretation of Bible prophecy. In response, he wrote *No Fear of the Storm* (Multnomah Publishers, 1992; now titled *Rapture Under Attack*). In the process of writing this book, Tim was impressed by the Christian leaders who, in Great Britain during the 1820s and 1830s, set up conferences for the purpose of discussing Bible prophecy. In 1992, Tim contacted Thomas Ice about the possibility of setting up similar meetings, which led to the first gathering of what is now known as the Pre-Trib Study Group in December 1992.

In 1993, Dr. LaHaye and Dr. Ice founded the Pre-Trib Research Center (PTRC) for the purpose of encouraging the research, teaching, propagation, and defense of the pretribulational Rapture and related Bible prophecy doctrines. It is the PTRC that has sponsored the annual study group meetings since that time, and there are now over 200 members comprised of top prophecy scholars, authors, Bible teachers, and prophecy students.

LaHaye and Ice, along with other members of the PTRC, have since produced an impressive array of literature in support of the pretribulational view of the Rapture as well as the literal interpretation of Bible prophecy. Members of the PTRC are available to speak at prophecy conferences and churches, and the organization has a monthly publication titled *Pre-Trib Perspectives*.

To find out more about the PTRC and its publications, write to:

Pre-Trib Research Center
Liberty University
1971 University Blvd.
Lynchburg, VA 24502

You can also get information through the Web site:
www.timlahaye.com